RECONSTRUCTING FEMINISM THROUGH CYBERFEMINISM

Studies in Critical Social Sciences Book Series

Haymarket Books is proud to be working with Brill Academic Publishers (www.brill.nl) to republish the *Studies in Critical Social Sciences* book series in paperback editions. This peer-reviewed book series offers insights into our current reality by exploring the content and consequences of power relationships under capitalism, and by considering the spaces of opposition and resistance to these changes that have been defining our new age. Our full catalog of *SCSS* volumes can be viewed at https://www.haymarketbooks .org/series_collections/4-studies-in-critical-social-sciences.

Reconstructing Feminism through Cyberfeminism

Edited by
Gözde Ersöz
Gökmen Kantar
Meltem İnce Yenilmez

Haymarket Books
Chicago, IL

First published in 2023 by Brill Academic Publishers, The Netherlands
© 2023 Koninklijke Brill NV, Leiden, The Netherlands

Published in paperback in 2024 by
Haymarket Books
P.O. Box 180165
Chicago, IL 60618
773-583-7884
www.haymarketbooks.org

ISBN: 979-8-88890-348-3

Distributed to the trade in the US through Consortium Book Sales and
Distribution (www.cbsd.com) and internationally through Ingram Publisher
Services International (www.ingramcontent.com).

This book was published with the generous support of Lannan Foundation,
Wallace Action Fund, and the Marguerite Casey Foundation.

Special discounts are available for bulk purchases by organizations and
institutions. Please call 773-583-7884 or email info@haymarketbooks.org for more
information.

Cover design by Jamie Kerry and Ragina Johnson.

Printed in the United States.

Library of Congress Cataloging-in-Publication data is available.

Contents

Preface

Reconstructing Feminism through Cyberfeminism examines how women have historically been underrepresented in the digital world, and the possibility for social change at the convergence of gender and technology.

The book investigates how digitalization has affected entrepreneurship, labour markets, financial markets, and women's empowerment, underlining the opportunity it presents for a more inclusive and equal society. It explores how technology changes and creates gender and the transformational potential it has for questioning conventional concepts of gender, drawing on the theories and critiques of cyberfeminism. It specifically examines the notion of "cyborg feminism," which rejects the binary conception of gender and welcomes the notion of the "cyborg" as a hybrid entity that defies conventional limitations. This book discusses how women's agency and power in establishing emancipated cyberspaces are critically impacted by Cyberfeminist conceptions of technical growth. Therefore, it intends to shed light on how technology may be a tool for women's empowerment and emancipation as well as how it might sustain current power imbalances and gender inequities by exploring cyberfeminism. It explores the nexus of gender and technology, examining the connections between gendered, classed, and digital activities. In addition, this book looks at how technology may either support current power relations or provide disadvantaged people with a chance to question and disrupt them.

This book also offers a thorough investigation of cyberfeminism while looking at the nuanced interaction between gender and technology. Therefore, it examines how women have historically been underrepresented in the digital world and the possibility of societal change at the convergence of gender and technology. In doing so, it speaks to the need to move past dogmatic ideas of digital empowerment and considers the many different ways that technology may both empower and marginalize women. The need for a more nuanced understanding of the digital world is highlighted by the critical examination of cyberspace's representation and commercialization. The book also underlines how crucial it is to think about how technology's ethical and political consequences relate to the creation and improvement of identities. So, it concludes with a thorough examination of cyborg feminism and its crucial implications for gender, power, and agency in the digital sphere.

Acknowledgements

The book is dedicated to my mother, Nilgün; my father, Mehmet; my sister, Hande; and my brother, Yasin. The book is also dedicated to our many wonderful teachers and students, past and present, from whom we have drawn inspiration and learned so much. I am also grateful to my friends, Meltem İnce Yenilmez and Gökmen Kantar, the co-editors of this book. Finally, I am indebted to the reviewers who contributed suggestions and feedback to ensure that the book is a success.

Gözde Ersöz

The book is dedicated to my mother Filize, my father Emrullah, my lover Gülderen, my children Işık Bürçe and Ali Osman. The book is also dedicated to our many wonderful teachers and students, past and present, who have been inspiring and from whom we have learned so much. I am also grateful to my friends Meltem İnce Yenilmez and Gözde Ersöz, the co-editors of this book. Finally, I am grateful to the reviewers who gave their suggestions and feedback to ensure the success of the book.

Gökmen Kantar

Words cannot express how grateful I am to my mother, father, mother-in-law, and father-in-law for all the sacrifices that they have made on my behalf and whose love and guidance are with me in whatever I pursue. They are the ultimate role models. I wish to thank my sisters. I have no words to describe the meaning of your love and support. Most importantly, I owe my deepest gratitude to my loving and supportive husband, Özgür, and my wonderful beloved son, Bryan Poyraz, who provides unending inspiration and is such a good boy who always cheers me up. You are the best thing that is still happening to me. Finally, I am so grateful to my dear friends and colleagues Gözde Ersöz and Gökmen Kantar, whose supportive approach and encouragement have guided me throughout the process.

Meltem İnce Yenilmez

This book is for all the women in the world who are the foundation stone and the architects of society.

Gözde Ersöz
Gökmen Kantar
Meltem İnce Yenilmez

Figures and Tables

Figures

Tables

Notes on Contributors

Yarkın Çelik
holds a master's degree in Corporate Communication from Anadolu University and New Media from Istanbul Aydın University. His fields of study are new media, communication sciences, new communication technologies, and visual communication design. Çelik worked at the Middle East Technical University Technopolis within the scope of various projects. He has been working as a Lecturer at Tekirdağ Namık Kemal University Media and Communication Program since 2018. (orcid.org/0000-0002-9615-7904)

Fatma Pelin Erel
is a Lecturer at Tekirdağ Namık Kemal University in Turkey. She received her Bachelor's Degree from Dokuz Eylül University in the Faculty of Administration. Erel completed her MSc and PhD degrees in Agricultural Economics at Tekirdağ Namık Kemal University. Her PhD dissertation, completed in 2021, is "The Evalution of Consumers' Nutrition and Health Professionals' Approaches to Functional Foods". In 2022, she presented her paper "Evaluation of Legal Framework of Functional Foods in Different Countries: A Literatüre Review" in Macedonia, XII International Conference on Economy, Business & Society in Digitalized Environment. Her paper "Evaluation of Health Professionals' Approaches in Strategic Marketing of Functional Foods" was published in *New Frontiers for Management and Strategy in the Post-Pandemic Era* (Ece Nur Degirmenci, Ed.) in 2022. Erel's research areas are: marketing, innovation, consumer behaviour. (orcid.org/0000-0003-2393-8096)

Gözde Ersöz
is an Associate Professor at the Department of Physical Education and Sports Teacher Education at Marmara University who specializes in sport management, behaviour science in sport, sport and exercise psychology. She has published 30 research articles and six book chapters and presented more than 100 papers at scientific congresses. Ersöz is the co-editor of the *Journal of Sport and Social Sciences* and *The Journal of Eurasia Sport Sciences Medicine*. She also serves on the editorial board of many journals published in the fields of Sports and Exercise Psychology, Sport Sciences and Recreation. Ersöz has served on the committees and boards of institutions and organizations such as the Turkish National Paralympic Committee, the Basketball Federation, the Triathlon Federation, the Exercise and Sports Psychology Association, the Sports Sciences Association, and the Sports and Physical Activity Association for Women. (orcid.org/ 0000-0002-4848-1929)

Oktay Hekimler

received his bachelor's degree in international relations from Istanbul University and completed his master's and doctoral studies at Istanbul University. Hekimler received his PhD degree in International Relations and Political Science with a study titled "Germany's New Eastern Policy in the Context of European Integration". Since 2008, he has been working as a lecturer at Tekirdag Namik Kemal University. Hekimler, who works in the field of International Relations and Political Science, has studies on European Integration, German Foreign Policy, Central and Eastern Europe, Turkish Foreign Policy, and Women in Foreign Policy. He also has published articles, book chapters and oral presentations in these fields. (orcid.org/ 0000-0001-7998-9699)

Meltem İnce Yenilmez

is a Professor at the Department of Economics at Izmir Democracy University who specializes in the economics of gender, labour economics and social work. She was a Visiting Researcher at the University of California, Berkeley between 2014–2015; was at Georg-Universität-Gottingen at summer school in 2015–2016; was Visiting Researcher at Lund University; was a Research Associate at the University of Massachusetts, Amherst in 2020–2022 and was Visiting Faculty at IIM Rohtak, India in 2022. İnce Yenilmez is a Visiting Professor at the University of Tohoku, Japan since 2021. She is an economist focused on labour economics, discrimination, sustainability, social policy, behavioural economics, and care work. İnce Yenilmez has eight books published by Routledge, Palgrave, Rowman, and Peter Lang; her next book projects on migration economy, and economy, ecology, and environment will be published in 2024. For more information, please go to İnce Yenilmez's personal website: www.melteminceyenilmez.com (orcid.org/ 0000-0002-4689-3196)

Ayşe Mine İşler

is currently a lecturer at Tekirdağ Namık Kemal University, Vocational School of Social Sciences, Department of Social Work and Counseling. She graduated from Hacettepe University, Department of Social Work in 2017. İşler worked at the Association for Solidarity with Asylum Seekers and Migrants and Turkish Red Crescent Gaziantep Community Center and worked in the field of migration and refugees. Afterwards, she worked at the Child Homes Coordination Center affiliated to the Ministry of Family and carried out professional work in the fields of social work with families, women and children, children in need of protection, child welfare, child neglect and abuse. Having completed her master's degree at Manisa Celal Bayar University, Department of Social Work and currently pursuing her PhD at the same university, İşler continues her academic studies in the fields of migration, social work with women and children and medical social work. (orcid.org/0000-0002-5386-0608)

Eylül Kabakçi Günay

holds bachelor's, master's and PhD degrees in Economics from Anadolu University. Her areas of research are economic growth, development economics and international economics. Throughout her career, Kabakçı Günay has taken part in various international and national projects, participated in seminars, and given lectures in diversified areas of economics. She serves as an Associate Professor at Izmir Democracy University. (orcid.org/ 0000-0001-5547-4316)

Gökmen Kantar

is an Associate Professor of political science, political communication, political discourse analysis, political history and politics at Tekirdağ Namık Kemal University, Department of Political Science and Public Administration. He gave lectures as a visiting lecturer in the field of political science at Esenyurt University Social Sciences Institute between 2018–2019 and 2019–2020 at Maltepe University. Since 2017, Kantar has been working as a visiting associate professor at Tekirdağ Namık Kemal University in Turkey. He is a political scientist focusing on political language, ideology, intercultural communication, social policy, democracy, feminism and modernization. Kantar has 12 international and two national books published by international publishing houses. In addition to his thirty national and international articles, Kantar has nearly 20 international oral presentations. (orcid.org/ 0000-0001-5120-110X)

Miray Özden

completed her undergraduate studies in the Department of Public Administration at Selçuk University Faculty of Economics and Administrative Sciences in 2009. She then completed her master's degree in Agricultural Economics at Tekirdağ Namık Kemal University Faculty of Agriculture in 2014. In 2020, Özden completed her PhD studies in the Department of Local Governments at Marmara University with her thesis titled *"Participatory Democracy and Participation in Local Governments: The Case of Thrace."* Since 2013, she has been working as a lecturer at Tekirdağ Namık Kemal University Vocational School of Social Sciences and currently holds the position of Assistant Professor. Özden's research primarily focuses on Citizen Participation, Participatory Democracy, Sustainable Development and Cities, Participation Methods in Local Governments, Governance, and the Relationship between Economic Development and Democracy. She has numerous published academic works both nationally and internationally. (orcid.org/ 0000-0001-7998-9699)

Kürşad Özkaynar
completed his undergraduate degree at Sivas Cumhuriyet University and his master's degree at Sakarya University. With his master's thesis, Özkaynar was awarded the Scientific Work of the Year Award by the Minister of Industry and Trade. In 2020, he completed his doctorate in Political Marketing at Sakarya University. Özkaynar is one of the editors of the international refereed journal *Studies on Social Science Insights* and also opened his exhibition on the History of Marketing and Advertising by compiling his collection of advertisements. Özkaynar is interested in political marketing, metaverse, artificial intelligence, and related marketing insights. (orcid.org/ 0000-0003-1683-9591)

Mehtap Polat
holds a bachelor's, master's and PhD in Public Administration from Karadeniz Technical University. During her master's and PhD studies, Polat worked as a researcher at Coventry University and Regent University with the Erasmus Internship Programme. Her research interests are women, migration and children in the context of social inequalities. Polat has been working as a research assistant and giving lectures at the Vocational School of Social Sciences, Local Management. (orcid.org/0000-0002-9294-4919)

Sedat Polat
holds a bachelor's degree in Sociology from Adnan Menderes University and both a master's degree and PhD from Atatürk University. He worked for a while as a lecturer at Trabzon Avrasya University, where he gave lectures in the field of social work. Polat completed his PhD in the field of "Poverty Studies" with a special scholarship programme "YÖK 100/2000 Doctorate Programme" in 2022. His research interests include poverty, social inequality, gender, and family. (orcid.org/0000-0002-6071-7252)

Gamze Yıldız Şeren
holds bachelor's, master's and PhD degrees in public finance from Marmara University. Her areas of research are public finance theory, public finance economics, public budget and gender. Throughout her career, Şeren has taken part in various international and national congresses, participated in seminars and workshops, and fulfilled national and international book editorships. She serves as an Associate Professor at Tekirdag Namık Kemal University. (orcid.org/ 0000-0002-5063-1172)

CHAPTER 1

Introduction

Meltem İnce Yenilmez

Technology is being used by the cyberfeminism movement to question conventional gender norms and stereotypes. Cyberfeminists hold that the internet can be a place where women can freely express themselves and develop new types of activism and communities.

The interaction of gender and technology is the focus of the 1990s-era social, cultural, and political movement known as cyberfeminism. The feminist movement that aimed to question gender norms and advance women's equality in the 1960s and 1970s is where cyberfeminism got its start. Contrarily, cyberfeminism expands on the traditional definition of feminism by utilizing the power of technology and the internet to provide new spaces for gender action and empowerment.

It is a large and diverse movement that includes many strategies and tactics for utilizing technology to advance gender equality. Cyberfeminism's fundamental goal is to use technology to challenge and undercut existing gender roles and power structures. The goal is to create new spaces for feminist engagement where women may challenge patriarchal expectations and claim their digital liberty.

The term "cyberfeminism" was first used in 1991 by Australian artist and scholar Susan Hawthorne to describe the development of feminist networks and online communities via the use of computer-mediated communication. Since then, cyberfeminism has grown to encompass a range of viewpoints and actions, from academic research and policy lobbying to online activism and artistic expression.

The term "cyberculture," which describes the cultural practices and identities that are developing in the digital sphere, is one of the fundamental ideas of cyberfeminism. Cyberfeminist tried to investigate how gender and sexuality are depicted in this new culture and to challenge the patriarchal systems that underpin these portrayals.

"Cyborg feminism" is a key phrase in cyberfeminism. This idea came from the work of feminist theorist Donna Haraway, who argued that technology has the power to break down old gender roles and restrictions. She saw the cyborg as a representation of this possibility – a hybrid being that blurs the distinctions between gender, nature, and society, as well as between man and machine.

Cyberfeminist claim that the cyborg represents a new kind of feminist identity that challenges conventional ideas about gender and the body.

The use of hacking and other forms of digital activism to advance social and political change is known as "hacktivism," and it has been related to cyberfeminism as well. Hacktivists have used technology to expose injustices, promote free speech, and subvert corporate and governmental power. The movement's leaders have been cyberfeminist, who have used their technological know-how and proficiency to oppose the gendered power structures that govern our digital world.

Cyberfeminism has not been without its challenges and critics, despite its many successes. Some critics claim that it unduly emphasizes the experiences of white women from the middle class while neglecting to address the demands and issues faced by women from disadvantaged backgrounds. Others claim that it has become excessively focused on technology and has forgotten about the greater social and political context in which it operates.

1   Emerging Topics and Concentration Areas

The convergence of technology and social justice is one of the most significant emerging concepts in cyberfeminism. Existing inequalities and disparities might get worse as technology gets more and more ingrained in our daily lives. Cyberfeminists are concentrating more and more on issues like algorithmic injustice, the digital divide, and online abuse. These issues demand a multidisciplinary strategy that considers the social, cultural, and political aspects of technology.

The use of technology for empowerment and resistance is a further focus of cyberfeminism. Technology may provide a forum for speech and activity while marginalized people continue to experience discrimination and persecution. There is no one definition of what it means to be a Cyberfeminist because the movement is varied and encompasses many different perspectives. All cyberfeminists, however, concur that the internet has the potential to be a potent force for social change. They want to build a more just and equal society for all people by using technology to challenge conventional gender roles and prejudices.

Some of the foundational ideas of cyberfeminism are as follows:
– Technology is a neutral instrument that may be employed for good or evil, according to the theory of technological determinism. Technology,

according to cyberfeminists, is not neutral and may be used to support or undermine established power systems.

- Cyberspace is a virtual environment produced by technology. Cyberfeminists contend that women may freely express themselves in cyberspace as well as develop new types of community and action.
- The concept of gender performativity holds that gender is not a fixed identity but rather something we perform via our interactions and behaviours. Cyberfeminists contend that women may defy conventional gender norms and experiment with new gender identities online.
- Hacktivism is the practice of using technology to advance social change. Cyberfeminists utilize hacktivism to oppose the ways that technology is applied to objectify and sexualize women as well as to spread awareness of gender-based violence and to promote laws that will safeguard women online.

On how we view gender and technology, cyberfeminism has had a huge influence. In addition to using technology to establish new communities and modes of activity, cyberfeminism has contributed to dispelling the myth that women are technologically innately less capable than males. Cyberfeminism is an effective force for social change, and it will undoubtedly continue to influence how we use technology in the years to come. Following are a few instances of Cyberfeminist activism:

- The Riot Girl movement, which promoted awareness of sexism and misogyny via zines, music, and other kinds of media.
- The Cyberfeminist International, an annual gathering of Cyberfeminist from all around the world to exchange concepts and tactics.
- The Yes Means Yes campaign, which aims to dispel rape culture and educate the public on consent.
- The #MeToo movement, which has increased understanding of sexual harassment and assault.

These are just a handful of the numerous ways cyberfeminism is utilizing technology to subvert conventional gender norms and stereotypes. Cyberfeminism is an influential societal force that will undoubtedly continue to influence how we use technology in the years to come.

2   Early Cyberfeminism

Cyberfeminism's early stages were characterized by a sense of hope and potential. Cyberfeminists viewed the internet as a brand-new platform for women to freely express themselves and develop new types of activism and communities.

They fought to make the world fairer and just for everyone by using technology to challenge conventional gender roles and prejudices.

The Cyberfeminist International was one of the most significant early cyberfeminism initiatives. It was an annual conference that brought together Cyberfeminists from all over the world to exchange concepts and tactics. Cyberfeminist International provided a forum for women to explore the potential and problems presented by the digital era and to devise new strategies for utilizing technology to advance women's rights.

The Riot Girl movement, which made use of zines, music, and other media to promote awareness of sexism and misogyny, was another significant early cyberfeminism endeavour. Inspiring a new generation of young women to use their voices to challenge the existing quo, Riot Girl was a potent force for change.

3   Cyberfeminism Today

In recent years, cyberfeminism has kept progressing. Cyberfeminists are employing technology to tackle a variety of problems today, such as gender-based violence, online harassment, and the digital divide. New kinds of art, activism, and community are also being created by them utilizing technology.

The emergence of online sexism is one of the biggest problems cyberfeminism is now confronting. Cyberfeminists are pushing for laws that will protect women online and are trying to end online harassment and violence against them. Additionally, they are aiming to make online places for women more inviting and inclusive.

Cyberfeminism is an effective force for transformation. This movement aims to make the world more just and equal for everyone by utilizing technology to question conventional gender roles and prejudices.

4   Central Themes and Principles of Cyberfeminism

Several key ideas and concepts that are significant to the philosophy and method of cyberfeminism are used to describe it. Here are a few illustrations:

1.   Intersectionality: Cyberfeminism recognizes the complex and varied experiences of power and marginalization that result from the interaction of several forms of oppression and privilege. It tries to address these

intersections in its advocacy and engagement, as well as to support settings that are more welcoming and equitable for underprivileged individuals and communities.

2. Cyberfeminism: Cyberfeminism considers technology to be both a tool and a setting for feminist intervention and engagement. It tries to use technology to support feminism and challenge patriarchal structures while also critiquing how it could support gendered and other forms of oppression.

3. Networked Activism: Cyberfeminism emphasizes the potential of networked and dispersed forms of activism, which enable decentralized and collaborative forms of social change resistance and change. It seeks to create feminist networks and communities on a worldwide and transnational scale through the application of digital technology.

4. Creative Resistance: Cyberfeminism frequently manifests as creative resistance, in which creators of art and other types of cultural output utilize their work to subvert accepted beliefs and narratives. It seeks to upend and subvert established power structures through humour, parody, and other forms of cultural intervention.

5. Openness and Access: Cyberfeminism advocates for open access to knowledge and information, free and open-source software, and universal access to digital technologies to advance openness and access in digital cultures.

5   Technology's Contribution

Technology has made significant contributions to the growth of cyberfeminism and will continue to do so. As new technologies arise, cyberfeminism must adapt and create fresh approaches to using them for social justice. For instance, the development of artificial intelligence (AI) has raised concerns about bias and discrimination in algorithmic decision-making. Cyberfeminists are searching for answers to these problems, such as increasing dataset diversity and developing moral AI frameworks.

Technology is also changing the way we see who we are and how we are embodied. Cyberfeminist are examining the effects on gender and other identities because of the blurring of the lines between the physical and digital worlds caused by virtual and augmented reality technology. As an illustration, some are using virtual reality to develop immersive experiences that challenge preexisting gender conventions and encourage fluidity and variety.

Opportunities of Cyberfeminism include:
- New forms of activism and community-building: The internet enables women to communicate with one another from all over the world, regardless of their geography or upbringing. For bringing women together and motivating them around common causes, this may be a potent weapon.
- Disprove conventional gender norms and stereotypes: Women can experiment with various gender identities and expressions online. This can assist in dismantling the binary thinking that frequently surrounds gender and in fostering an environment that is more welcoming to women.
- Access to information and resources: Women have easy access to a plethora of data and tools online that may help them lead better lives. This covers details regarding rights, health, work, and education.
- Economic empowerment: The internet may help women become more economically independent. Women may create their enterprises, offer their goods and services, and look for jobs online.
- Political participation: Women may use the internet as a tool for political engagement. Internet access enables women to research political topics, get in touch with elected officials, and take part in political campaigns.

6   Challenges of Cyberfeminism

Among the difficulties facing cyberfeminism is gender-based violence, which can take the form of abuse, stalking, and harassment of women online.
- Accessibility: Not all women have the same level of access to the internet. This is caused by several things, such as poverty, lack of knowledge, and poor infrastructure.
- Computer divide: The gap in computer literacy between men and women may widen because of the internet. This is because males are more likely than women to have access to the internet and utilize it for a variety of purposes.
- Cybersecurity: Cybersecurity attacks tend to target women more frequently. This is because they utilize less secure gadgets and are more inclined to divulge personal information online.
- Underrepresentation: In the tech sector, women are underrepresented. This indicates that fewer women are involved in the design and development of the technology that we use. This could result in technologies that don't take women's demands into account.

Cyberfeminism is a strong force for social change despite these obstacles. Cyberfeminism uses technology to disprove gender norms and stereotypes, build new communities and movements, and advance the status of women all over the world.

7   Conclusion

Cyberfeminism has expanded and flourished since its start in several different ways. Cyberfeminism has evolved beyond its early stages in part due to its participation in a wider array of social justice issues. Recognizing the linkages between gender, racism, class, and other forms of oppression, cyberfeminism has started to use digital technology to address a wider range of social justice issues.

For instance, several cyberfeminists have addressed issues relating to abuse and harassment online, particularly in the context of social media platforms. They have developed methods to stop online harassment and protect underrepresented groups online. Cyberfeminism has also been working to promote technology access and digital literacy among groups who have traditionally been shut out of or marginalized from it.

Interaction with different forms of activism and cultural production is another way that cyberfeminism has developed. From digital art and literature to performance and film, cyberfeminism has embraced a variety of artistic mediums. Cyberfeminism may explore the complex and occasionally contradictory relationships among technology, gender, and power using these tools, as well as create new modes of feminist expression and representation.

There has been a growing recognition of the importance of intersectionality in feminist activism beyond the early years of cyberfeminism. Cyberfeminists have been more active in a wider range of social justice issues because of this awareness, and they have also adopted more inclusive and diversified approaches to feminism.

For instance, many cyberfeminists have tackled issues of disability justice, seeing how ableism interacts with other forms of oppression to uphold injustices in digital contexts. Additionally, a lot of cyberfeminists have worked to create inclusive and accessible digital tools and platforms because they understand how important accessibility and universal design are for achieving social justice and digital equality.

The future of cyberfeminism is both intriguing and challenging. Cyberfeminism must take the initiative to address emerging issues and find novel ways to employ technology for social justice as it develops and influences our environment. By focusing on the convergence of technology and social justice and taking the initiative to keep up with emerging technologies, cyberfeminism may be able to have a significant impact on society and the tech industry in the future.

CHAPTER 2

Revisiting Cyberfeminism

Mehtap Polat and Sedat Polat

This chapter explores the re-formation of the Cyberfeminist field by examining the impact of feminist theory on digital technology and the transformation of digital environments. Drawing on the historical development of cyberfeminism, its conceptual map and current developments, this study aims to understand the complex relationships between gender, technology, and social equality in the digital age.

The cyberfeminism movement emerged as feminist activism shifted to the digital sphere with the spread of the internet and the development of digital technology. This movement has focused on the interactions between technology, gender, and social change. These interactions influenced the work of the pioneers of cyberfeminism and played an important role in shaping the principles and values of the movement. The interplay between technology, gender and social change has shaped the historical evolution and current position of cyberfeminism.

Today, the position of cyberfeminism is determined by the gender inequalities that exist in the digital space. Issues such as online gender violence, the transformation of digital activism, and the reproduction of gender roles are called digital inequalities and are among the current issues of cyberfeminism. Cyberfeminism reveals its potential and limits by evaluating these issues and problems considering current debates. It also aims to provide suggestions for policymaking and the future of the cyberfeminism movement by drawing attention to possible gender inequalities in the digital space.

This study defines cyberfeminism and discusses the historical development of the movement. It then focuses on theoretical foundations such as feminist theory and technology, intersectionality in cyberfeminism, posthumanism and cyborg feminism. Cyberfeminism addresses issues of gender, identity, and representation in cyberspace with sub-headings such as gendered online identities and performances, digital activism, and online communities, Cyberfeminist art and digital expression. In terms of power and inequality in the digital age, subheadings such as gendered digital division and access, online harassment, and gender-based violence, algorithmic bias and discrimination are examined in detail.

This study aims to provide a resource for academics, activists and researchers who want to understand the current state of cyberfeminism and contribute to issues such as gender equality and digital activism. Analyzing the past and present of cyberfeminism provides a comprehensive framework for understanding the relationship between gender and technology in the digital age.

1   Introduction

This chapter examines the re-formation of the Cyberfeminist field by focusing on the transformation of feminist theory in digital technology and its digital environments. In light of the historical development, conceptual mapping and current developments of cyberfeminism, the study aims to understand the complex relationships between gender, technology and social equality in the digital age.

With the spread of the Internet and the development of digital technology, feminist activism has shifted its attention to the digital sphere, and cyberfeminists have seen this technological development as an important platform for art and politics. The Cyberfeminist movement that emerged in the 1990s focused on the interactions between technology, gender, and social change. These interactions influenced the work of the pioneers of the Cyberfeminist movement and played an important role in the formation of the principles and values of the movement. The interaction between technology, gender and social change has also determined the historical evolution and current position of cyberfeminism.

Along with technological progress, the current position of cyberfeminism is determined by gender inequalities in the digital space. Issues such as online gender violence, transformation of digital activism, and reproduction of gender roles are defined as digital inequalities and these digital inequalities are among the current issues of cyberfeminism. Cyberfeminism reveals its potential and limits by evaluating these issues and problems considering current debates. In addition to these issues, cyberfeminism aims to offer suggestions for policy-making and the future of the Cyberfeminist movement by drawing attention to possible gender inequalities in the digital space. In this respect, cyberfeminism also sets a certain direction for future studies.

In this study where cyberfeminism is re-evaluated, the definition of the Cyberfeminist movement will be made. After the definition of cyberfeminism, the historical development of the concept will be discussed and analyzed and then the theoretical foundations of cyberfeminism will be discussed under the subheadings of feminist theory and technology, intersectionality in cyberfeminism, posthumanism and cyborg feminism. Under the title of gender, identity, and representation in cyberspace, gendered online identities and performances, digital activism, and online communities, Cyberfeminist art and digital expression will be evaluated from various perspectives. In the fourth section, which deals with power and inequality in the digital age, the subject will be presented in detail with the subheadings of gender-based digital division and access, online harassment, and gender-based violence, algorithmic bias, and discrimination. This study aims to provide a resource for academics, activists and researchers who want to understand the current state of cyberfeminism and contribute to issues such as gender equality and digital activism. By analyzing the past and present of cyberfeminism, it provides a comprehensive framework for understanding the relationship between gender and technology in the digital age.

2   Defining Cyberfeminism

Cyberfeminism as a feminist theory and practice represents a field that has developed with the emergence of digital media and new communication technologies. It is a concept first introduced in 1991 by the Australian artist group vns Matrix under the title "cyberfeminist manifestos for the 21st century". Cyberfeminism was coined in 1994 by Sadie Plant, director of the Cybernetic Culture Research Unit at the University of Warwick in the UK, to describe the work of feminists interested in theorizing, critiquing, and using the Internet, cyberspace and new media technologies in general (Consalvo, 2002: 1).

Cyberfeminism encompasses a wide range of feminist practices. These practices can take place in fields as diverse as high theory, political techno-art, science fiction writing, game design and activism. Cyberfeminism provides a platform for feminist theory and practice to explore the interactions of gender, technology, and digital media. It is a social and political movement whose point of departure is the internet. Cyberfeminism aims to make visible and rebel against gender inequality in the digital sphere. Cyberfeminism is seen to promote gender equality online (Arias-Rodriguez and Sánchez-Bello, 2022).

Cyberfeminist projects can often be associated with two intersecting axes. The first is the distinction between "theoretical" and "practice-based" cyberfeminism. Theoretical cyberfeminism analyses the impact of feminist theory on digital technologies and media, while practice-based cyberfeminism focuses on feminist actions with the aim of actively combatting digital media use and promoting change. The second intersecting axis is the relationship between "third wave" and "second wave" feminism. Cyberfeminism emerged from second-wave feminism's struggle for gender equality and women's rights and adapted to the prioritized issues of third-wave feminism. This intersection shows the place and evolution of cyberfeminism in the history of the women's movement (Sundén, 2008: 1). In conclusion, cyberfeminism is an area where feminist theory intersects with digital media and communication technologies. This concept provides an important tool for understanding the relationships between gender, technology, and digital media, questioning inequalities, and bringing feminist practice into the digital world. Cyberfeminism is recognized as an important field for understanding and navigating technology-related social change by bringing together feminist ideas from different disciplines and practices.

On the other hand, there is little consensus on the meanings and boundaries of the concept. If, as the Old Boys Network (OBN) declared at the first Cyberfeminist International in 1997, everyone can and should invent their cyberfeminism, the concept may seem fluid enough to accommodate almost any reference (Paasonen, 2011: 336). The Cyberfeminist International agreed not to define cyberfeminism and instead produced the "100 anti-thesis of cyberfeminism" (100 things cyberfeminism is not) (OBN, 1997).

3   Historical Overview of the Cyberfeminist Movement

Before asking what cyberfeminism is, let us briefly remind gender and feminism. Gender is a concept based on masculinity and femininity roles different from biological sex. In patriarchal societies, masculinity and femininity are considered the norm, while other gender identities are excluded. The man in the subject position tends to exert pressure in society. In society, women are subjected to various injustices and injustices because they are women. Feminism is a movement that fights against gender-based inequalities. Finally, the most important thing we should know about patriarchy is that all societies living in the world have their own patriarchy. In countries with different patriarchies, the levels of gender inequality are also different.

The issue of gender inequality, which is the building block of feminist theory, continues to exist as a problem that will not be solved in the short term. To see the dimensions of this inequality, it is necessary to look at the Global Gender Equality Gap Index data. The Global Gender Gap Index provides a detailed analysis in four main categories to examine the gender equality gap. These categories are economic participation and opportunities, participation in education, health and survival, and political empowerment. According to the gender gap report, it is estimated that it will take approximately 100 years for inequalities between women and men to be eliminated. Closing inequalities, especially in the fields of economy and health, involves the most challenging processes. It is estimated that it will take another 217 years to close the gender gap in the economic sphere. In health, some progress has been made, but more work is needed to achieve full equality. The gap in education is projected to narrow further within 13 years. Progress in women's access to education is a promising indicator for reducing inequality in this area. The dimension of political empowerment is currently the area where the gender gap is widest. Nevertheless, while some progress has been made in recent years, the pace of progress appears to have slowed down. Nevertheless, it stands out as the dimension where the most progress has been made and it is estimated that this gap can be closed in about 99 years (WEF, 2017: 25). Of course, cyberspace also exhibits a patriarchal structure and inequalities we experience in social life spill over into this field.

Prior to the emergence of cyberfeminism, feminist technology studies tended to examine how technological developments were socially and culturally constructed. One of the main arguments of these studies was the positioning of technology as part of masculine culture. That is, the idea that technology was something that men were interested in, that they were successful at, and therefore more engaged in than women. Although in the past women have played an active role in the development of new technologies, feminists have argued that technology is still perceived as a masculine creation. For example, although women were involved in the creation and development of the computer, their contributions were often marginalized and their participation was often ignored or erased from history (Consalvo, 2002: 1).

In the early 1990s, cyberfeminism emerged as a critical arena for exploring the gender-technology nexus, especially in connection with the rise of the Internet as a mass media. Academics, activists, and artists formed networks with different interpretations of cyberfeminism and its compatibility with feminism (Paasonen, 2011: 335). For example, cyberfeminist activities in Germany developed through the Old Boys Network (OBN). OBN organized the Cyberfeminism Internationals (First in 1997, Next in 1999 and very in 2001), providing platforms for people interested in cyberfeminism to connect, explore and critique digital technologies and their embedded discourses (Paasonen, 2011: 339).

There are important texts that laid the foundations for the idea of cyberfeminism and contributed greatly to the development of the movement. There are many more influential texts and works in the field of cyberfeminism. The following texts reflect the diversity and richness of the movement.

1.   "A Cyberfeminist Manifesto for the 21st Century" by: VNS Matrix
     (Josephine Starrs, Julianne Pierce, Francesca da Rimini) and Virginia
     Barratt. This manifesto explains the principles and goals of the
     Cyberfeminist movement and presents a framework that interrogates
     the relationships between the female body, technology, and digital
     environments.

2.   "Cyberfeminism" written by: Sadie Plant, in Sadie Plant's *Zeros +
     Ones: Digital Women and the New Technoculture*. This article addresses
     cyberfeminism through women's participation in technology and the
     transformation of gender roles in digital environments. According to
     British cultural theorist Sadie Plant, as machines become smarter, women
     become liberated. Sadie Plant is a leading figure in cyberfeminism
     and argues that technology is fundamentally feminine, not masculine.
     According to Plant, cyberspace can also be considered an emancipatory
     space for women, which can have a wide range of postmodern subjec-
     tivities. This is because the internet has inherently "feminine" qualities.
     Plant argues that with the development of technology, women will be
     liberated, and cyberspace can offer opportunities for women (Paasonen,
     2011: 338).

3.   "The Cyborg Manifesto" by: Donna Haraway. This iconic article is an
     important text that forms the foundations of cyberfeminism and defines
     the concept of "cyborg". In exploring the relationships between gender,
     technology, and the body, Haraway emphasizes the emergence of inter-
     sectional identities that blur boundaries. Haraway provides a new defini-
     tion of feminism by putting forward various views on the advancement
     of technology. According to her, the blurring of the boundaries between
     man and machine will make the categories of man and woman redun-
     dant. Saying that she would rather be a cyborg than a goddess, Haraway
     imagined a world of thought without gender. She also asked feminists to
     stop emphasizing gender and adopt a gender-insensitive approach (Hall,
     1996: 147).

4.   "Hacking the Futures: Feminist Pedagogy and Technological Innovation"
     by: Faith Wilding and subRosa Collective. This paper addresses
     Cyberfeminist practice and digital activism, combining feminist peda-
     gogy and technological innovation. By combining the political and ped-
     agogical dimensions of the movement, it examines how feminist values
     can be blended with digital technologies.

It is argued that cyberfeminism begins as an idea but can develop into a practice and a movement through its indirect reflection in mass culture facilitated
by technological progress. Put more simply, without advances in biological,

medical, and cybernetic technologies, cyberfeminism would have remained a utopian concept limited to the world of science fiction (Afanasov, 2022: 89). Cyberfeminism works in theory and practice to raise awareness of horizontal networks and their potential, arguing that the age of the cyber citizen poses new and significant risks of marginalization and new forms of empowerment based on gender and other factors (Youngs, 2005: 69). In the age of cyber citizenship, cyberfeminism points to the emergence of new risks of marginalization and new forms of empowerment based on factors such as ethnicity, sexual orientation, class, disability as well as gender. With the widespread use of digital technologies, the effects of these factors are also seen in online environments and problems such as gender inequality are also encountered in the digital space.

Today, cyberfeminism has been subjected to some criticisms. Firstly, it is criticized that cyberfeminism has a utopian approach and ignores the limitations in the real world. It is stated that women do not intervene sufficiently in the production process of digital technologies and that women's access to these technologies is still limited. It is also criticized that cyberfeminism ignores other social inequalities, does not politicize women, and has sexualizing tendencies that reproduce traditional gender stereotypes. However, despite all these criticisms, cyberfeminism can be considered as a part of studies aimed at understanding the new experiences that enter our lives with digital technologies. It is emphasized that cyberfeminism can be used as a conceptual tool in the process of analyzing the gender codes of cyber culture, which still has masculine qualities (Varol, 2014: 231). In conclusion, it is understood that cyberfeminism has been subjected to criticism and has some shortcomings. However, it is also stated that cyberfeminism can make a valuable contribution to understanding the experiences associated with digital technologies and discussing gender. It is thought that a continuous discussion and development process is needed to be aware of the criticisms and to make cyberfeminism more inclusive.

4   Theoretical Foundations of Cyberfeminism

4.1   *Feminist Theory and Technology*
Feminist theory and technology encompass many subfields and topics. These include digital inequality, how gender-based violence manifests on online platforms, women's access to and use of technology, increasing women's representation in technology, how technology shapes gender norms, and the interactions between gender identity and technology. Feminist theory and technology

also explore how traditional gender norms are reflected in the design of technological products and how these products affect women. For example, issues such as the use of products based on a male-dominated perspective or digital platforms that exclude or endanger women are addressed in this field.

Early feminist theorists expressed pessimism regarding the masculine nature of technology, but this perspective shifted in the 1990s to an unfounded optimism about its emancipatory potential for women. The association between technology and male privilege was seen as broken in the digital age. Feminist theories of technology highlight the mutual shaping of technology and gender, emphasizing the need for feminist technology policies to achieve gender equality. While early feminism recognized the entanglement of technology with capital and patriarchal relations, cyberfeminism views the virtual space and the internet as liberating for women by challenging the corporeal basis of gender difference. Wajcman (2006) acknowledges the evolving gender-technology relationship, attributing it to feminist politics rather than technology itself.

Furthermore, feminist theory and technology also examine how technology can contribute to feminist movements and how women can use it for digital activism and empowerment. In this context, studies are conducted on the impact of social media on the feminist movement, examples of digital feminist activism and the potential of technological tools in the struggle for gender equality. Technofeminist approaches, which avoid both technological determinism and gender essentialism, see the gender-technology relationship as fluid and flexible and argue that the key to gender equality is not the technology itself but feminist policies (Wajcman, 2007: 287).

Feminist theory and technology is a broad interdisciplinary field and is closely related to disciplines such as sociology, communication, information and communication technologies, computer science, media studies and women's studies. There is a diversity of theoretical frameworks, research methods and practices in this area of academic endeavor.

4.2   *Intersectionality in Cyberfeminism*

Intersectionality is a perspective in which different identities and experiences intersect and influence each other. In cyberfeminism, intersectionality refers to the critical insight that gender, as well as ethnicity, class, sexual orientation, disability, and other social identities, are not mutually exclusive, but mutually constructed phenomena that shape complex social inequalities (Collins, 2015: 2).

In the 1970s, Afro-American women in Boston formed an initiative called the Combahee River Collective. The main goal of this initiative was to develop a social justice project that could be considered within the framework of black feminism. In 1982, the members of the Combahee River Collective published a statement called "A Black Feminist Statement" in which they argued that systems of oppression, which are claimed to be different from each other, are in fact intertwined. The intersection point of issues such as gender, race, social class and sexuality is that all of these issues involve the experiences of unequal approaches and practices applied to women of color (Collins, 2015: 12). Black women who struggled for their rights within second wave feminism in the USA were ignored by the reactionary forces, racist and elitist circles within this movement, and their participation in the movement was hidden. The non-egalitarian approach even within the feminist movement forced black women to build a separate organization, the National Black Feminist Organization (Taylor, 2017). Even in the second wave of feminism, which corresponded to a more advanced level in the struggle for women's rights, there was a division based on power relations. Even within this movement, white women and other elites did not see women of color on an equal footing. In this sense, intersectionality in cyberfeminism expresses the intersectionality between these different identities by pointing out that women are subjected to various oppressions ranging from their skin color to their racial affiliation and class origins.

Intersectionality in cyberfeminism emphasizes analysing the intersection of multiple identities and experiences rather than a one-dimensional perspective of feminism. This approach recognizes that women's experiences are not only limited to gender but also combine with other social factors and influence each other. Intersectionality in cyberfeminism provides an important framework for understanding how different social positions and experiences influence each other, and in this way aims to provide a more inclusive and equitable analysis.

4.3   Posthumanism and Cyborg Feminism

Posthumanism and cyborg feminism are two interrelated concepts that explore the intersections between technology, feminism, and the boundaries of the human subject within academic discourse. Posthumanism challenges the traditional understanding of the human as a fixed and bounded entity and instead explores the idea that humans are intertwined with and shaped by their relationships with technology, non-human beings, and the environment. It questions binary distinctions between human and non-human, nature and culture, and challenges anthropocentrism. From a feminist perspective, posthumanism emphasizes the ways in which gender and sexuality intersect with the technologically mediated world and how these intersections shape subjectivity, embodiment, and power dynamics.

Theoretically, orientated cyberfeminism brings together feminist theory and technoscience studies to offer a sophisticated framework for understanding gender's interaction with technology and science. This approach emphasizes that gender is a socially constructed and malleable concept and suggests that gender norms and binaries need to be questioned. Through cyborgs and other theoretical concepts, cyberfeminism promotes transformation at the intersection of gender and technology and fights for gender equality and social justice.

Cyborg feminism celebrates the idea of the cyborg as a hybrid figure that blurs the boundaries between human and machine, challenging the notion of a fixed and natural gender identity. It rejects essentialist and biological determinist views of gender and advocates a fluid and intersectional understanding of identity.

Cyborg feminism investigates how technology affects gender relations and provides avenues for empowerment and resistance. It places a focus on online environments, digital art, and cyberspace that have the potential to subvert established hierarchies and open up new avenues for female activity. Cyberfeminism is a theory that is compatible with third-wave feminism and operates at a complicated and advanced level of feminist theory and technoscience studies. Cyborg feminism explores the confluence of technology, gender, and identity and was influenced by Donna Haraway's seminal article "A Cyborg Manifesto." Traditional ideas of femininity and gender binary are questioned. Donna Haraway, a feminist scientific historian, coined the term "cyborg" in 1991. It is seen as a symbolic representation. Cyborgs are used by Haraway to symbolize the erasure of dichotomies like mind/body, organism/machine, culture/nature, and civilized/primitive. While the cyborg is frequently used as an illustration of strict masculinity in conventional science fiction, Haraway approaches the cyborg in a different perspective. For him, being a cyborg means advancing toward a world in which gender is irrelevant, or at least is significant in a new manner. Cyborg seeks to dismantle conventional gender binaries by blurring the lines between human and machine (Sundén, 2008: 1). It does this by connecting the feminine body and identity with technology.

Both posthumanism and cyborg feminism critically engage with the ways in which technology intersects with gender, challenging normative understandings of the human and offering new ways of understanding subjectivity, embodiment, and social relations.

5   Gender, Identity and Representation in Cyberspace

5.1   *Gendered Online Identities and Performances*

"Gendered Online Identities and Performances" is a concept that explores how gender is expressed and performed in online environments. This concept examines how individuals represent themselves on online platforms, mimic gender roles, or challenge existing gender norms. An example of such research is the study of Maloney et al. (2018). In that study, research examining the gender performances and constructions of male actors on YouTube emphasizes the emergence of increasing levels of complexity in the construction of contemporary masculine identities.

Online identities are the identities that a person creates and presents in a virtual environment. These identities may be represented through avatars, usernames, profiles or other digital representations. Gendered online identities are choices made to express an individual's gender or to mimic behaviors, appearance or characteristics associated with gender.

Performances are when individuals play a specific gender role or behave in accordance with gender expectations in online environments. These performances may involve conscious actions to represent a particular gender identity by exhibiting behaviors that conform to gender norms, or to question and transform existing gender norms.

Online gaming platforms provide individuals with the opportunity to adopt gendered online identities and behaviours. These digital spaces allow for the exploration of alternative gender identities, challenging traditional norms. Crowe and Watts (2014) argue that these platforms offer a means for young people to understand gender identity. Eklund (2011) conducted a study on gender and sexuality in World of Warcraft, highlighting the significance of contextual factors in the construction of gender identity within the game. The study found that while gender performances were influenced by the game's rules and social relations, there were possibilities for queer performances and alternative gender expressions.

Gendered online identities and performances are an important analytical tool for examining the many dimensions in which gender is socially and culturally constructed and for understanding how it is expressed in online platforms. These concepts are used in research to understand the complexity and diversity of gender in online environments, to question gender norms, and to contribute to online gender equality studies. Analyzing online identity performances in this way informs a better understanding of the social construction of gender and racial identities more generally, not just in relation to online interaction (Kendall, 2000: 256).

5.2   *Digital Activism and Online Communities*

The concepts of digital activism and online community refer to forms of activism realised using digital technologies and communities created in online environments. These concepts include actions taken to promote social or political change, raise awareness or fight for social justice through digital tools such as the internet, social media, digital platforms and communication technologies, and online communities created for these actions. Digital activism refers to activism activities carried out by online platforms and digital tools. These activities can take various forms such as social media campaigns, online petitions, hashtag activism, digital protests, and hacktivism. Digital activism utilizes digital tools to promote social or political change, raise awareness, expose inequalities, or fight against injustices.

Between third-wave feminism and practice-based cyberfeminism, there are online counterparts of feminist groups such as Guerilla Girls and Riot Girls. In the artistic sphere, the "girls" have come together internationally to participate with ironic force in the struggle for representation. Braidotti describes their position as "the politics of parody" and points to the irony of being able to play with various options for addressing femininity. This online politics is characterized by a mix of active resistance, fun and enforcing their own rules among the girls. They are "bad girls", smart and proud of their tech skills. By mentoring other women online, they encourage self-expression, empowerment and codification (Sundén, 2008: 2).

The Australian artist group VNS Matrix, located on the cyberfeminist map, occupies a position that moves between art, politics and theory, using strategies such as irony, parody and sexual obscenity. VNS Matrix shares the idea that technology is feminine and sexual, while at the same time making literary efforts to connect technology with corporeality. Phrases such as "A direct line to the clitoris matrix" in their manifesto were not only considered provocative language but also criticized the traditionally male-dominated field of computer technologies attributed to women.

Online communities are groups of people who come together on online platforms around a specific topic, purpose, or interest. These communities may come together for digital activism and aim to achieve common goals, share information, and experience, and promote solidarity or social change. They interact through social media groups, forums, blogs, online campaign platforms or other online communication channels. For example, Momstown Mothers have facilitated an online community of mothers through a social networking site to experience technologically supported motherhood and leisure time. These mothers, sometimes referred to as "cyber mothers", are mothers who remain "constantly connected" to other mothers and to technologies that change connectivity. The interaction between mothers and technologies has blurred ideologies, including the distinction between public and private spheres and restrictive ideologies about motherhood. In response to contemporary challenges of increasing social isolation and anxiety-inducing culture, cyber mums are embracing new possibilities of connectivity and opening new leisure spaces for women (Valtchanov et al., 2016: 15).

Digital activism and online communities offer the potential to reach wider audiences using the communication and organization capabilities of digital technologies. These tools make it easier for activists to express their opinions, share information, build communities, and contribute to social change. These concepts are an important area of research to examine the effects of the digital world on social mobility and political participation and to understand communities fighting for social justice on online platforms.

5.3   Cyberfeminist Art and Digital Expression

The gap between digital life and real life continues to shrink, and nowhere is this more evident than in the contexts of art and culture (Giannini and Bowen, 2016: 237). The development of digital, information and communication technologies has created a complex corpus called cyberculture, and (multi)media art has played an important role in analyzing the new social relations created by these technologies, making it a successor to the avant-garde movement (Kluszczynski, 2005: 124).

"Cyberfeminist Art and Digital Expression" refers to the intersection between feminist art and digital technologies. It explores how artists who identify with cyberfeminism use digital tools and platforms to create artworks that address gender, sexuality, identity, and technology.

Cyberfeminist art embraces the ethos of cyberfeminism, challenging traditional gender norms, power structures and inequalities in the digital space. It criticizes and subverts patriarchal and male-dominated aspects of technology while promoting inclusion, diversity, and empowerment. Cyberfeminist artists often engage with themes such as cyborg identities, virtual bodies, online communities, and the impact of technology on gendered experiences.

Digital expression in cyberfeminism art encompasses a variety of forms and media, including but not limited to

Digital Installations: Artists create immersive experiences using interactive technologies, projections, virtual reality, or augmented reality to explore feminist themes and engage audiences in critical reflection.

Network Art: Artists use the internet as a medium to create artworks that often blur the lines between art and online activism. They may use websites, blogs, social media platforms or online collaborations to address feminist issues and challenge traditional narratives.

Video and Multimedia Art: Artists use video art, animation, or multimedia installations to explore the intersections between gender, technology and society. They may use digital editing techniques, visual effects, or digital manipulation to convey their message. For example, one study suggests that the use of femininity and voice in digital art practice has a strong potential to create provocative spaces in the new technoculture (Gilson-Ellis, 2001: 77).

Performance Art: Artists incorporate digital elements into live performances or use live streaming platforms to explore gender identity, virtual embodiment, or social interaction in the digital age.

Through cyberfeminist art and digital expression, artists seek to critically examine and disrupt gender norms, explore new forms of self-expression, challenge dominant narratives and envision more inclusive and egalitarian futures. These artistic practices not only provide a platform for feminist voices but also contribute to broader debates surrounding technology, society and gender politics.

6   Power and Inequality in the Digital Age

6.1   *Gender-Based Digital Divide and Access*

Cyberfeminism tends to involve women who are young, tech-savvy and from Western, white, middle-class backgrounds (Consalvo, 2002: 1). As mainstream cyberfeminism is considered to have failed to address the complexity experienced by women in the South, demystification of technology is thought to be necessary, but not sufficient, for empowerment (or re-empowerment, a preferred term) (Gajjala, 1999: 619).

Another type of cyberfeminism, situated between second-wave feminism and practice-based cyberfeminism, has a significant awareness of information inequality and seeks to create online spaces of private women's resistance that seek to network with women worldwide. One such example is the "Women Working on the Net" alliance between UNESCO and the International Development Association. This project considers how women in academic, activist and professional circles in industrialized countries can extend their online opportunities to other women, especially in developing countries. While theoretically oriented cyberfeminism has been criticized for excluding women who do not belong to the white, Western, middle-class, inner circle of theoretical cyberfeminism, this type of cyberfeminism aims to integrate women from many different ethnic backgrounds (Sundén, 2008: 2).

The Gendered Digital Divide and Access refers to the differences and inequalities between genders in terms of access and use of digital technologies. It emphasizes the different opportunities, resources and experiences that individuals of different genders face when interacting with digital platforms, online services and information and communication technologies (ICTs).

The concept of the Gender Digital Divide recognizes that gender plays an important role in shaping individuals' digital experiences and outcomes. It emphasizes that access to technology is not equally distributed between genders, resulting in unequal participation and representation in the digital space. There are two statistically significant gender differences in internet access and use. The access gap is not the product of gender-specific factors but is explained by socioeconomic and other differences between men and women. The usage gap is the result of a combination of both socioeconomic and underlying gender-specific phenomena. About half of the "digital divide" between men and women on the Internet is fundamentally gender-related (Bimber, 2000: 868).

The Gendered Digital Divide can manifest in several ways:

Inequality of Access: This refers to differences in physical access to digital technologies such as computers, smartphones, and internet connectivity. Women and girls, especially in low-income or marginalised communities, may face barriers in accessing these technologies due to factors such as affordability, availability, or cultural norms.

Patterns of Use: The Gender Digital Divide also encompasses differences in the way individuals of different genders use digital technologies. For example, research has shown that men tend to have higher levels of internet use, engagement in certain online activities and digital skills compared to women. This difference in usage patterns can be influenced by social and cultural factors, gender stereotypes and unequal opportunities for digital literacy and education.

Digital Skills Gap: The Gender Digital Divide includes differences between genders in digital literacy and skills. Women and girls may face limited opportunities or support to acquire digital skills such as coding, programming, or technical knowledge. This can exacerbate inequalities in employment opportunities, entrepreneurship and access to digital resources and opportunities.

The "digital divide" debate primarily focuses on access to technology and is prominently discussed at the policy and political level, such as the World Summit on the Information Society (WSIS). The WSIS recognizes the stark digital divide between wealthy and impoverished nations, and ICTs are positioned within the broader framework of the Millennium development goals. These goals include eradicating poverty and hunger, achieving universal education, promoting gender equality, reducing child mortality, improving maternal health, combating diseases, ensuring environmental sustainability, and fostering global partnerships for a better world (WSIS-03/Geneva/Doc/4-E).

A study from India, using data from a large-scale nationally representative sample, shows that the gender digital divide is significant. The study found that factors such as caste, household size, marriage and family structure affect women's computer self-efficacy and thus influence the gender digital divide. The study revealed inequalities in women's computer skills and access to digital technologies in India. Social factors such as caste system, household size, marriage and family structure influence women's level of computer self-efficacy. For example, women living in certain caste groups or large families face more challenges in developing digital skills and accessing technology. Furthermore, marriage and family structure also influence women's level of digital divide. For example, women who are married or have children may have more difficulty developing computer self-efficacy and accessing digital technologies due to family responsibilities. These findings reveal the complexity and diversity of the gender digital divide in India. Gender inequality not only affects women's access to digital skills and resources but is also linked to the social structure of society. Therefore, efforts towards gender equality should take into account social and cultural factors and support women in accessing and using digital technologies (Vimalkumar et al., 2021).

A study conducted in Rwanda shows that despite the government's intensive efforts to eliminate the digital divide, a gender-based digital divide still exists. This study revealed that there are various barriers to women's access to and use of ICT. Among these barriers, emotional factors such as women's lack of self-esteem, lack of self-confidence and lack of appropriate education are prominent. Women's lack of self-confidence towards digital technologies may limit their interest and abilities in this field. In addition, lack of educational opportunities can make it difficult for women to develop their digital skills and access technology. Social, economic and cultural factors also affect women's access to ICTs. Intense domestic responsibilities may prevent women from devoting their time and energy to digital technologies. Computer anxiety is also an important factor; women may hesitate to use ICTs because of their concerns and fears about technology. These findings highlight the existence of a gender-based digital divide in Rwanda and the barriers women face in accessing digital technologies. In order to overcome these problems, women's self-esteem needs to be raised, educational opportunities improved, and support provided to overcome barriers such as computer anxiety. It is important that all segments of society raise awareness and develop policies for gender equality. Women's access to and use of digital technologies should be encouraged to ensure social and economic development (Mumporeze and Prieler, 2017).

The debate on women's access to and use of digital Information and Communication Technologies (ICTs) in developing countries has not yet reached a satisfactory conclusion. Some argue that women are more technology-averse and that men use digital tools better, while others argue that women enthusiastically embrace digital communication. However, the reason why women access and use ICT less is directly linked to unfavourable conditions in terms of employment, education, and income. When these variables are controlled for, it turns out that women use digital tools more actively than men. This enables the alleged digital gender to divide to be turned into an opportunity. Given women's interest in ICT and the potential of digital technologies to improve living conditions, ICT offers a tangible and concrete opportunity to overcome long-standing problems of gender inequality in developing countries. This opportunity can be utilised to improve the situation of women in areas such as employment, income, education, and access to health services. In this context, women's access to and use of digital technologies should be encouraged, and the necessary resources and training opportunities should be provided for equality. ICT is an important tool for empowering women, enabling them to achieve economic independence and interactively reshape their social roles. However, more efforts should be made to combat gender inequality and policies and programmes should be developed to remove the barriers women face in using ICT (Hilbert, 2011).

Addressing the Gender Digital Divide and Access involves recognising and eliminating barriers that impede gender equality in the digital space. It requires initiatives and policies aimed at improving digital literacy programmes, promoting equal access to technology, fostering diversity and inclusive representation in digital spaces, and promoting an inclusive and empowering online environment for individuals of all genders. By closing this gap, we can strive for a more equitable and inclusive digital future for all.

6.2 *Online Harassment and Gender-Based Violence*
"Online Harassment and Gender-Based Violence" refers to various forms of abusive and harmful behaviour towards individuals based on their gender identity or perceived gender online. It encompasses harassment, threats, intimidation, discrimination, stalking and other forms of violence that occur through digital platforms and communication channels. The visible and audible harassment of women shows that cyberspace, once heralded as a new, democratic, public space, suffers from similar gender inequalities as the offline world. Rather

than online abuse being a form of communication, it should be considered as a form of abuse or violence against women and girls (Lewis et al., 2016: 1462).

Online harassment and gender-based violence can manifest in various ways:

Cyberbullying: This involves the use of digital platforms such as social media, messaging apps or online forums to target individuals based on their gender. It can include the spread of derogatory comments, offensive language or humiliation aimed at degrading or belittling one's gender identity.

Revenge Porn: This refers to the sharing of explicit or private content, often of a sexual nature, without the person's consent. It disproportionately affects women and marginalized genders and is intended to shame, humiliate, or exert power and control over them. Such sharing can have serious consequences for victims' work, family and social relationships and can cause psychological trauma. Revenge porn, because of the digital age, can spread on online platforms and quickly reach large audiences. This can put victims in a difficult situation and expose them to severe harassment and attacks. Many countries have legally criminalized revenge porn and perpetrators of such acts may face legal consequences. In addition, measures such as community awareness-raising efforts and support services play an important role in combating this problem. Revenge porn is an example of digital sexual violence and highlights issues of violation of sexual privacy, gender inequality and digital safety. Combating such acts, raising public awareness, and providing support to victims are important steps towards creating a safer environment in the digital world.

Online Sexual Harassment: Involves unwanted sexual advances, explicit messages, sexually explicit messages, or the distribution of sexually explicit content without consent. It can create a hostile online environment and contribute to the objectification and commodification of individuals based on their gender.

Doxing and Online Stalking: These involve the non-consensual public disclosure of personal information, including addresses, phone numbers or workplace information. It can lead to offline harassment, threats or physical harm and is often used to exert power and control over individuals based on their gender.

Hate Speech and Online Misogyny: This involves the use of sexist, misogynistic or discriminatory language and expressions to target individuals or groups based on their gender. It perpetuates harmful stereotypes, reinforces gender inequalities, and creates a hostile online environment.

Bullying and cyberbullying are associated with societal norms that put girls at risk of harassment, violence, abuse and discrimination (Mishna et al., 2020: 403). Online harassment against women exemplifies behaviors that cause great harm to women in the twenty-first century but are often ignored or even trivialized. This harassment includes rape threats, posting manipulated photos of women drowning, revealing women's home addresses with suggestions to subject them to sexual assault, and technological attacks that shut down blogs and websites. This prevents women from fully participating in the online world, taking them offline and undermining their autonomy, identity, dignity and well-being.

The trivialization of these incidents of harm to women is not new. In fact, there was not even a term to describe sexual harassment of women in the workplace until the 1970s. Ignoring these situations, whose harms uniquely affect women, carries an important social meaning – it sends the message that abuse of women is acceptable and tolerated behavior. Tackling the downplaying of cyber gender harassment is a crucial step in understanding and combating the harm it causes. It is crucial to recognize cyber harassment as gender discrimination, educate the public about gender-based harms, enable women to publicize their complaints, persuade perpetrators to end their online attacks, and ultimately transform online subcultures of misogyny into subcultures of equality (Citron, 2009: 373).

A study by Vitis and Gilmour (2017) focuses on women's use of non-traditional forms of resistance to online sexual harassment. Taking Anna Gensler's Instagram art project "Instagranniepants" as an example, the research examines how women use the language and practices of cyberspace to their advantage to expose online sexual harassment and create a critical, comic, and playful resistance. Drawing on interdisciplinary literatures such as testimony, satire, and shaming, the paper explores how Gensler not only documents harassment, but also uses techniques such as resisting, engaging with, and punishing harassers. In this way, the article questions the view of women as merely passive victims in online public spaces and criticizes popular discourses that portray online spaces as merely a risky environment and position women as natural victims of online violence. It is pointed out that a narrative focused on risk and victimization undermines the emancipatory potential of the online space. For this reason, it is emphasized that women's experiences of online spaces need to be understood and examined in more depth. As a result, it is concluded that with a more detailed understanding of women's struggles and interactions in the online space, there is a need for a more inclusive narrative to evaluate the potential of the online space and ensure women's empowerment.

Addressing online harassment and gender-based violence requires a multifaceted approach that includes awareness, education, policies, and legal frameworks. It includes promoting digital literacy, supporting respectful online behaviors, implementing stronger community guidelines and content moderation practices on digital platforms, providing support and resources for victims, and advocating for legal measures to hold perpetrators accountable. Creating safer and inclusive online spaces is essential to combat gender-based violence and promote a more equitable digital environment for all individuals.

6.3   *Algorithmic Bias and Discrimination*

"Algorithmic Bias and Discrimination" refers to the inherent biases and discriminatory consequences that can result from the use of algorithms in various fields such as artificial intelligence, machine learning and automated decision-making systems. Algorithms are sets of instructions or rules used to process data and make decisions or predictions. However, they can be influenced by societal biases, prejudices, or unequal data representations, and can lead to biased outcomes that disproportionately affect certain groups. Algorithmic bias is a problem that arises from seemingly innocuous models of information processing, making it difficult to identify, reduce or evaluate using standard resources in epistemology and ethics, and does not accept a purely algorithmic solution (Johnson, 2020).

Algorithmic bias refers to the systematic errors or injustice that can occur when algorithms produce results that are discriminatory or favor certain groups over others. These biases can arise from biased training data, biased design choices, or the reinforcement of existing societal biases in algorithmic decision-making. There is widespread concern that the increasing use of machine learning algorithms in important decisions may reproduce and reinforce existing discrimination against legally protected groups (Rambachan et al., 2020).

Discrimination in algorithmic systems refers to differential treatment or adverse impact to individuals or groups based on protected characteristics such as race, gender, age or socio-economic status. Algorithms may unintentionally perpetuate or reinforce societal biases, leading to discriminatory outcomes in areas such as recruitment processes, credit approvals, criminal justice systems or content recommendation systems. While algorithms are procedures or a set of precise instructions that facilitate automated decision-making, bias is a byproduct of these calculations and harms historically disadvantaged populations (Lee, 2018).

Academic research and analyses of algorithmic bias and discrimination seek to identify, understand, and mitigate these problems. Academics and researchers examine the underlying causes of bias in algorithmic systems, assess the impacts on marginalized communities, and propose strategies to reduce bias and ensure fairness. This includes exploring methods to improve data quality and diversity, developing justice-sensitive algorithms and evaluation metrics, implementing transparency and accountability measures, and promoting ethical guidelines and regulatory frameworks. There is a need for more workplace diversity in technology industries and public policies that can detect or mitigate the possibility of racial bias in algorithmic design and implementation (Lee, 2018).

On the other hand, studies have shown that the belief that the choices made by the machine will be made without bias is high and that people will therefore turn to less legal processes or that anger situations can be minimized as a result of trust in the artificial machine. When discrimination is caused by an algorithm (compared to a human), people are less likely to find the company legally responsible (Bigman et al. 2020). Algorithmic decisions that create gender or racial inequality are perceived as less biased than human decisions (Bonezzi and Ostinelli, 2021).

The study of algorithmic bias and discrimination highlights the ethical and social implications of relying on algorithms in decision-making processes. It underlines the importance of critically examining and addressing biases in algorithms to achieve fair outcomes and minimize the persistence of discriminatory practices.

7   Conclusion

This study reassessed the history and current state of cyberfeminism. By reviewing the basic tenets of cyberfeminism and the evolution of the movement, we sought to understand the complex relationships between gender, technology, and social equality in the digital age.

Today, cyberfeminism faces significant challenges with technological advances and changes in digital spaces. Issues such as digital inequalities, online gender violence, the reproduction of gender roles and the transformation of digital activism are shaping Cyberfeminist thought and practice.

This study analyses the current state of cyberfeminism and current debates, revealing the movement's potential and limitations. Cyberfeminism plays an important role in promoting gender equality and justice in the digital age. However, the effectiveness and impact of cyberfeminism requires ongoing study in an environment where digital inequalities still persist.

As a result, more research, policymaking, and activism in the field of cyberfeminism is needed. More efforts should be made to promote gender equality, reduce digital inequalities, and ensure a safe and inclusive environment in online communities. Future work should aim to explore research and new strategies to further deepen understanding of the relationship between gender and technology in the digital age.

By revisiting the cyberfeminism movement, this study aims to promote progress in this field and to build a more equitable and inclusive future for gender equality in the digital world. The continuing importance of cyberfeminism should not be overlooked. Cyberfeminism plays an important role today for the following reasons:

1. Digital Inequality: There are still issues of digital inequality around the world. Women are lagging in accessing and using digital technologies compared to men. Cyberfeminism provides an important framework to recognize, analyze and address these inequalities.

2. Online Violence: Women face harassment, threats, attacks, and other forms of violence online. Cyberfeminism offers awareness-raising, advocacy, and policy recommendations to combat online violence and ensure women's digital safety.

3. Gender Norms and Stereotypes: Gender norms and stereotypes continue to be prevalent in digital environments. Cyberfeminism offers a feminist perspective to question, refute and change these norms.

4. Gender Inequality in the Creation Process of Technology: Women are still in the minority and underrepresented in technology and software development processes. Cyberfeminism is a movement that strives to combat gender inequality in the creation process of technology and to encourage greater participation of women.

5. Digital Activism and Communities: Cyberfeminism is an important component of digital activism. Digital tools and social media platforms have become powerful tool for discussing feminist issues, raising awareness, and conducting activism activities. Cyberfeminism plays a pioneering role in this field.

For these reasons, cyberfeminism still plays an important role today. It is an important movement and current of thought to address the challenges women face in terms of equality, security and representation in the digital world and to combat gender inequality.

References

Afanasov, N. (2022). Cyberfeminism as science fiction. Drawn in Japan. *Galactica Media: Journal of Media Studies*. https://doi.org/10.46539/gmd.v4i1.248.

Arias-Rodriguez, A., & Sánchez-Bello, A. (2022). Informal learning with a gender perspective transmitted by influencers through content on YouTube and Instagram in Spain. *Social Sciences.* https://doi.org/10.3390/socsci11080341.

Bigman, Y., Wilson, D., Arnestad, M., Waytz, A., & Gray, K. (2020). Algorithmic discrimination causes less moral outrage than human discrimination. *Journal of Experimental Psychology. General.* https://doi.org/10.31234/osf.io/m3nrp.

Bimber, B. (2000). Measuring the gender gap on the Internet 1. *Social Science Quarterly,* 81, 868–876.

Bonezzi, A., & Ostinelli, M. (2021). Can algorithms legitimize discrimination? *Journal of Experimental Psychology. Applied.* https://doi.org/10.1037/xap0000294.

Citron, D. (2009). Law's expressive value in combating cyber gender harassment. *Michigan Law Review,* 108, 373–415.

Collins, P.H. (2015). Intersectionality's definitional dilemmas. *Annual Review of Sociology,* 41(1), 1–20. https://doi:10.1146/annurev-soc-073014-112142. (Erişim Tar: 18.07.2023).

Consalvo, Mia. "Cyberfeminism." *Encyclopedia of New Media.* Ed.. Thousand Oaks, CA: SAGE, 2002. 109–10. SAGE Reference Online. Web. 4 Apr. 2012.

Crowe, N., & Watts, M. (2014). 'When I click "ok" I become Sassy – I become a girl'. Young people and gender identity: subverting the 'body' in massively multi-player online role-playing games. *International Journal of Adolescence and Youth,* 19, 217–231. https://doi.org/10.1080/02673843.2012.736868.

da Rimini, F., Starrs, J., Pierce, J., & Barratt, V. (1991). *Cyberfeminist Manifesto for the 21st Century.* Adelaide, Australia: VNS Matrix.

Eklund, L. (2011). Doing gender in cyberspace: The performance of gender by female World of Warcraft players. *Convergence,* 17, 323–342. https://doi.org/10.1177/13548 56511406472.

Gajjala, R. (1999). 'Third World' perspectives on cyberfeminism. *Development in Practice,* 9, 616–619. https://doi.org/10.1080/09614529952774.

Giannini, T., & Bowen, J. (2016). Curating digital life and culture: Art and information, 237–244. https://doi.org/10.14236/EWIC/EVA2016.46.

Gilson-Ellis, J. (2001). Low and behold: voice ghosts in the new technoculture. *Digital Creativity,* 12, 77–88. https://doi.org/10.1076/digc.12.2.77.6860.

Hall, Kira (1996). "Cyberfeminism". Herring, S.C. (Ed.) *Computer-Mediated Communication: Linguistic, Social and Cross-Cultural Perspectives.* Amsterdam: John Benjamins Publishing Company, 147–170.

Haraway, D. (1991). A cyborg manifesto: Science, technology, and socialist feminism in the late twentieth century. At http://www.stanford.edu/dept/HPS/Haraway/Cybo rgManifesto.html, accessed September 12, 2006.

Hilbert, M. (2011). Digital gender divide or technologically empowered women in developing countries? A typical case of lies, damned lies, and statistics. *Development Economics: Women*. https://doi.org/10.1016/J.WSIF.2011.07.001.

Johnson, G. (2020). Algorithmic bias: on the implicit biases of social technology. *Synthese*, 198, 9941–9961. https://doi.org/10.1007/s11229-020-02696-y.

Kendall, L. (2000). "Oh no! I'm a nerd!". *Gender & Society*, 14, 256–274. https://doi.org/10.1177/089124300014002003.

Kluszczynski, R. (2005). Arts, media, cultures: Histories of hybridisation. *Convergence*, 11, 124–132. https://doi.org/10.1177//1354856505061059.

Lee, N. (2018). Detecting racial bias in algorithms and machine learning. *Journal of Information, Communication and Ethics in Society*. https://doi.org/10.1108/jices-06-2018-0056.

Lewis, R., Rowe, M., & Wiper, C. (2016). Online abuse of feminists as an emerging form of violence against women and girls. *British Journal of Criminology*, 57, 1462–1481. https://doi.org/10.1093/BJC/AZW073.

Maloney, M., Roberts, S., & Caruso, A. (2018). 'Mmm … I love it, bro!': Performances of masculinity in YouTube gaming. *New Media & Society*, 20, 1697–1714. https://doi.org/10.1177/1461444817703368.

Mishna, F., Schwan, K., Birze, A., Wert, M., Lacombe-Duncan, A., McInroy, L., & Attar-Schwartz, S. (2020). Gendered and sexualized bullying and cyber bullying. *Youth & Society*, 52, 403–426. https://doi.org/10.1177/0044118X18757150.

Mumporeze, N., & Prieler, M. (2017). Gender digital divide in Rwanda: A qualitative analysis of socioeconomic factors. *Telematics Informatics*, 34, 1285–1293. https://doi.org/10.1016/j.tele.2017.05.014.

Old Boys Network (1997). 100 Anti-theses of cyberfeminism. Electronic document at http://beingres.org/front-page/cyberfeminisminternational_web/.

Paasonen, S. (2011). Revisiting cyberfeminism. *Communications*, 36(3). https://doi.org/10.1515/comm.2011.017.

Plant, S. (1997). *Zeros + Ones: Digital Women + the New Technoculture*. New York: Doubleday.

Rambachan, A., Kleinberg, J., Ludwig, J., & Mullainathan, S. (2020). An economic perspective on algorithmic fairness. *AEA Papers and Proceedings*, 110, 91–95. https://doi.org/10.1257/pandp.20201036.

Sundén, J. (2008). Cyberfeminism. *The International Encyclopedia of Communication*. https://doi.org/10.1002/9781405186407.wbiecc178.

Taylor, K. (2017). *How We Get Free: Black Feminism and the Combahee River Collective*. Haymarket Books.

Valtchanov, B., Parry, D., Glover, T., & Mulcahy, C. (2016). 'A whole new world': Mothers' technologically mediated leisure. *Leisure Sciences*, 38, 50–67. https://doi.org/10.1080/01490400.2015.1043414.

Varol, S. F. (2014). Kadınların Dijital Teknolojiyle İlişkisine Ütopik Bir Yaklaşım: Siberfeminizm. *The Journal of Academic Social Science Studies.* 27, 219–234. http://dx.doi.org/10.9761/JASSS2463.

Vimalkumar, M., Singh, J., & Gouda, S. (2021). Contextualizing the relationship between gender and computer self-efficacy: An empirical study from India. *Information & Management*, 58, 103464. https://doi.org/10.1016/J.IM.2021.103464.

Vitis, L., & Gilmour, F. (2017). Dick pics on blast: A woman's resistance to online sexual harassment using humour, art and Instagram. *Crime, Media, Culture: An International Journal*, 13, 335–355. https://doi.org/10.1177/1741659016652445.

VNS Matrix (1991). Cyberfeminist manifesto for the 21st century. At http://www.obn.org/reading_room/manifestos/html/cyberfeminist.html, accessed July 17, 2007.

Wajcman, J. (2006). Technocapitalism meets technofeminism: Women and technology in a wireless world. *Labour & Industry: A Journal of the Social and Economic Relations of Work*, 16, 20–7. https://doi.org/10.1080/10301763.2006.10669327.

Wajcman, J. (2007). From women and technology to gendered technoscience. *Information, Communication & Society*, 10, 287–298. https://doi.org/10.1080/136911 80701409770.

Wajcman, J. (2010). Feminist theories of technology. *Cambridge Journal of Economics*, 34, 143–152. https://doi.org/10.1093/CJE/BEN057.

WEF (2017), The Global Gender Gap Report, http://www3.weforum.org/docs/WEF_GG GR_2017.pdf (15.10.2019).

WSIS-03/Geneva/Doc/4-E (2003) 'Declaration of principles. Building the information society: a global challenge in the new Millennium', [online] Available at: http://www.itu.int/wsis/ docs/geneva/official/dop.html.

Youngs, G. (2005). Ethics of access: Globalization, feminism and information society. *Journal of Global Ethics.* https://doi.org/10.1080/17449620500103849.

CHAPTER 3

From Cyberization to Feminization

Cyberfeminism

Oktay Hekimler

The transformation that has made itself felt in all areas of social and political life has also had a profound impact on social movements. Feminism, which advocates the view that women should no longer be an object but a subject in the writing of history and fights against sexism, gender exploitation and all forms of sexist oppression, has also had its share. Cyberfeminism, which entered our lives with digitalization and digital activism, has also seen technology as a tool to liberate women, based on the argument that digital technology is not as masculine as industrial technology. In this way, a new perspective has been brought to the relationship between gender and technology.

Cyberfeminism considers the transgender status offered by cyberspace as an advantage and focuses on the question of how digital technologies influence existing gender policies. Nevertheless, approaches that are sexist and marginalizing do not only exist at the local and national levels but also at the global level. It is impossible to establish peace unless we improve the situation of marginalized groups of people, those who are forced to live under oppression and domination. The processes of peace and democratization, the construction of security, universal human rights and minority rights are only possible through the implementation of policies that are free from all forms of sexism. Indeed, this fact necessitates breaking not only the patriarchal traditions that shape social relations but also the masculine character of international relations. Therefore, this justifies the arguments that foreign and development policies should also be feminized and that world peace can only be created in this way.

In this chapter, how cyberization affects feminist debates and how it transforms them has been evaluated. In this context, first, the relationship between feminism and cyberfeminism is introduced, and then, in the following sections, it tries to present how this transformation affects different fields by including sample texts and discussions in the literature in the light of cyberfeminism theories and perspectives. In conclusion, the influence of digital transformation on the debate on the feminization of foreign policy is evaluated, considering the masculine character of the international system.

1   Introduction

In today's world where the world and technology are in constant change, a broad range of fields from international politics to human rights are affected by this transformation, and feminism and feminist struggle have also been influenced by this change. The internet today is everywhere and used by everyone. In this regard, the internet (for the sake of consistency – others are used in lowercase) is not only a source of communication and information but also a new pillar of public deliberation. Nowadays, an individual's post on social media, a picture they publish or a tweet they tweet can reach a wide audience, thus paving the way for a digital but multidimensional debate. As internet use moves out of the computer and from the table to the palm of our hands through phones, the feminist struggle cannot be kept independent from this transformation. Moreover, the opinion that foreign policy should be feminized has now moved into the virtual world and turned into an issue discussed by large masses.

Nowadays, social media also hosts feminist debates, and a post, a message written, or a comment made under a photograph can lead to new discussions. Therefore, the struggle against the male-dominated understanding that now exists in the public domain also finds its counterpart in the virtual world. The male-dominated society and the gendered understanding normalized by it are thus attempted to be broken through social blogs and media accounts in this new field of negotiation. This technology change has also made it possible for a much wider range of people to take part in the debate, and to be involved in the negotiations. In other words, the voice of the street is carried to the virtual space and the virtual space to the street (Candemir, 2020: 158). In this way, gender, which is a derivative of social inequalities that constitute the background of many problems today, has become more questioned with technology.

Another question sought to be answered in the relationship between technology and social inequality is whether technology has a gender. In other words, it addresses the question of the impact of technology on the formation of existing inequality. The common perception is that technology is shaped by men, and as such, the technology that exists to this day legitimizes gender and inequality. That is, as each technology is recreated, it essentially renews the existing patterns in society and serves to normalize them. In this way, it deepens gender stereotypes.

The Feminist movement, which until recently had a negative approach to technology, attributing a masculine character to it, acknowledges that virtual technology has an emancipatory effect on women, albeit with its shortcomings.

Furthermore, it argues that technology is not masculine but feminine and that the muscle power that dominated technology in the past has been replaced by brain power. According to this self-described cyberfeminism movement, digital technology has taken on an increasingly feminine character, and it has even been possible to establish a relationship between women and machines. From this perspective, this study attempts to explain how feminism has evolved and how the cyber-feminist movement has established a link between women's emancipation and technology. In the conclusion of the study, it is tried to reveal how these developments are reflected in the idea that a feminist foreign policy should be created.

2   The Beginning of the Road: Feminism

In the narrowest sense, feminism can be defined as a doctrine that aims to expand the role and rights of women in society and fights for it. In this sense, it is a movement focused on eliminating all forms of inequality, sexism, gender exploitation and gender-based domination relations (Varol, 2014: 221). Feminism is a movement that aims to change the power relationship between men and women, a political project that aims to eliminate all forms of oppression, exploitation, and inequality (Altınbaş, 2010: 22). Feminism, which started as a mere doctrine in the early days, soon included activism, and over time turned into an organized action movement, and nowadays, digital activism has been added to this. In this way, feminism has become not only a suffragette movement, as Şirin Tekeli puts it, but also a multifaceted and long-term movement fighting for the emancipation of women and people, rather than a short-term movement focused on a single goal. In other words, it has been a movement that reacts to oppression, oppressed and all kinds of oppression relations, especially oppressed women (Saygılıgil and Berber, 2020: 14). Meanwhile, feminism is the biggest reaction to the exclusion of women from the public sphere and their confinement to the private sphere, to the distinction between public and private spheres. In this context, feminism also aims to keep the past debates, struggles for rights and political boundaries of women and all segments that support this idea alive, to keep these struggles alive and constantly negotiate, to keep the struggles in this field alive, to pass them on to new generations and to carry them to much wider platforms.

Despite the fact that feminism is a movement focusing or which focused on ending all forms of sexist oppression and domination, it is not possible to speak of a single type of feminism. While feminism struggles for the acceptance of women's existence through various types of feminism such as liberal feminism, socialist feminism, and radical feminism, today a new type of feminism has been added to this genre, which is defined as digital feminism, cyberfeminism or internet feminism. Liberal feminism is the first type of feminist struggle that emerged in the 19th century. Liberal feminists, influenced by liberalism, argue that women are human beings like men and that they have rights. In this context, it argues that as the importance and rights given to human beings improve, the situation of women will also improve (Altınbaş, 2010: 24). However, it also argues that inequality between men and women is in prominent contrast with liberal democracy and therefore women should be recognized as equal subjects. On the other hand, socialist feminism, which does not only focus on gender to explain the position of women, also focuses on the economic and social class position of women. In this regard, socialist feminism tries to explain the oppression, exploitation, and inequality of women in the capitalist system, which has patriarchal characteristics, with the division of labour in terms of gender (Özdemir, 2017: 399). Radical feminism, which argues that women are subjected to male oppression simply because they are women because of their gender, argues that patriarchal oppression against women, who build society, is at the root of all the evils in society. According to them, the only way to change this is to eliminate all existing gender roles and male-dominated understanding. As such, radical feminism aims to create a world without gender-based roles, characteristics, and behaviours among people (Çağıl, 2020: 7).

Likewise, feminism is a movement that transforms over time, developing in waves. Although there are opinions that its roots go back to the 16th century, the first wave of feminism corresponds to the 19th and early 20th centuries. Giving the right to vote for women and opening civil society to women are the prominent goals of this period. Although second-wave feminism began to emerge after World War II, it was not until the 1960s that it reached a certain maturity and became an organized movement. While the opening of the working life, in which women had been limitedly involved until then, the ability to perform different professions, and equal pay were the issues discussed, women's right to decide over their own bodies was perhaps the most prominent debate of this period. Third-wave feminism, which emerged as a reaction to and criticism of second-wave feminism, also acts as a spokesperson for women of different identities. The third wave, which draws attention to and includes women of different nationalities, ethnicities, religions, skin colours and cultures, is both a reaction to the second wave and a movement that complements its shortcomings. A prominent feature of this wave, which developed in the 1990s and beyond, is that it is now in a much more intense relationship with technology. Developments in the field of technology and the fact that women are more closely connected with information and communication technologies have brought the relationship between technology and women into question. In other words, the gender of technology and women have been discussed (Stoltenhoff and Raudonat, 2018: 131).

Feminists also address international relations and criticize the masculine structure and character of the international system and point to this as the source of the current conflictual situation. According to feminists, the theories that try to explain the international system try to understand events and phenomena with an extremely male-dominated perspective (Sönmezoğlu, Güneş, & Keleş, 2017: 58). This attitude has resulted in international relations being influenced by gender-blindness for many years and an understanding that ignores women. The main argument of feminist opposition in international relations is that women's lives and experiences have been and continue to be ignored in the analyses of international relations (True, 2014: 320). In an environment shaped by this understanding, where women are ignored, not accepted as subjects and not accepted as actors in political actions, it is not possible to build equality, peace or a system. In this world where women are ignored, there is only room for the concepts of war, independence, power and interest, and the construction of security, which are identified with masculinity, and have become generally accepted as symbols of masculinity. In this way, feminists not only unify the private and public spheres but also react to the distinction between domestic and foreign policy. According to feminists – security building is not only about military methods and politics, but security is also closely related to identities, namely gender and gender equality. Security is no longer a phenomenon that has only military and economic dimensions, but an organization in which all forms of violence and all forms of sexual violence are not permitted. Therefore, as long as a state allows inequalities, sexual discrimination, sexism, exploitation and oppression, it will not be possible to ensure peace and security either in the foreign policy of that country or in international relations. This makes it essential for the feminist struggle to be reflected on a broad scale extending to international politics, for foreign policy to be touched by women's hands and, moreover, for foreign policy to be feminized because the application of the ethical principles of feminist international relations to the global practices of policymakers and volunteers has still not reached the desired level (True, 2014: 316). The desired progress has still not been achieved on this matter. This fact shows how important it is for digital activism and digital feminism to bring every feminist struggle into the digital environment and thus discuss it on a much wider platform.

3   From Digital Activism to Cyberfeminist Manifesto

The widespread use of the internet is also reflected in social movements today. Digital activism can be narrowly summarized as the use of digital tools to create political change or resistance (Candemir, 2020: 158). This movement, which is called by different names such as cyber activism, internet activism, online activism, e-activism, etc., is first and foremost recognized as paving the way for a much more effective political participation to change the existing power relations in society. Digital activism is thus considered to complement traditional activism and make a positive contribution to the path of struggle. According to this view, digital activism means that the reception of protests in the online space has increased, the number of participants is higher than the number of offline protest participants, it is trackable, and this increases motivation. On the other hand, the negative criticism of digital activism is that it allows oppressive governments to maintain existing relations of domination and increase repression. According to the pessimistic view, the internet somehow liberates individuals, but at the same time it enables oppressive and authoritarian governments to crush, control and persecute dissenters. This situation deepens the existing inequality in the existing oppressor-oppressed relationship. Moreover, considering that access to digital technology and the internet varies from country to country, and that the biggest obstacle to becoming digitally literate is economic poverty, it is another fact that this opportunity is not open to all country populations. Another negative attitude towards digital activism is that it transforms individuals into passive individuals who are distant from the real world, abandoning the physical act of leaving the real public sphere where they struggle only at a desk. Another criticism is that digital activism, although it makes traditional activism easier and improves it, cannot radically change the existing power relations in societies and produce new types of effective activism (Candemir, 2020: 158).

This new movement, also known as digital feminism or virtual feminism, e-feminism, or online feminism, is the meeting of developments in information and communication technologies and the feminist struggle. The widespread use of virtual platforms and forums, news channels, virtual newspapers and magazines has made them easily accessible to Internet users, and discussions on the streets have been brought into the halls. Although non-virtual organizations and actions have continued in this new era, with the widespread use of digital technologies, this struggle has now been supported by virtual actions. In other words, two-way activism has emerged.

When it comes to the relationship between the use of technology and feminism, cyber feminists have been the most prominent in this debate. Donna

Haraway's "Manifesto for Cyborgs" and Sadie Plant's *Zeros + Ones* signaled the beginning of a new era in this direction. Donna Haraway laid the foundations of cyberfeminism in her Manifesto for Cyborgs, first published in 1987. Haraway, who made a new definition of feminism here, based on the relationship between humans and machines, argued that if this relationship becomes increasingly ambiguous, genders, that is, the categories of men and women, will become inactive (Reiche, 2018: 45). Haraway, who dreamed of a world without genders, "preferred to be a cyborg instead of a goddess", thus advocating an approach that is blind to gender rather than gender-emphasizing icons (Haraway, 1995: 35). For this reason, Haraway's attitude towards the gender debate has also been defined as Cyborg Feminism (Varol, 2014: 222). Cyborg, a combination of machine and organism, a fictional and hybrid entity, is a cybernetic organism. Cyborg is formed from the combination of human and non-human actors. Cyborg is a figure of today's politics of both domination and struggle (Bozok, 2019: 139). In Cyborg, the boundaries between machine and organism have disappeared, and, in the future, everyone will turn into a hybrid being consisting of machine and organism. With this state, Haraway argues that in the future, everyone will become Cyborgized and transform into a transgender being (Stoltenhoff and Raudonat, 2018: 131). Haraway has paved the way for the possibility of being transgender through Cyborg. The gradual blurring of existing borders has allowed the fragmented structure of identity to be recognized. It has now made it possible for gender to coexist with nationality, ethnicity, class, skin colour, religion, culture and similar inequalities.

In contrast, Sadie Plant referred to the gender of technology and argued that technology also has a gender. According to Sadie Plant, technology is not identical to man and does not have a masculine character, as has been argued so far. On the contrary, technology has a feminine character. Therefore, there is a close relationship between technology, machines and women. In her words, "As machines become smarter, this will lead to the liberation of women" (Plant, 1996: 232). The reason for such a conclusion is that modern technology, especially digital technology, is now feminine. The fact that the Internet has a feminine character will pave the way for women's emancipation in this context (Daniels, 2009: 104). According to Plant, technology will transform women's lives and thus liberate them. Inspired by the basic programming language of computers, the author refers to the feminine with zeros and the masculine with ones. As the virtual world takes on an increasingly feminine character, zeros will replace ones in the future, so an environment built on a sense of shame will be replaced by a non-linear environment (Daniels, 2009: 104). Sadie Plant's *Zeros + Ones* and Sandy Stone's *The War of Desire and Technology* are important and even the starting points of cyberfeminism. Sadie Plant claims that if the internet is not used as a tool of oppression, that is, as long as it is not monitored and regulated, it contributes to the weakening of male-dominated oppression and hegemony. As such, digital technology and the internet will liberate women and the world constructed by male-dominated and masculine values will lose its influence. Cyberfeminism is therefore a righteous rebellion and revolt of women against the patriarchal order that has oppressed them with digital technology, computers, and the internet. In other words, with the new technology, women were able to shake the foundations of this patriarchal system that had been trying to keep them in line until then.

4   Cyberfeminism as a Concept and Its Development

Cyberfeminism is conceived of as a heterogeneous field of theoretical-artistic positions and projects with roots in the 1990s (Mauß and Schrader, 2020: 39). This new deliberative field offered to users by the internet culture created by digital technology is described as a space where concepts such as gender, gender inequality, sexuality, decision-making over the body, taking your own future into your own hands and social equality meet. In this context, the cause of womanhood, which is as old as the history of humanity, meets with technology and the issues that feminism has been discussing since the past and the struggle for rights is now being carried to a new and multidimensional medium. Cyberfeminism is a combination of the words cybernetics and feminism that brings feminist struggle into the digital environment today. Although cyberfeminism also refers to the electronic environment of feminism, according to cyberfeminists, it is not correct to limit the theory in this way. Cyberfeminism can be interpreted as a posthuman revolt against the patriarchal system that brings women and computers together (Ateş, 2022: 2). In this way, feminism, which developed as a reaction to all kinds of exclusionary policies against women and fought for the visibility of all women, serving the purpose of women regaining the dignity they deserve and realizing their own historiography, is now moved to a wider and accessible supra-gender platform. Approaches in this direction, notably Donna Harvey's Cyborgs, inspire this new form of action, and the debates that have existed since the past are negotiated in a genderless transgender space. Issues related to identity, technology and the body are the focus of the Cyberfeminist movement, which aims to ensure that innovative media technology contributes to the construction of an egalitarian society (Stoltenhoff and Raudonat, 2018: 129). Sadie Plant's view of cyberfeminism conceptualizes the Internet as a structure compatible with women's fluid identities by shaking the traditional patriarchal character of technology

(Candemir, 2020: 160). In contrast to Susanna Paasonen, who describes cyberfeminism as a type of feminism that explores the relations between gender
and technology in digital media, Liesbet van Zoonen conceptualizes this new
type of feminism as academic and artistic practices that focus on the internet
and existing new technologies (Varol, 2014: 224). Susan Hawthorne and Renate
Klein point out that cyberfeminism is a philosophy formed by feminists who
argue that there is a power and power differential between men and women
in digital negotiations and struggle to change this situation (Hawthorne and
Klein, 1999: 131). So, what are the foundations of Cyberfeminism or Feminist
internet politics today? According to Waltraud Ernst, political action can never
be considered independent of feminist struggle. Although political action has
been left to institutional oblivion over time, there has recently been a growing
number of consciously activist feminist projects. This activist struggle takes
place both online and offline, that is, in the online as well as offline space. This
raises the question of how feminists use the digital world and networks as a
tool and instruments of struggle. According to Ernst, the important thing here
is not only to use these technologies as a means of liberating the digital world
from the dominance of the analogue world, which is closely intertwined with
the digital world, but also to use them as a means to bring this war to a victorious conclusion. This requires a deep knowledge of how relations of domination and power are created and imposed, and how they can be changed and
ultimately destroyed (Ernst, 2020: 528). In this context, Chela Sandoval recognizes cyberfeminism as a struggle for survival. In doing a methodology of the
oppressed, she argues that the infrastructures of media technologies should be
questioned and changed (Ernst, 2020: 528).

   In this way, cyberfeminism, which was born because of the widespread and
more accessible use of computers and the internet with the third-wave feminism movement, has reached a certain maturity with the fourth-wave feminism
movement. With this new era, the cyber environment has become a new space
for women to struggle for their rights with the development of social media
and the mobilization of technology. In other words, the public sphere has now
expanded to include the digital sphere and women's search for rights has been
carried to this wider platform and responded to here. What is remarkable is
that this is now a genderless, supra-gender platform. This means that the masculine character of the public sphere is now transformed into a genderless form
as much as possible. On platforms such as social networks, Instagram, Twitter,
etc., which are now a reflection of the current society, the user moves out of an
identity normalized by patriarchal gender inequality and assumes a genderless and even supra-gender identity. In this way, cyberfeminism becomes the

equivalent of a struggle on the digital platform against the mentality that has normalized gender inequality until then.

Like Sadie Plant and Donna Harvey, VNS Matrix is one of the most important sources influencing the development of cyberfeminism. Founded by four feminist women artists, VNS Matrix pioneered theory-based activism focused on women and technology. The main debates focused on the influence of women in technology and art, and a guerrilla-style feminist struggle based on art and poetry was adopted. VNS Matrix focuses on examining society, identity and gender relations in cyberspace stating that its aim is to analyze the narratives of domination and control surrounding technological culture (Erek, 2009). The movement, which argues that women are active in the production and use of digital technologies, in other words, they are subjects in the production and use of digital life, has pointed out that women are still underrepresented in this arena (Ganz and Meßner, 2015: 62). The VNS Matrix has declared war on the male-dominated order and its symbols, starting from the fact that women are subjects, not objects, but that this continues even in the world of digital technology within the framework of existing stereotypes. The method of this war is to eliminate all the patterns, discipline, ethical values, prohibitive morality, ideas, and values of this male-dominated order. The traditional system is built with male-dominated patterns and all kinds of dilemmas that are part of it are the topics that need to be fought. If an egalitarian order is desired, it is essential to abolish the ambivalent distinction in which the intellect is superior to the emotions and the masculine is superior to the feminine. The text of this idea is the "Cyberfeminist Manifesto of the 21st Century" published by VNS Matrix (Ganz and Meßner, 2015: 68). The essence of the manifesto published by VNS Matrix is to break the masculine character and negative effects of technology and to prevent anything that ignores or alienates women in electronic art projects (Erek, 2009).

A milestone in the development of cyberfeminism was the first International Conference on Cyberfeminism. Held on September 20, 1997, in Germany, this first international organization of cyberfeminism started with the question of what cyberfeminism is and added a new impetus to the women's movement by seeking answers to this question (Reiche, 2018: 45). What is noteworthy is that while the question of what cyberfeminism is was sought to be answered, the answer was that what cyberfeminism is not. The answers found were between ambiguity and versatility. Perhaps the most important conclusion reached at this conference, where it was agreed that there is no single and common definition of cyberfeminism, was "Cyberfeminism is not a woman alone". It was the Old Boys Network (OBN), which claimed that it was a real and virtual coalition, that spearheaded the convening of the International Conference on

Cyberfeminism. Moreover, OBN, which is considered as the first international alliance of cyberfeminism, was the movement that brought the gender debate to the new media plane (Ganz and Meßmer, 2015: 70).

In this framework, cyberfeminism, on the one hand, focuses on the gender problem brought about by industrial gender, which has so far assumed a masculine character, and seeks an answer to the question of whether technologies have gender. Today, it examines the impact of digital technologies, which it argues have a feminine character, on gender. This framework focuses on the advantages of ambiguous gender or genderlessness in the digital environment where brain power replaces muscle power and their impact on women's struggle for rights. With the increasing number of websites and e-publications, a new space of freedom is being created for women in the virtual world, which is considered a kind of freedom space, and above all, it recognizes that the reconstruction of society and thus the reconstruction of women's freedom is possible in this genderless environment.

Cyberfeminism, which coincided with the growth and development of the internet and digital culture during the period when the fourth wave of feminism gained power, also developed and transformed in waves within itself. Cyberfeminism, just like feminism, had two waves because of differentiations (Başpınar, 2016). While the first wave of cyberfeminists argued that there was an innate relationship between women and machines, they brought discussions on gender and identity politics to the digital world. On the other hand, those who now recognize themselves as the second wave of cyberfeminism have primarily rebelled against the term feminism (Schmidt, 2020: 3). As such, while the first wave of cyberfeminism was a kind of liberal cyberfeminism movement, the second wave can now be read as radical cyberfeminism. While the first one sees technology as a tool that liberates women in the digital space, the second one is embodied in groups that are open only to women, which men cannot enter, and which are formed by women against male attacks (Kuni, 2002).

5   Cyberfeminist Strategies and Digital Actions

Cyberfeminist activist individuals or groups have developed and implemented different methods and strategies from the very beginning of the movement. The creation of numerous digital platforms, primarily aimed at reaching and spreading this heterogeneous and international movement to a wider audience, has been a prominent way of doing so. In addition to the ones that still exist today, it was also possible to create a wide network through websites such as FACES and X Xero, which no longer exist today (Stoltenhoff and Raudonat, 2018: 132). In addition, other platforms, such as the Old Boys Network, which is predominantly German-speaking, and Dolores' Bulimic Breakfast, have made the aims, objectives and means of cyberfeminism visible. Most of these internet-initiated groups are artistic in nature. While VNS Matrix or the anonymous group Guerilla Girls, which are frequently mentioned in the study, are examples of this, another example is the SubRosa movement. Initiated by US writer and artist Faith Wilding, this group is made up of artists and scholars who support the cyberfeminist movement. Both Old Boys and SubRosa offer the possibility of organizing, exchanging and presenting cyberfeminist projects. SubRosa's work is more multimedia and multiperspective, focusing on Bio and Reproduction technologies (Stoltenhoff and Raudonat, 2018: 132). While feminism has reached its fourth wave as a result of this collaboration with digitalization, the increased use of social media tools, especially by women, has enabled them to create an effective and efficient online movement. Women now initiate online protests individually or in groups, paving the way for discussions that reach very large masses in cyberspace. Days of Choice, No More Page, Everyday Sexism Projekt, Slut Walk protests are some prominent examples (Candemir, 2020: 161). Perhaps one of the most striking actions in this direction is the "'Gather your legs and don't occupy my seat' protest" in Turkey. According to Candemir's quotation from Tuğçe Eda Sarıgül, a member of the Istanbul Feminist Collective who initiated the action, the action was first initiated as a reaction to men sitting with their legs open, and photographs of the action were taken and hung on public transportation vehicles (minibuses) travelling between some districts of Istanbul. In this way, they tried to draw attention to this attack on women, male harassment and occupation. However, the movement did not stop there, the photos in question were hashtagged on social media channels with the slogan "Gather your legs and don't occupy my space". This way, the post, which reached a wide audience in a very short time and was retweeted, enabled this issue to be widely discussed online and offline. Many women showed solidarity against a violation against themselves that they were uncomfortable with, angry about but could not speak out against. As such, this issue, which had been the subject of outrage, but which could not be discussed with a wider audience, has been able to spark a collective outrage and desire for struggle through social media. It is a simple (#) sign that gives a boost to the spirit of solidarity and collective struggle among women, but its broad inclusiveness demonstrates once again the importance of digitalization and feminist solidarity. Jutta Weber questions the use of the female body in pornographic sites on the internet, based on the movement Women with Beard in her project "Irony, Erotics and Techno-Politics: Cyberfeminism as a Virus in the New World Order". The Dutch movement Women with Beard initiated the debate on whether images of people should not often follow a heteronormative logic in order to be considered erotic, both in mass media and in art (Weber, 2001: 94).

The cyberfeminist and internet activist artist Cornelia Sollfrank, founder of the Old Boys Network, not only drew attention to the exclusion of women in the art scene, but also to the conservatism of the field, even though it portrays itself as pro-change. In 1997, the Hamburg Art Gallery in Germany organized the Internet Art "Extension Competition", to which many women artists in the field of avant-garde art applied. However, the commission awarded the first three money prizes to male artists and did not include any of the women artists in this category (Vorkoeper, 1999). However, what the commission would learn much later, and what it would find unethical, would be Sollfrank's method of what would come to be known as hacking activism. Cornelia Sollfrank has enabled 127 women artists (Fake artists), whose identities, names, postal addresses and e-mail addresses she created with the support of other women artists through a hacking program she wrote, to participate in the NetSanat competition organized by the Hamburg Art Gallery. In this way, she increased the number of women participants. However, despite this number of women participants, only male artists, not any women, won the first three prizes and the cash prize. Through this incident, she protested against inequality in the art community and drew attention to the sexism there.

6   Internet (Cyber)feminism: an Answer to the Need for a New Feminism?

Today, many women are now supporting struggles in cyberspace and fighting for their existence with a slogan that can be summarized as "The Internet is feminine, and we are increasingly political". Indeed, "equality" as understood by feminists or progressives has still not been achieved today. The feeling of not having been able to create a reaction to this despite all the struggles, like everyone and everything marginalized and marginalized by the media, politics and society, discharges this disappointment on the internet. The internet now serves this kind of mission because political protests and movements are organized here before they take to the streets. In other words, they meet here before acting on the streets (Bücker, 2011). Although Teresa Bücker welcomes this development as "Welcome Network/Internet Feminism," she does not recognize it as a new trend or wave of the women's movement. Internet Feminism is not a new type of game for the women's movement. According to her, this child that has already been born has already been baptized long ago: Cyberfeminism. However, Feminist Web/Internet Culture, Pop Feminism, Queer Feminist Blogs, or Girls on Web Society ... are just new labels for internet feminism that brings together activists around the world. In this way, people were given a new stimulus to "stand up and change things" (Bücker, 2011). This has worked in a similar way with internet politics. The phenomenon of talking politics and discussing politics on the internet, which at first was only in the hands of low-level parties, but voluntary and engaged, has evolved into a modern political space fostered by the commitment of large numbers of people. "While politics is boring, network politics is sexy and fun. While politicians wear grey suits and beige suits, online politicians can wear hoodies or high heels" (Bücker, 2011). With the opportunity provided by the Internet, political debates are now being moved to this modern political space, and the reason behind this is that it is inclusive, attractive, and pluralistic for a wide range of people. According to Annekathrin Kohout, contemporary feminism consists of two poles. The first is classical written theoretical feminism. The second is focused on images and the visual and expresses itself more through artistic devices and social networks. In this way, for example, a picture of a (naked) woman breastfeeding her child can trigger a new debate. For some, this picture is a symbol of women's liberation/emancipation. The opposite side may read this as confining women to the classic role of motherhood. Or whether a t-shirt with the words Girl-Power on it symbolizes an innocent naive young girl or brings a new question mark (Kohout, 2019: 32). As can be seen, a simple picture shared on social media such as Twitter, Instagram, etc. can suddenly start a huge debate on a woman's will to exist.

Internet feminism encompasses on the one hand a critical feminist perspective on internet politics and on the other hand it includes different activists who bring different feminist issues into the online space and fight for them. The latter can often be subjected to sexist if not outright misogynistic, comments. In Laurie Penny's words, "A woman's opinion here can become the miniskirt of the internet." Indeed, harassment that exists offline continues to exist in the online space (Aigner and Schiff, 2023).

This new form of feminism is united in purpose with the other. Both aim to create, as Virginia Woolf argues, "a room for women". They both want to share knowledge and experience, break down established stereotypes, build solidarity and dispel existing misconceptions. Internet feminists do not claim to fight for a better feminism than the women's movements of previous eras and previous generations. On the contrary, this movement and the platform on which it takes place are open to everyone. The prevailing understanding here is not to exclude, ignore and discriminate, but instead to be open and inviting to all. There is no centre (base), no board of directors, and no leadership status. In fact, this political movement is not directed from a centre, nor is it dependent on it. Moreover, this environment has enabled women of all ages and movements to come together. Women of all age groups, social classes and professions can come together to discuss and debate. Most importantly, online feminism brings together people who have never had any feminist affiliation because there are no places that offer this opportunity, especially to young people. Apart from the internet, neither the media nor other places offer young people a pluralistic discussion environment where gender equality is dominant. Many young people are familiar with and have grown up with the now clichéd views of Alice Schwarzer, Monique Wittig and others, symbolic figures of the feminist struggle, who advocated the now clichéd views of the lie that women are equal, that women must be liberated, and so on. However, for the first time, the internet has shown these people, who are sensitive to these issues and even filled with a certain anger and reaction, that they are not alone through social media. It showed them that the anger and excitement that had accumulated inside them was not only experienced by them but also by others, that there were others who thought and felt like them, that they were not crazy. The internet told them that there are thousands of others who think and feel like them and showed them that they are not alone.

The fact that many women and men are sensitive to feminist issues and advocate for them has become increasingly visible through social networks. Even if this is sometimes a conscious act, sometimes mere coincidence can draw someone into a debate and make them a party to it. In this context, the principle of coincidence is extremely effective in connecting internet users with important feminist debates. For example, countless users have created a kind of "feminist wish list" of their feminist wishes in the form of a tweet. This list was created with the hashtag #Feministwishlist, and in a very short period, the event generated numerous demands and opinions with a global perspective through a very high number of participants. This is how digital activism and its derivative, online feminism, are gaining more and more adherents. In times and on issues where it is not enough just to change laws to achieve gender equality, especially when politics is not brave enough, it is almost an important tool in this struggle. Equality is first and foremost about eliminating stereotypes and enabling different attitudes and new values and discourses (Martin, 2011). For this reason, online debates have for years been an important contribution to the offline struggle for feminist work by different groups. It reinforces this struggle in the 2000s because the struggle is here: the activism on the internet, web pages, tweets, a "like". ... The debate here contributes to the creation of a new consciousness, to draw attention to issues, to discuss values and to put pressure on decision-makers (Martin, 2011). This requires feminists to build new alliances, to focus on new issues and debates, and to finance these activities. After a certain point, the support provided only by volunteers, even online, is insufficient for the effectiveness of negotiations and actions (Bücker, 2011). Moreover, it is contrary to the spirit of feminism, which demands equality for all, that the struggle in this direction should be carried out only by a small, privileged group of people with a certain level of income and access to all kinds of technological tools and equipment. It is unacceptable that those who have the financial means and the free time to engage in political debates are given the opportunity to fight for this cause, while those who do not have the means are completely forgotten and left to their fate. Therefore, it is only with strong financial support that this struggle can be for and inclusive of everyone. Internet politics is nowadays "en vogue" (Bücker, 2011). Digital activism has become a kind of healing prescription for those who want to win back young, informed and educated voters. Politicians, who are aware of how active young people are and that they are potential voters, are therefore paying more and more attention to their demands to win them over. This is also an advantage for internet feminism, a form of digital activism.

Women who are committed to the feminist struggle not only promote themselves on their own blogs or web pages, but also join their strengths through the www, creating solidarity, as in the case of Feministing or Featurette. They can also, for example, fight for more widespread use of the contraceptive pill through online petitions such as Change.org or draw attention to malnutrition through a link published in high-rated publications such as Germany's Next Model (Knop, 2014). According to Susanne Klingler, the effectiveness of such petitions depends on the fact that they contain concrete demands (Reim, 2008: 2). However, campaigns do not always bring direct results, especially when a problem has been around for a long time and is complex and controversial. The debate on prostitution is a case in point (Knop, 2014). The under-utilization of other tools in women's research and projects, such as crowdfunding, is also a disadvantage according to Magdalena Köster, author of "Watch-Salon". Therefore, it is important to take the struggle to traditional media as well as online, to negotiate on a wide platform without #hashtags or #hashtags, in order to achieve the goal, because they take into account social networks and the discussions there. The fact that there is no longer a single talk show where Twitter comments are not read and taken into account is the most concrete evidence of this (Köster, 2017). According to Susanne Klingner, the nomination of feminist internet projects for the Grimme Online Award is another development in recent years, which she sees as a turning point for feminist struggle (Knop, 2014).

However, despite all these positive developments, there is a flip side to the coin. In the digital struggle, women are often confronted with insulting or threatening counter-messages. The reaction here varies from person to person. Some respond, some ignore the comment, some delete the message entirely or file a criminal complaint. One example is to publicize any insulting message and draw attention to this harassment. The widespread perception is that people's websites or blogs are private, like a home, and therefore it is up to the individual to decide who can and cannot access them. In other words, "I now decide who and how to litter in front of my house." The other negative side of the coin is that not everyone benefits equally from the opportunities offered by the web. Although cyberfeminists argue that digital technology is feminine and that the masculine character of industrial technology has been eroded, not everyone can benefit equally from this opportunity. Moreover, beyond connectivity/technological constraints, many factors – religion, social or ethnic identity, financial status, and education – can limit or even make it impossible for women to take advantage of this gift. Not all people have equal resources and opportunities to participate in different deliberative forums where they can express themselves. In 2013, for example, a number of activists launched a campaign under the title #Call for Sexist Deliberation (Aigner and Schiff, 2023). Although the aim was to draw attention to all kinds of sexist treatment that women are subjected to in their daily lives, the most vulnerable groups (transsexuals, asylum seekers and socially excluded women) were not included for the reasons (Aigner and Schiff, 2023). Moreover, this desperate situation continues to this day.

7   The Contribution of the Virtual World to Feminist Foreign Policy Making

In this way, many women take a position against inequality and discriminatory policies and try to draw attention to themselves and the world they live in. In this way, they question both the society in which they try to exist, which has so far failed to take them into consideration, and the existing inequitable structure of the international system. Indeed, it is not only society that is inequitable, but also the international community and the international system, hence international politics.

If the present conflicts, wars and power and interest-oriented international conflicts are the result of this system, which is always constructed with a masculine character, this reaction, this counter stance should extend from the bottom up. In this context, there is now a movement called internet or network feminism in which women can question the entire international system and have broad participation. The support from all over the world for Mahsa Amini, who was forced to die in Iran because she did not comply with the compulsory dress code imposed by a male-dominated system men drew the shape, can perhaps be considered one of the biggest actions of internet users in recent years. The support of sisters around the world for an unknown country and an unknown woman (human being), and the impact of the campaign on other sisters in Iran demonstrate the power of not only digital activism but also online feminism. As a result, the target was not only to draw attention to a violation of women but also to a regime and its practices that contradict the norms and universal values of the international community. In this way, the women of the free world were able to reach out through the internet to their sisters in other parts of the world who did not have this right. The online world succeeded where the offline world could not, and women around the world drew attention to the lawlessness of the international system based on their sisters (Mahsa Amini and others). This large solidarity network that women have created through the internet has shown the truth of the statement "If women could share stories they would find patterns. They could be allies instead of rivals". Women are everywhere and even the spirit of time has had to adjust itself to this solidarity between technology and women.

However, it is not only women in Iran who are resisting regimes that oppress and even ignore them, exclude them with discriminatory policies up to the death penalty, and demand a free world. In Afghanistan, Ukraine, Belarus, Colombia, and many other places around the world, women are fighting against patriarchal violence and wars with all their bodies and strength at the risk of their lives. And all this while feminist demands such as gender equality, human rights for women and LGBTIQ people or anti-racism are not yet fully on the agenda of international human rights and peace policies, neither in the United Nations nor in national politics. This fact shows that foreign policy must also be feminized, otherwise, it is not possible to build a non-sexist and non-equalitarian order in the international community. Yet feminist movements have always been the driving force behind social change and changes in national and international politics. Every small step has somehow led to major victories for gender equality and democracy. One of these is the Women, Peace and Security Agenda adopted by the United Nations Security Council, which recognizes prominent gender perspectives and forms of gender-based violence in war. Similarly, the adoption of a feminist foreign and development policy by a number of countries are the important achievement of recent years.

Even though the first foundations of a feminist and democratic foreign policy can be traced back to the 1915 resolution of the international women's peace organization, Women's International League for Peace and Freedom (WILPF), there is a growing demand for it. Feminist Foreign and Development Policy is gaining more and more adherents around the world. WILPF was founded at the first Women's Peace Conference, which resisted World War I and the patriarchal world order, demanding disarmament, an end to the arms trade, more peace education, the democratization of foreign policy and the fair representation of women in (foreign) political decisions. In 2014, 99 years after these demands, Sweden became the first country to declare a feminist foreign policy with the declaration of its Foreign Minister Margot Wallström. In 2023, Canada, Mexico, France, Spain, Luxembourg, Chile, Germany and the Netherlands also adopted feminist forms of foreign and development policy, paving the way for women's rights in conflicts and wars, the fight against women's poverty and, above all, for women to be more present at the political negotiating table and in decision-making positions (Heinrich Böll Stiftung, 2021).

Over time, there has been a strong political and social momentum for feminist approaches, practices and positions in foreign and development policy. However, the effectiveness of these measures taken by states in the transformation process is a matter of debate. It is not easy for a state to eradicate the inequitable values inherited by a society built on a patriarchal foundation and to build feminist politics. Therefore, the feminization of foreign policy is ambivalent (Scheyer, 2023). On the one hand, decades of struggle, resistance and lobbying have made feminist issues visible at the level of government and foreign affairs. On the other hand, feminist foreign policy is still far from bringing about the systematic transformation demanded by feminist movements. In fact, the right-wing government established in Sweden in 2022 abolished the feminist foreign policy resolution. This shows that the future of this project is uncertain but still essential for world peace.

Nevertheless, sufficient steps towards the feminization of foreign policy, as in the case of gender equality, have still not been taken. There are many reasons for this. One of the reasons behind this is the current global anti-gender (in)equality attitude, but another reason is the reluctance of governments to gain expertise in technology, innovation, and digital education. One of the most concrete indicators of this is the case of Germany. Although the German Federal Government has declared a feminist foreign policy, it has not shown sufficient commitment to involve civil society (Menninger, 2023).

The UN Commission on the Rights of Women (CSW) takes important initiatives in this direction and draws attention to this issue both online and offline. The UN Commission on the Rights of Women (CSW) takes important initiatives in this direction and draws attention to this issue both online and offline. At its 67th session, held on March 6–17, 2023, the CSW discussed the digitalization of education in the digital age, as well as the development of innovation and technological change to achieve gender equality and empower all women and girls (wilpf.de). Members of the Women's International League for Peace and Freedom (WILPF), who participated in the session from different parts of the world, drafted a statement focusing on gender-based online violence, weapons technology, and the ecological impact of technological advances, but still made limited progress. According to Jennifer Menninger, the biggest shortcoming is the lack of a policy that advocates for global justice and strengthens the rights of everyone, including LGBTIQ people, in the final declarations of such meetings. Violence prevention is addressed at the individual rather than the collective level. This ignores the global concentration of power of big tech companies and mass surveillance by states. As a result, alternatives to, for example, the lifelong retention of personal data and the development of data capitalism have not yet been developed (Menninger, 2023). Similarly, while the Final Declaration emphasized the implementation of Resolution 1325 "Women, Peace and Security", the negative impact of new warfare technologies (e.g., cyber, drones, autonomous weapon systems) on women and human rights was either not addressed at all or not sufficiently.

The real negotiation is still on the street, where brave women are fighting for this cause all over the world and demanding a systemic transformation. Despite different contexts, reactions and perceptions of threats, they are all opposed to masculine violence, exploitative relations, and the waste of resources in ways that touch on environmental and climate policies. Feminist foreign and development policies, therefore, need to focus more on these issues, support movements that struggle for them, and ensure that states take more responsibility for them, because women's power and capacity to do so, and their bargaining space, are limited. Civil society and critical (feminist) voices must be well coordinated, and resources and energy must be pooled effectively to fill feminist foreign policy with content and practice, so that the decisions taken are not politically emptied or instrumentalized by decision-makers. This requires a struggle both online and offline. Therefore, more discussion of this struggle in the digital environment will contribute positively to the creation of a feminist foreign policy. Moving this struggle to the digital environment, where technology is now free from the oppression of the masculine gender, will bring it closer to its goal through the establishment of an effective network system. The aim of such a network should be to support intersecting feminist foreign and development policy, create an effective information network, build mutual solidarity, and create a strong lobby. Furthermore, civil society will be more actively involved in this process. This would bring together a wide range of organizations, individuals and groups working for peace, justice, anti-discrimination, gender equality, the fight for the rights of all (including LGBTIQ) and anti-racism and create a broader space for deliberation that includes the citizen in the street. Moreover, those who do not identify as Feminists will also be able to take part in this negotiation.

8   Conclusion

Today, society, which is built on a male-dominated foundation, still continues to put pressure on women and all kinds of others. However, the number of individuals using digital technologies is increasing day by day. This development has enabled the problem that exists in society to move from the offline to the online sphere and to meet with a much wider audience. Technology is no longer only a means of maintaining the status quo but also serves to transform it. In this context, changing technology and how it contributes to women and the women's question, and to what extent it contributes to the emancipation of women, and indeed all kinds of "others", has been a topic of debate for the last few years.

In this context, cyberfeminists ascribe a special mission to digital technology and see it as a tool to save women. Cyberfeminists, who attribute the oppression and authoritarian attitude in society to the patriarchal structure, see industrial technology, which has a masculine character, as a collaborator of this domination relationship in society. Therefore, the path to women's freedom requires technology to be freed from its masculine character. However, digital technologies and the virtual world have created a whole new space for women. They have paved the way for women to have a space beyond the "room of one's own" that Virginia Woolf desired for every woman: a space for negotiation where gender is not determinative.

However, the reality invites us to think a little more because today, not all women benefit from digital technologies at the same rate. It is a fact that this digital saviour, which has been entrusted with such a sacred mission, does not extend the same hand to all others, and does not carry them to an equal and free world. Differences in levels of development, income distribution, education, and technical infrastructure mean that not all women benefit equally from digital technology. Many discriminatory and exclusionary treatments are still unknown or ignored. Moreover, even those who can benefit from the blessings of digital technology are still not fully free from the harassment and oppression of the dominant culture and masculine values of society. At the same time, digital technology, which is seen as a saviour for women and others, continues to transmit the traditional patterns, and oppressive and sexist policies of those who marginalize them to those who give them credibility. Moreover, there is still a profound difference between the virtual world and the real world. Therefore, it is necessary to recognize the offline and online space, rather than limiting the struggle and action to a single space. The struggle will continue both on the street and in the digital space. In this struggle, which extends from the international community to the family, women will continue to need the support of the state, but also their own virtual and real rooms.

References

Aigner, İ. & Schiff, A. (2023) Netzfeminismus und seine Grenzen, *Wir Frauen*, Frühjahr, 1/2023, https://wirfrauen.de/netzfeminismus-und-seine-grenzen/, (17.05.2023).

Altınbaş, D. (2010). Feminist Tartışmalarda Liberal Feminizm, *Kadın Araştırmaları Dergisi*, Sayı: 9, s. 21–52.

Ateş, T.N. (2022). Siberfeminizm Üzerine Bir İnceleme, https://thepentacle.org/2022/09/18/siberfeminizm-uzerine-inceleme-elestiri, (02.05.2023).

Başpınar, E. (2016). Bir Siberfeminist Manifestosu. Siber Feminizm Nedir? http://elonse.blogspot.com/2016/09/bir-siberfeminist-manifestosu.html, (02.05.2023).

Böll Stiftung, H. (2021). Ed: Meike Fernbach, Feministische Aussenpolitik ein Leitfaden zur Praktischen Umsetzung, s. 6.

Bozok, N. (2019). Herkesle ve Kimsesiz. Türler Arasında ve Kökensiz Siborg: Donna Haraway'in Düşüncesinde Feminist Bir Beden Politikasının İmkanları, Vira Verita E-Dergi, Sayı: 9, s. 128–148.

Bücker, T. (2011). Viele neue Wellen: Der Netz Feminismus, *Frankfurter Allgemeine*, 17. November. 2011.

Candemir, D.M. (2020). 2000'lerde Feminizm: Türkiye'de Feminist Hareketler ve Dijital Aktivizm, içinde, *Modern Türkiye'de Siyasal Düşünce: Feminizm*, İletişim Yayınları, s. 159–183.

Çağıl, A. (2020). Feminizm ve Politika İlişkisi Bağlamında Radikal Feminizm, *Ağrı İslami İlimler Dergisi*, Sayı: 6, s. 136–146.

Daniels, J. (2009). Rethinking cyberfeminisms: Race, gender and embodiment. *Women's Studies Quarterly*, C: 37, s. 101–124.

Erek, A. (2009). Siberkültürün Olduğu Yerde Siberfeminzme de İhtiyaç Vardır, https://yenimedya.wordpress.com/tag/siber-feminizm/, (03.05.2023).

Ernst, W. (2020). "Feministische Netzpolitik und Netzaktivismus". In Ed: Tanja Thomas ve Ula Wischermann, *Feministische Theorie und und Kritische Medienkulturanalyse*, Transcript Verlag, 523–539. doi.org/10.1515/9783839440841-051.

Ganz, K. & Meßmer, A.K. (2015). "Anti Genderismus im İnternet, Digitale Öffentlichkeiten als Labor eines neuen Kulturkampfes". İn Ed: Sabine Hark &Paula

İrene Villa, *Anti Genderismus: Sexualität und Geschlecht als Schauplältze Aktüeller Politischer Auseinandersetzungen,* Bielefeld, s. 59–77.

Haraway, D. (1995). "Ein Manifest für Cyborgs". In Ed. Carmen Hammer & İmmanuel Sties, *Die Neuerfindung der Natur. Primaten, Cyborgs und Frauen,* Frankfurt, Campus Verlag, s. 33–72.

Hawthorne, S & Klein, R. (1999). *Cyberfeminism. Connectivity, Critique and Creativity,* Melbourne, Spinfex Press, s. 131.

Knop, A. (2014). Netzfeminismus-die jüngste Welle der Frauenbewegung, https://watch-salon.blogspot.com/2014/06/netzfeminismus.html.

Kohout, A. (2019). *Netzfeminismus,* Wagenbach Verlag, Berlin, s. 32.

Köster, M. (2017). Feministisch Alter Werden: Wie Geht Das? *Watch Salon,* https://watch-salon.blogspot.com/2017/11/Feministisch-aelter-werden.html, (09.05.2023).

Kuni, V. (2002). Kreuz-und Que(e)rfahrerinnen im Cyberspace. Schöne Neue Welt, https://www.querelles-net.de/index.php/qn/article/view/171/179, (08.05.2023).

Martin, C.E. (2011). You are the NOW of now. The future of online feminism, *The Nation,* https://www.thenation.com/article/archive/you-are-now-now-future-online-feminism/, (19.05.2023).

Mauß, B. & Schrader, G. (2020). Computerisirung und Frauenarbeitsplätze:Feministische Perspektiven auf İnformations und Kommunikations Technologien, *Expertise für den Dritten Gleichbestellungsbericht der Bundesrepublik,* Berlin, s. 39–42.

Menninger, J. (2023), CSW67 Verpasste Chance für eine gerechte Politik im Digitalen Zeitalter, 31.03.2023, https://www.wilpf.de/csw67-verpasste-chance, (19.05.2023).

Özdemir, Ö. (2017). İki Sistemli Kuram Olarak Sosyalist Feminizm, Karadeniz Sosyal Bilimler Dergisi, Cilt: 9, Sayı: 2, s. 395–417.

Plant, S. (1996). On the Matrix: Cyberfeminist Simulations," in *Cultures of the Internet: Virtual Spaces, Real Histories, Living Bodies,* ed. Rob Shields (London: Sage, 1996), 170–183.

Plant, S. (2020). "On the Matrix: Cyberfeminist Simulations", In Ed: Tanja Thomass ve Ulla Wischermann) *Feminnistische Theorie und Kritische Medien Kulturanalyse,* De Gruyter Verlag, s. 232.

Reiche, C. (2018). Cyberfeminismus: Was Soll das Heissen? https://www.gender.hu-berlin.de/de/publikationen/gender-bulletin-broschueren/bulletin-texte/texte-24/texte24pkt4.pdf, (01.05.2023).

Reim D. (2008), Alpha Mädchen und İkonen des Feminismus, https://www.nomos-elibrary.de/10.5771/1866-377X-2008-3-159.pdf?download_full_pdf=1&page=0, (09.05.2023).

Saygılıgil, F. and Berber, N. (2020). Modern Türkiye'de Siyasi Düşünce: Feminizm. Cilt 10, İstanbul: İletişim.

Scheyer, V. (2023), Feministische Aussenpolitik: Ein ambivalentes Projekt, (31.03.2023), https://www.wilpf.de/feministische-aussenpolitik-ein-ambivalentes-projekt/, (05.05.2023).

Schmidt, F. (2020). Digital Policy: A Feminist İntroduction, https://eu.boell.org/sites /default/files/20212/Digital%20Feminist%20Policy_Introduction_Conclusion.pdf, (08.05.2023).

Sönmezoğlu, F., Güneş, H. & Keleş, E. (2017). Uluslararası İlişkilere Giriş, DER Yayınları, İstanbul, s. 58–59.

Stoltenhoff, A.K. & Raodonat, K. (2018). Digitalisierung (Mit)gestallten: Was Wir Vom Cyberfeminismus Lernen Können, GENDER, Heft: 2, s. 128–141.

True, J. (2014), "Feminizm". In Uluslararası İlişkiler Teorileri, Ed: Scott Burchill ve Andrew Linklater (çev. Muhammed Ağcan & Ali Aslan), Küre Yayınları, İstanbul, 315–344.

Varol, S.F. (2014). Kadınların Dijital Teknolojiyle İlişkisine Ütopik Bir Yaklaşım: Siberfeminizm, International Journal of Social Science, 27, s. 219–234.

Voerkörper, C. (1999). "Programmierte Verführung". In: Telepolis. Magazin für NetzkulturInstitut für Moderne Kunst, Nürnberg, s. 128–131.

Weber, J. (2001). İronie, Erotik und Techno-Politik: Cyberfeminismus als Virus in der neuen Weltordnung, Die Philosophin: Forum für feministische Theorie und Philosophie, Jg. 12, Nr. 24, 81–97.

CHAPTER 4

From Individual to Dividual

Women Ecology and Scientific Revolution

Eylül Kabakçi Günay

The feminist connection between women and nature has engaged with debates in environmental ethics and politics and has attempted to counter human domination over women and nature through political activism. The concept of ecofeminism shows the interrelationship of women and nature based on the fact of their sharing a common inferior position, a parallel conceptual and evaluative structure is applied to each. In addition, as seen in our research, the visibility of science in human life has increased with the scientific revolution, and this visibility has surrounded us just as nature has surrounded us. Scientific theories, which seemed to belong only to scientists in the past, started to affect daily lives with discoveries and inventions, and it was inevitable for women to have a say in this movement. In an intellectual sense, women can't be kept away from science at the point where they are positioned by being inspired by nature. The influence of feminist economics and feminist views on women's achievement of these gains is undeniable. Academics, thought groups and policymakers should continue to take steps to strengthen women's place in the world of science, and women's natural relations with science as a result of their relevance to nature arising from their existence should also be considered.

1 Introduction

The transition from perceiving individuals as separate entities to understanding them as interconnected parts of a larger whole has profound implications for various aspects of human society, including women's role in ecology and the scientific revolution. This shift in perspective, often referred to as moving from the "individual" to the "dividual," recognizes the complex interdependencies and interactions that exist between individuals, communities, and the environment. On the other hand, accepting gender stereotypes like nature is feminine because of the reproductivity of women, creates another point of view. In the Age of Enlightenment, which is the period in which the organic bond in the human-nature relationship is broken and the approaches in which this bond is broken and human-centred are accepted and justified, the idea that everything is created for humans and that humans are superior to all living things is dominant. In this understanding, which makes the human mind superior, nature is instrumentalized.

The understanding that discrimination between men and women by gender and social roles has elevated the man with reason while transforming the feminine nature into an entity that must be controlled and managed. Francis Bacon (1561–1626), who laid the foundations of the Enlightenment's view of nature, stated that nature is feminine, and science is masculine. He defined nature with feminine features and put that "Man understands nature and dominates it. He does this by looking at both the objects and the mind" (Bacon, 2012: 15). In fact, Bacon summarizes the perspectives of masculine dominance, from Plato to the present, against women and nature.

Then, with industrialization and urbanization, a managed and directed tool has been transformed into a shared slave with colonialism. Along with the deterioration in nature caused by human beings, technological developments have completely distanced the people of the city from nature (Erdoğdu et al., 2020).

It is accepted that the destruction in nature and its devastating consequences, in short, the struggle with nature to ensure the continuation of human existence has become more aggressive, and therefore the questioning of the relationship between nature and nature began in the 1960s for the first time. At the global level, environmental problems were mentioned for the first time at the "United Nations Conference on the Human Environment" held in Stockholm in 1972. Exactly 20 years later, in 1992, the "United Nations Conference on Environment and Development" was held in Rio de Janeiro. While the states participated in the conference, known as the Rio Conference, with their high-level representatives, non-governmental organizations also participated intensively. At the conference, five main topics "Climate Change", "Convention on Biological Diversity", "Rio Declaration", "Agenda 21" and "List of Principles for the Protection and Development of Forests" were discussed. The principles adopted at the conference increased environmental efforts at both – national and international levels. However, despite the above-mentioned conferences and other global measures, the problems of our elderly world continue to increase. Our world today-is struggling with many problems from desertification to acid rain, from depletion of the ozone layer to the reduction of biodiversity, from climate change to poverty. (Ersoz, 2022).

When examining the relationship between women, ecology, and the scientific revolution, it is important to consider how this transition has impacted their roles and contributions. Historically, women's contributions to scientific and ecological endeavors have often been overlooked or marginalized. However, as the understanding of interconnectedness has deepened, there has been a growing recognition of the valuable insights and knowledge that women bring to these fields.

In the context of ecology, women have long played vital roles in understanding and conserving the natural environment. Their deep connection with nature and their local communities has enabled them to develop unique perspectives and insights into ecological systems. Women have traditionally been involved in activities such as farming, herbal medicine, and sustainable resource management, which have contributed to the preservation and sustainability of ecosystems.

Furthermore, the recognition of interconnectedness has led to a greater appreciation for the importance of diversity and inclusion in scientific research and innovation. As more women have gained access to education and opportunities in the sciences, their contributions have become increasingly recognized and valued. Women scientists have made significant discoveries and advancements across various disciplines, including biology, environmental science, and ecology. Their research has shed light on important issues such as biodiversity, climate change, and sustainable development.

The scientific revolution, characterized by a shift towards empirical observation, experimentation, and the development of scientific methodologies, has also been influenced by this transition from the individual to the dividual. The acknowledgement of the interconnected nature of the world has challenged reductionist approaches that isolate phenomena from their broader contexts. Instead, a more holistic and systemic understanding has emerged, recognizing the intricate relationships between scientific disciplines and the need for interdisciplinary collaboration.

Women have contributed to this paradigm shift by bringing diverse perspectives and methodologies to scientific research. Their experiences as members of marginalized groups have allowed them to question existing paradigms and propose alternative frameworks that consider the interconnectedness of social, cultural, and environmental systems. Additionally, women have played key roles in advocating for ethical and inclusive scientific practices, ensuring that the benefits of scientific advancements are accessible to all.

While progress has been made, it is important to acknowledge that systemic barriers and gender inequalities still persist within scientific fields. Efforts are needed to address these issues and create more inclusive and supportive

environments for women in ecology and the scientific revolution. By recognizing the importance of diversity, embracing interdisciplinary approaches, and
fostering collaboration, we can further enhance our understanding of the complex ecological challenges we face and work towards sustainable solutions that
benefit both individuals and the broader interconnected web of life.

2   Women and Ecology: a New Approach from Feminism to Ecofeminism

Considering the evolution of the genders of men and women in the historical
process, the division of labour between men and women in primitive times
contains much sharper boundaries. In primitive times, unlike today, women
were either pregnant or caring for children for most of their adult lives. Due
to the physical bond of the newborn and the infant in early childhood the
mother, and women were concerned with childcare, and men were concerned
with issues related to nutrition, shelter and survival. Thus, while men became
hunters, shepherds, or warriors; women stayed at home, looked after the children, did agriculture and ran the household chores. This differentiation of
roles spread over time to all aspects of life. After all, while men are generally
identified with brave, strong, independent and adventurous, in short, extro-
verted character traits; women began to be seen as warm, passive, quiet and
caring (Vatandaş, 2007).

    Although the division of roles originating from the differences in physical
creation, which is an extension of the primitive ages, has been used in the construction of the patriarchal order, it has formed the cornerstone of the patriarchal structure, despite the development of technology and the fact that the act
of survival has become much easier compared to previous ages. Exploitation
against nature also begins with the masculine mind seeing itself as superior
and accepting nature as an enemy to be overcome. The bond established
between nature and women also supported this impulse. Nature and women,
which are trying to be taken under control, have been exposed to exploitation with different possibilities of each period. However, after the Industrial
Revolution, the destruction of nature became visible and it became difficult
to compensate.

    All these exploits have started to cause wars of rights and freedoms, which
are demanded in many fields in terms of law, in the 20th century. Ecofeminism,
which emerged with the second-wave feminist movement, also struggled
against the exploitation of women and nature in the theoretical and operational field.

The concept of feminism first emerged in England in the 18th century and entered the academic field for the first time with Mary Wollstonecraft's *A Vindication of the Rights of Women*, published in 1792 (Sevim, 2005: 7–8). Feminism is a social movement that encompasses struggles for the emancipation of women, the prevention of their oppression, and equal rights with men in the public or private sphere. Since its inception, feminism has not progressed in a single direction but has emerged differently in different countries. Influenced by the periodical socio-political events, it showed itself in the phases called waves. The first wave of feminism sprouted from the positive effects of values such as equality, freedom and human rights that took the western world under its influence after the French Revolution and lasted until the 1960s. In the second wave feminism, which emerged in the 1960s and continued until the 1980s, the struggle was fought mostly on equal rights and gender inequality at the constitutional level. Third wave feminism, which emerged under the influence of postmodernism in the 1980s, "focused less on the law and the political process and more on individual identity" (Özdemir and Aydemir, 2019: 1708).

Ecofeminism emerged in the 1970s when the archaic-based bond between women and nature came to the fore and was first used as a concept in the book *La Feminisme ou la Mort (Feminism or Death)* published in 1974 by the feminist and activist Françoise d'Eaubonne. In this study, "a connection was established between oppression against women and oppression against nature, and it was claimed that the freedom of both women and nature would go together" (Tong, 2006: 432). In the early 1980s, ecofeminism gained a dimension based on theoretical foundations in the academic community and attracted attention with the workshop titled "Women and Life in the World: Ecofeminism in the Eighties," held in the United States by a women's coalition (Öçal, 2011: 79). Ecofeminism establishes important links between the oppression of women and the oppression of nature. Understanding the status of these ties is imperative for any attempt to comprehend the oppression of nature as well as the oppression of women. It emphasizes the necessity of feminist theory and practice to include an ecological perspective. They have a point of view that solutions to ecological problems should include a feminist perspective (Ferry, 2000: 161).

Another important portrayal of ecofeminism belongs to Charis Thompson. According to Thompson (2006), ecofeminism is a feminist theory that explores the relationship between women and nature, and how both have been historically oppressed and exploited by patriarchal systems. It argues that the domination of nature and women are interconnected and that the exploitation of the environment is often linked to the exploitation of women. Ecofeminism also emphasizes the importance of valuing and protecting the environment and advocates for a more sustainable and equitable relationship between humans and nature.

3   Key Aspects of Ecofeminism

Ecofeminism encompasses a range of perspectives and approaches, but there are several key aspects that are commonly associated with the movement. These include:

Intersectionality: Ecofeminism recognizes that systems of oppression intersect and interact with one another. It acknowledges that women's experiences of oppression differ based on factors such as race, class, ethnicity, and sexuality. Therefore, ecofeminism aims to address multiple forms of discrimination and advocates for inclusivity and justice for all marginalized groups.

Valuing interconnectedness: Ecofeminism emphasizes the interconnectedness and interdependence of all life forms. It rejects the notion of human superiority over nature and promotes an ecological worldview that recognizes the intrinsic value of the natural world and the need for harmony and balance in human-environment relationships.

Critique of patriarchal systems: Ecofeminism critiques patriarchal systems that perpetuate hierarchical power structures. It argues that the domination and exploitation of women and nature stem from similar root causes and must be addressed together. Ecofeminism seeks to challenge and transform these oppressive systems, advocating for gender equality and social justice.

Revaluing women's knowledge and experiences: Ecofeminism seeks to reclaim and value women's traditional knowledge and practices related to ecological sustainability. It recognizes the historical roles of women in nurturing and caring for communities and advocates for the inclusion of women's perspectives in decision-making processes related to the environment.

Environmental activism: Ecofeminism often involves active engagement in environmental and social justice movements. It encourages collective action, community organizing, and sustainable practices to challenge destructive systems and work towards a more equitable and sustainable world.

Ethics of care: Ecofeminism emphasizes the importance of ethics of care in our relationship with the environment. It highlights the nurturing, interconnected, and reciprocal aspects of caring relationships, emphasizing the need for empathy, responsibility, and stewardship towards the natural world.

Eco-spirituality: Some strands of ecofeminism incorporate spiritual or religious perspectives that emphasize the sacredness of nature and the interconnectedness of all beings. Ecofeminist spirituality often promotes reverence for the Earth and a sense of ecological interconnectedness.

These aspects of ecofeminism provide a framework for understanding and addressing the interconnections between gender inequality, environmental degradation, and social justice. By recognizing the ways in which oppression operates on multiple levels, ecofeminism seeks to create a more sustainable and equitable world for all. Besides, according to ecofeminism, it is a crucial point to investigate the linkage between women and nature. Most of the researchers believe that mother nature and creature of feminine have a common share, "productivity". Producing a new plant, a new human being and giving life to seeds are unique, that's why soil defines as "feminine", and characterized what a feminine should have. Another issue that we cannot underestimate is the merits of collaboration and other intangible atmospheres of ecofeminism.

In this context, ecofeminism has different pillars through different levels of development between countries. For example, in a developed country debate on ecofeminism is generally in a more philosophical and skeptical form of mindset. But ecofeminism has a more tangible sphere and is more related to gender roles in a developing country. It is possible to say portraying ecofeminism in a developing country looks like taking a photo instead of painting.

4   Scientific Revolution and Ecology

The Scientific Revolution, which occurred primarily between the 16th and 17th centuries, brought about significant changes in the way people understood and interacted with the natural world. While the Scientific Revolution is often associated with advancements in physics, astronomy, and mathematics, its influence extended to the field of ecology, albeit indirectly.

During the Scientific Revolution, there was a shift from traditional, supernatural explanations of natural phenomena towards a more empirical and evidence-based approach. This shift in thinking laid the foundation for the development of modern scientific methodologies, such as observation, experimentation, and the formulation of testable hypotheses. As a result, scientists began to systematically investigate the natural world, including its living organisms and ecosystems.

Ecology as a distinct scientific discipline emerged much later, in the late 19th century. However, the Scientific Revolution played a crucial role in setting the stage for ecological studies by promoting a reductionist approach and mechanistic worldview. The focus on breaking down complex systems into their constituent parts and understanding the laws governing their behaviour allowed for a better understanding of ecological processes.

For instance, as scientists gained a deeper understanding of the principles of energy transfer and the interconnectedness of ecosystems, they were able to study topics such as nutrient cycling, predator-prey relationships, and the interdependence of species. The scientific methodologies and advancements in fields like botany, zoology, and geology that emerged during the Scientific Revolution provided the groundwork for later ecological studies.

Furthermore, the Scientific Revolution contributed to the exploration and cataloguing of biodiversity. Expeditions and scientific voyages undertaken during this time expanded knowledge of the natural world and its diverse ecosystems. These expeditions laid the groundwork for the study of biogeography and the understanding of how organisms are distributed across different regions.

However, it is important to note that the ecological implications of the Scientific Revolution were not uniformly positive. The emphasis on exploitation and resource extraction that accompanied the rise of industrialization and capitalism during this period had detrimental effects on ecosystems. The mechanistic view of nature and the pursuit of economic growth often disregarded the long-term consequences of environmental degradation, leading to the depletion of natural resources and ecological imbalances.

There are some crucial viewpoints to understand the linkage between the scientific revolution and ecology. For instance, the second of the three themes in *The Death of Nature's* subtitle, "Women, Ecology, and the Scientific Revolution," (Merchant, 1989) was ecology's role in the revolution. In fact, Mitman's work (1992) has been at the forefront of these connections.

In summary, while the Scientific Revolution did not directly give rise to the discipline of ecology, it provided the intellectual and methodological framework that laid the foundation for ecological studies. The shift towards empirical observation, experimentation, and reductionist thinking during this period contributed to our understanding of ecological processes and paved the way for further exploration of the natural world. However, it is essential to acknowledge that the environmental consequences of the Scientific Revolution highlight the need for a more holistic and sustainable approach to scientific inquiry and ecological understanding in the modern era.

5   Conclusion

The feminist connection between women and nature has engaged in debates in environmental ethics and politics and has attempted to counter human domination over women and nature through political activism. The concept of ecofeminism shows the interrelationship of women and nature based on the fact of their sharing a common inferior position, a parallel conceptual and evaluative structure is applied to each.

In addition, as seen in our research, the visibility of science in human life has increased with the scientific revolution, and this visibility has surrounded us just as nature has surrounded us. Scientific theories, which seemed to belong only to scientists in the past, started to affect daily lives with new discoveries and inventions, and it was inevitable for women to have a say in this movement. In an intellectual sense, it is not possible for women to be kept away from science at the point where they are positioned by being inspired by nature. The influence of feminist economics and feminist view on women's achievement of these gains is undeniable. Academic thought groups and policymakers should continue to take steps to strengthen women's place in the world of science, and women's natural relations with science as a result of their relevance to nature arising from their existence should also be considered.

References

Ersöz, A. (2022). Vandana Shiva'nin Ekofeminizme Katkilari Üzerine Bir Değerlendirme. *Uluslararası Anadolu Sosyal Bilimler Dergisi,* 6 (4), 1374–1385.

Ferry, L. (2000). *Ekolojik Yeni Düzen.* İstanbul: Yapı Kredi Yayınları.

Öçal, A.K. (2011). Dişil Dil Ve Ekofeminist Bağlamda Latife Tekin Ve Muinar. (Yüksek Lisans Tezi, Ankara Üniversitesi, Sosyal Bilimler Enstitüsü, 2011).

Özdemir, H. & Aydemir, D. (2019). Ekolojik Yaklaşımlı Feminizm/Ekofeminizm Üzerine Genel bir Değerlendirme: Kavramsal Analizi, Tarihi Süreci ve Türleri. *Akdeniz Kadın Çalışmaları ve Toplumsal Cinsiyet Dergisi,* 2 (2), 261–278.

Özgenç Erdoğdu, N, Karaalioğlu, O, Ömür, İ. (2020). Kadın ve Doğa İlişkisi Bağlamında Ekofeminizmin Sanata Yansıması. Sanat Dergisi, (36), 33–50.

Sevim, A. (2005). *Feminizm.* İstanbul: İnsan.

Thompson, C. (2006). Back to nature? Resurrecting Ecofeminism after poststructuralist and third-wave feminisms. *Isis,* 97(3), 505–512.

Tong, P.R. (2006). Feminist düşünce (çev. Z. Cirhinoğlu). İstanbul: Gündoğan.

Vatandaş, C. (2007). "Toplumsal cinsiyet ve cinsiyet rollerinin algılanışı". *Journal of Economy Culture and Society,* Sayı 35, 29–56.

CHAPTER 5

Ecofeminism

Lessons on Ecology and the Environment

Gamze Yıldız Şeren

Ecofeminism is based on the relationship established between women and the environment. In this context, it defends the idea that the patriarchal capitalist system has negative effects on women and the environment. Therefore, ecofeminism has taken its place in feminist literature as not only a feminist approach but also an approach that includes the environmental factor and draws attention to the relationship between women and nature. This approach considers the destruction of the environment and the secondary position of women as interrelated problems and considers patriarchy as the main factor of this problem. At this point, it argues that raising awareness of women and the dissolution of patriarchal systems will reduce environmental destruction. In this context, patriarchy in ecofeminism is problematized with nature and the analysis of the problems that feminism seeks answers to gains a deeper structure. Ecofeminism, which started in the 1970s, has been divided into various branches over time.

This study aims to discuss the validity of the propositions of ecofeminism in the context of the environment and ecology in the context of the 21st century. Although ecofeminism is frequently criticized in the literature, as it lays the groundwork for the reconstruction of gender perceptions it can be considered as an alternative policy in the face of the climate crisis in the world. In light of the findings obtained from the study, it is concluded that women are more affected by environmental problems than men. This situation reveals the importance of an environmental struggle in which women will be the pioneers. Ecofeminism, which draws attention to the disadvantaged position of women with its criticisms of environmental problems, can be considered as a vision for sustainable environmental policies.

1   Introduction

The ecofeminism movement, which connects environmental and women's issues with each other, aims to draw attention to two basic problems.

Accordingly, the patriarchal system is responsible for both the secondary position of women and environmental problems. Therefore, the fragmentation of patriarchal codes may be instrumental in building a way that can prevent both environmental and women's problems. According to ecofeminists, who argue that women have a special relationship with the environment, women can also play a role in correcting the damage done to the environment. Opinions that criticize as well as support ecofeminism are frequently seen in the literature. Accordingly, the traditional roles of women, such as collecting food, water, farming, and the use of women's intuitive approaches to establish the bond between women and nature lead to the reproduction of gender codes.

In the study, ecofeminism was handled conceptually, and it was questioned whether there are lessons to be learned from ecofeminism in the face of 21st-century environmental problems. Accordingly, educating women through awareness-raising activities, based on the connection that ecofeminism establishes between women and the environment, can lead to both a solution to patriarchal domination and an effective struggle against environmental problems. Ecofeminism should be seen as a tool for sustainable environmental policies and sustainable approaches to take action. The study is designed in three main sections. Accordingly, the excessive use of "accordingly" in the first section, ecofeminism was discussed conceptually. In the second section, connections were revealed from the perspective of the 21st century, starting from the relationship between the environment and women. In the third section, country examples from ecofeminist struggles were given and it was questioned whether ecofeminism could be used as an active solution to environmental problems.

2   A Critical Stance within the Framework of the Environment, Women and Patriarchal System: Ecofeminism

2.1   *Historical Process and Basic Arguments*
Feminism dates back to Ancient Greece. In the modern sense, it first emerged in 17th-century Europe and evolved into a systematic way of thinking during the French Revolution. Feminism, which emerged as a reaction to the rights that women could not obtain, advocates the need for women to have equal social and political rights with men. Accordingly, the destruction of the system of values that leads to inequality between women and men will lead to the desired result of the women's movement (Vural and Kantar, 2022: 36). Feminism is concerned with the social injustices brought about by the patriarchal system that renders women worthless. Although feminism is not consistent within

itself, it has been divided into various branches over time and has laid the groundwork for the formation of different ideas. Ecofeminism, on the other hand, is based on the idea that man and the world are threatened by the same "enemy". Accordingly, it is the control mentality of the same domination that harms the environment and women (Pompeo-Fargnoli, 2018: 1). The branch of feminism, which establishes a connection between women and the environment based on their similarities, is called "Ecofeminism" and the ecofeminist movement began to develop in the 1970s (Çetin, 2005: 63–64). In other words, ecofeminism is a social movement and theoretical research form that produces social egalitarian policies and resists the formation of domination (Carlassare, 2000: 89). At this point, the ecofeminist approach combines the environment and feminism, examines the problems faced by people and produces solutions (Pompeo-Fargnoli, 2018: 1).

According to ecofeminism, women are closer to nature than men. The closeness of women to nature makes them interested in their environment. Some argue that this intimacy derives from biological qualities of women, while others argue that it stems from historical and cultural circumstances. Ecofeminism, powered by the feminist movement of the 1960s-1970s, acts for the dissolution of the patriarchal system by examining the means and methods that subjugate people under the control of the authority (Anjum, 2020: 847–848).

The term ecofeminism was first used in 1974 by Françoise d'Eaubonne in her book *Le Feminisme ou la Mort* (*Feminism or Death*). Accordingly, under the term "ecofeminism" lies social and cultural concerns about the relationship of oppressed women with the deteriorating nature (Ojha, 2021; Salman and Iqbal, 2007: 853). It is thought that the first ideas on this subject also took place in Mary Daly's *Gyn/Ecology: The Metaethics of Radical Feminism* (1978) (Daly, 1978; cited in Cuomo, 2002: 2). Ecofeminism focused on ecology beyond human relations with the world and revealed a synthesizing philosophy in terms of nature, philosophy and culture (Cuomo, 2002: 2). The subjugation of the environment and women began with Western patriarchy some 5000 years ago. Patriarchy, on the other hand, is based on dualism, which separates human from mind, man from woman, and finally man from nature. This division of assets into two creates a power imbalance. Ecofeminism seeks to combine politics and spirituality in opposition to the system that generates an imaginary other. (Salman and Iqbal, 2007: 853).

After the Second World War, the pressures of population growth on natural resources, the increase in the use of industrial products by developed countries, and the environmental pollution caused by the use of nuclear energy left humanity alone with environmental problems. The fact that human actions are responsible for the environmental destruction created here has brought different approaches in different branches. Accordingly, the way of thinking that brings a feminist perspective to environmental problems is ecofeminism. Ecofeminism is an approach that addresses environmental issues by blending them with women's issues (Çetin, 2005: 63).

Ecofeminism, which is the combination of the words eco and feminism, embodies both the ecological protection movement and the women's liberation movement. Based on the aforementioned combination, the idea of ecology-oriented feminism underlies ecofeminism. Ecofeminism, which has a variety of meanings, can be considered in spiritual, and social meanings. According to spiritual ecofeminists based on ancient matriarchal thought, woman and nature is a sacred religious belief. Spiritual ecofeminism, on the other hand, considers God and his religion as patriarchal. Social ecofeminists, on the other hand, argue that the relationship between nature and women is socially constructed. Here nature is the victim of oppression, while man is the oppressor. A similar situation occurs in women because in a situation where the man becomes the subject, the woman becomes the object of domination. Spiritual ecofeminism has been criticized by social ecofeminists (Ottuh, 2020: 168).

Ecofeminism has a unique history. Based on the experiences of women in developed and developing countries, ecofeminism also emphasizes the ecological dimension of the situation. It encourages a new synthesis against urban theory paradigms such as Marxist, poststructuralist, liberal and radical. Accordingly, ecofeminism deals with both man's relationship with woman and human's relationship with nature (Salleh, 1992: 197–198). According to Western culture, while women have been associated with the inferior animality, materiality and nature in the historical process, men have been associated with mind, culture and reason. In this context, nature has been feminized and a way of thinking has emerged in order to understand the oppressions against women. According to critical ecofeminism, the human-nature dichotomy is the key to ecological failures (Plumwood, 2004: 43–44).

According to ecofeminists, the patriarchal system is built on environmental destruction, class exploitation, racism and sexism. In this context, ecofeminists protest the exploitation of nature and women. The world must therefore be reconceptualized in a non-hierarchical way. The basic assumption here is that the environmentalist and feminist movement represent equal and non-hierarchical systems. Ecofeminists shape the emancipation of women by overcoming their secondary roles in society, and that it is related to the emancipation of nature, according to these three main arguments (Anjum, 2020: 846):
- Access to public decision-making systems
- The division of labor is based on gender
- Property rights

The insatiable pursuit of wealth by the modern capitalist economic model causes both women and the environment to be detrimental. In this respect, ecofeminist theory takes a critical stance against the patriarchal and capitalist model. Establishing a bridge between feminism and ecology, ecofeminism offers solutions to create a sustainable world. Of course, although it cannot be claimed that women are more naturally connected to nature than men, at the international level women take a more active role in the defense of the environment and animals. The fact that women do not have access to weapons in the historical process, traditionally taking care of the sick, children and elderly, and fulfilling household duties (cooking, cleaning) are the main reasons that establish this relationship at this point (Puleo, 2017: 27).

While in the 1980s ecofeminism was a broad umbrella rooted in cultural (essentialist) feminisms and developed in different ways, in the 1990s ecofeminist theories developed and refined their analysis on international, intersectional, and economic grounds. The development in question has an ongoing process (Gaard, 2011: 32).

2.2   What Does Ecofeminism Hope to Achieve?

Ecofeminism aims to connect the movements and thoughts about these concepts by evaluating the feminist and ecological perspectives in the same pot. In addition, ecofeminism aims to criticize elements such as the lack of ecological awareness in the women's movement and the sexist nature of the green movement (Plumwood, 2004: 43). There are studies in the literature examining the relationship between women and nature since the 1970s (Ruether, 1975; Griffin, 1978; Merchant, 1981; Salleh, 1984; Warren, 1990). As a result, ecofeminist thinkers researching the cultural and conceptual linkages between women and nature have had a variety of focal points while examining the relationship between women and nature. The first ecofeminist thinkers, which can be described as early ecofeminism, developed immanence spiritualities by opposing the dual soul concepts. Contemporary ecofeminism, on the other hand, has focused on the analysis of deep distinctions such as spirit-matter, male-female, mind-body, for gender and ecological danger zones (Plumwood, 2004: 43).

Ecofeminism can also be considered in terms of liberal, radical and spiritual approaches. While ecofeminists do not reject the equal participation of liberal feminists in society, they use this access to bring about fundamental changes in different institutions and values, just as radical feminists do. Both radical feminism and feminist spirituality have shaped the analytical approach of ecofeminism. Thus, both the feminist discourse and ecological ethics have been expanded by elaborating on the self-society-nature. With ecofeminism, the male-centered culture is problematized together with the natural world, taking feminism beyond the pursuit of social justice and deepening the analysis of problems from different perspectives. Thus, it criticizes the dysfunctional value system of the male-centered society and shares its commitment to improve the negative consequences of people's alienation from nature. (Pompeo-Fargnoli, 2018: 5). In ecofeminism, the main issue is not men in terms of individuals, but the patriarchal structure. The emancipation of women can only be possible with the ecological revolution that will take place under the leadership of women. The aim in this transformational process is the reformulation of the social order, and this does not mean the replacement of male power with female power (Çetin, 2005: 63–64). Ecofeminism seeks human reality in the depths of ecological realities in the face of worker exploitation, women's oppression, ecological degradation and racism. Ecofeminism with normative claims aims to draw attention to links to forms of oppression such as environmental degradation and sexism (Cuomo, 2002: 1). Although feminism is mainly divided into various branches, it essentially aims at the recognition of equality for women. In this context, very different analyzes and ideas have been put forward on what equality includes or should cover. In this context, ecofeminism includes ecology and deals with the equality of women in terms of different needs and problems (Plumwood, 2004: 49–50).

Ecofeminism has to be ecological because ecofeminism has an ecological perspective. Emphasizing the interdependence of ecosystem elements, ecology also emphasizes the mutual interactions, differences and dependencies of individuals. According to ecofeminism, all living things on nature are connected. Therefore, ecofeminism opposes the reductionist and discriminatory dualist way of thinking. Ecofeminism instead prefers an integrated and multidimensional way of thinking. The mentioned relationship emphasizes the bond between dopa and human and tries to prevent conflict and division. This multidimensional perspective, on the other hand, avoids all forms of domination and offers a holistic perspective. Thus, the individual and the whole relationship are handled dialectically, avoiding abstract individual perspectives (Ling, 2014: 71).

According to ecofeminism, ecological problems are also cultural and social problems. Social changes that support egalitarian social relations are required for an ecologically healthy society. Accordingly, in a world where the basic relationship model is the patriarchal domination model, ecological degradation and oppression of women are linked. Thus, ecological threats are also feminist issues. While ecofeminists acknowledge the link between women's oppression and ecological degradation, debate continues as to what the link is (Carlassare, 2000: 90).

Ecofeminism, which aims to eliminate the patriarchal structure, also high-lights the importance of women in the ecological movement. Ecofeminism argues that both regional and global liberation movements should exhibit a whole structure in order to ensure the social freedom of women. The success of ecofeminism is dependent not only on the implementation of feminist prin-ciples but also on the assimilation of ecological theories. Thus, it makes great efforts for the solution of ecological crises, feeds on regional-global ecologi-cal movements and establishes a new relationship between human-society-nature (Ling, 2014: 71–72).

2.3   Criticism of Ecofeminism

Ecofeminism, which was founded in the 1970s and formulated in the 1980s, started to come to the fore in the 1990s. Although it was criticized for being essentialist in the previous periods, this situation was actually abandoned, and the term ecofeminism started to develop at the intersections of the environ-ment and feminism. After the criticism of gender essentialism, it was renamed and terms such as ecological feminism, feminist environmentalism, critical feminist ecosocialism, social feminism were developed (Gaard, 2011: 26–27).

According to ecofeminism, domination in the natural world, is a branch of domination patterns. In this context, patterns of domination need to be elimi-nated in order to make progress on the environment. The main challenge facing ecofeminism is how to fully understand the link between human domination over humans and human domination over nature. Issues such as how they are related, whether they can be considered as parallel developments, and the con-nections between forms of domination are both the starting point of criticism of ecofeminism and the main topics of disagreement (Ottuh, 2020: 177).

Ecofeminism cannot be generalized easily. The fact that it covers these different perspectives has caused ecofeminism to be seen as an inconsistent approach (Carlassare, 2000: 89). The inconsistency of ecofeminism also stems from the incompatibility of cultural and socialist perspectives. Ecofeminists have differing views on the interplay of gender, patriarchy, class, imperialism, and race with ecological degradation. Despite all these differences, the area where ecofeminism is united is the survival of the planet and the end of the pressures on ecology (Carlassare, 2000: 89). According to critical ecofeminism, ecofeminism criticizes the view that women are part of nature or are closer to nature than men. Accordingly, both men and women live in the same nature and culture. Therefore, the opposition of women and nature emerges as an issue that needs to be considered again (Plumwood, 2004: 50).

Another fundamental criticism of ecofeminism is that equating women with nature reproduces gender norms. But the main philosophy of feminism is not to reinforce gender norms (Regan, 2020). Associating women with nature can be a labor mediated by nature on behalf of men, even if all legal measures are taken. Under the capitalist patriarchal system, women undertake complex tasks such as childcare, cooking, cleaning and shopping in the household. These tasks in a way secure the "second sex" part of men and become a secondary part of the agreement between labor-capital-government (Salleh, 1995: 28). According to another criticism, politically active, essentialist, and biologist ecofeminism is not only inconsistent but also lacks in certainty. Despite the debates on the certainty and effectiveness of ecofeminism, the potential of this thought should not be ignored (Sargisson, 2001: 52).

The problem of inconsistency, which is most criticized in ecofeminism, can be viewed as a wealth of thought rather than rejecting ecofeminism altogether. This inconsistency also highlights the fact that ecofeminism's ability to act for an ecological future is based on a shared ideology. Therefore, the criticism of inconsistency directed at ecofeminism overlooks the fact that ecofeminism paves the way for a formation that allows different perspectives (Carlassare, 2000: 103).

Since ecofeminism is a complex discourse, it is necessary to determine the lines of questioning. According to some branches of ecofeminism, it romanticizes women's closeness to nature and does this to justify the feminist point of view. However, this theory only focuses on women and nature, assuming the roles assigned to women. This is rooted in second-wave feminism, which focuses on heterosexual white women. Conceptually narrow ecofeminism has been expanded by LGBTIQ and Black Native People of Color (BiPoC). In this context, it is believed that in order for ecofeminism to be effective, it should not be binary and should adopt an intersectional approach (Heidegger et al., 2021: 19).

According to some, the proposal of ecofeminism already includes ideas that are against women. According to this view, the consequences of an ethical understanding based on more biological characteristics, such as feeding and caring, can become more destructive for women. The establishment of women's relationship with nature on the nature of women is criticized on the grounds that it does not include reason, science and freedom in this respect. In line with the roles assigned to women, the fact that women have the character traits needed to protect the environment also makes women more qualified to "save the world". This may mean that men are excluded from restoration projects and their participation is not expected because, according to this view, men do not have the nature sensitivity that women have. In such a situation, women may return to their traditional roles as "nurturing mothers" in a way, as they are responsible for cleaning the global pollution. In such a framework, it is not thought that the consequences of ecofeminist ethics will reinforce women's freedom (Archambault, 1993: 21). The gender differences put forward in ensuring environmental sustainability are based on the characteristics of men and women. Accordingly, this role has been associated with women because the party (women) who is concerned about the environment should be a more self-sacrificing, more empathetic gender. Since women think more about the future, they may be more dependent on the environment, especially if they have children, and they may be more sensitive to safety and health issues. But it can also be a cliché and encourage men to avoid environmentally friendly activities in order to protect their sexual identity (Brough et al., 2016: 568).

3   Environmental Problems and Ecofeminism

From the time since Françoise D'Eaubonne first used the term "ecofeminism", ecofeminism has been questioned from various perspectives and different orientations have been defined. Therefore, it does not seem possible to talk about ecofeminism singularly today. Especially after the identification of women and nature and the discriminatory attitude of the first advocates of ecofeminism, different dimensions were discussed. Environmental problems such as air and water pollution in the world, excessive population growth, and extinction of plant and animal species affect women more. Therefore, ecofeminism has also been addressed with alternative names such as ecological feminism, eco-womanism, and global feminist environmental justice (Estévez-Saá and Lorenzo-Modia, 2018: 123). With the new millennium, human-centred feminism has begun to dominate in feminist thought. Therefore, situations such as energy security, climate justice, food security, habitat loss have both ecological and feminist dimensions (Gaard, 2011: 32).

The deep relationships that women form with the environment are rooted in the conventional roles that women are allotted by society. unnecessary Women are also more sensitive to environmental changes as a result of these responsibilities. Noticing the temperature of the air, perceiving the change in the smell of water makes women more intertwined with nature due to the assigned roles. From the point of view of the global economy, women are also at the forefront compared to men in agricultural matters (such as collecting wood, carrying water, weeding, collecting food from the forests) (Salman and Iqbal, 2007: 855–856). In this context, the ecofeminist argument sees the domination of women and nature as fundamentally ideological. Its origins stem from representations of values, beliefs and ideas that hierarchically place women and the world under the domination of men. In the relationship between ecofeminism and the environment, ways to reconceptualize the relationship between men and women both with each other and with the world in a non-hierarchical way are sought (Agarwal, 1992: 120).

The issue of achieving a sustainable development without harming the environment was brought to the agenda at the Environment and Development Conference in Stockholm in 1974. Examples pointing to the close bond of women with nature are in the historical process. Therefore, women are in a closer connection with nature due to their domestic roles and responsibilities (Ojha, 2021). Ecofeminism, which reveals the nature-labor-woman relationship as a contradiction, examines the analysis of all pressures on the basis of an ecological problematic. At this point, ecofeminists, like other branches of feminism, defend gender justice, while also addressing the issue of global sustainability as a problem (Salleh, 1995: 26). However, according to ecofeminism, it is women who will shape the new ideals of humanity (Plumwood, 2004: 49–50). Today's climate crisis and gender inequalities are intertwined. As an increasing number of data and research reveal this relationship, the link between climate change and women's empowerment has become more involved in global climate action (Unwomen, 2022). Natural disasters caused by climate change affect not just specific geographical locations, but also take on a global scale. In this scenario, the world's situation necessitates individuals becoming more aware. At the intersection of feminism and environmentalism, a feminist approach does not always come out, and feminism may not always show an ecological sensitivity. According to Puleo (2017), although the environment and feminism are still "two worlds with their backs to each other", ecofeminism is a theory at this point that promises that the combination of both elements will enrich the dialogue (Puleo, 2017: 28). Historically, women have been associated with nature and emotion, while men have been associated with culture and reason. It is accepted that nature is not made by people while culture is. Accordingly, if women are seen closer to nature, they are placed in a lower position than men. While women represent nature, the public sphere (commerce, politics) is associated with men. In ecofeminism, the domination of women is the domination of nature, and the controlling patriarchy has led to the destruction of the environment. Underlying this lies the bond established between nature and the oppression of women, and the patriarchal system as the main cause of oppression (Aziz, 2021: 21–22).

The roles of women and men, their economic strengths, differences in social expectations can also help to understand how they are affected differently in the face of climate change. For example, women are responsible for 65% of household food production in Asia, 45% in Latin America and the Caribbean, and 70–80% in sub-Saharan Africa. In addition, women are more vulnerable to climate change, as they are largely responsible for water collection. Climate changes affect human health; climate change threatens with reasons such as deterioration in water resources, decrease in drinking water, decrease in agricultural production and warming. Considering that women are generally the primary caregivers in families, increasing diseases also increase women's responsibilities. However, the low access of women to medical care, especially in underdeveloped countries, turns the process against women. The effects of climate change on women are as follows (Canadian International Development Agency, 2002: 2):

- Climate-related changes in production structure and resources may increase women's workload by affecting women's income.
- Rising sea levels may affect livelihoods.
- Decreased access to natural resources can limit or even eliminate women's rights to resources.

Considering the development of ecofeminism in the 1970s, there have been major policy changes in the field of environmental sustainability and gender inequality. Here, it can be thought that the gender mainstreaming policies of the European Union and other international initiatives are decisive. The fact that feminism debates are handled in the orbit of environmental concerns (Buckingham, 2004: 146) should be interpreted as a sign that the climate crisis is not gender neutral. Women's livelihoods are experiencing the most adverse effects of climate change, which threatens their safety and health, and this situation further deepens gender inequalities. It is known that while women are more dependent on natural resources, their access is limited. For example, women take on disproportionate roles in fuel, water and food in many places. Therefore, agriculture is an important area of employment for women, especially in lower middle and low-income countries. Changes in the climate indirectly put agricultural workers in a more difficult situation and threaten their income sources. It is the girls who have to drop out of school to help the mothers who are in a difficult situation. Climate change causes conflicts in the world, and the main target of these conflicts is women (such as violence, human trafficking). In the event of disasters, women are more likely to be injured and less likely to survive due to gender inequalities. The emergence of health problems of women threatens the health of mother and child in case of difficulty in accessing health. For example, extreme heat increases stillbirth rates, climate changes accelerate the spread of some epidemics (Unwomen, 2022).

Considering the history of ecofeminism, it can be said that important steps have been taken to include the issue of gender in some policy areas, both locally and globally. International agreements and local practices are the situations that strengthen this argument. What needs to be done is to provide

structural changes so that feminist concerns can become a part of environmental decision-making processes (Buckingham, 2004: 153). Because the idea
that patriarchy is the main cause of ecological crises is now being discussed.
Men's control over nature and women has led to both population growth and
the destruction of nature. In this context, the role/importance of gender comes
into play for the solution of the climate crisis today, which is an agenda item
(Ojha, 2021).

4 Ecology and Environment: Evaluations within the Scope of Women's Struggle and Ecofeminism

Although ecofeminism is shaped around the woman-society-nature relationship, it is not the right approach to limit women's perspectives on the environment and society with a feminist approach. Beyond this, the inclusion of
women in public life at the national/international level is a very important
factor in the success of the movement. Historically, environmental movements, especially in Western industrial countries, started to develop at the end
of the 19th century and have a structure that continues until today (Salman
and Iqbal, 2007: 857–858). The fact that ecofeminists, who have made important contributions to environmental ethics and philosophy (Ottuh, 2020: 177)
bring the issue of nature to the agenda (Salleh, 1995: 26) makes it necessary
to evaluate the issue from the perspective of the 21st century. Because one of
the most important goals of ecofeminism is to redefine societies' perspectives
on nature and women's productivity. Accordingly, ecofeminist actions evaluate
the production-reproduction contradiction. At this point, it is aimed to prevent social/biological reproduction attacks on production. Thus, it also challenges mainstream society to reproduce gender roles (Anjum, 2020: 847–848).

4.1 Examples of Ecofeminist Movement

Although ecofeminism does not exhibit an organized structure, it has a mass
that can be considered important. Due to its structure that brings together the
environment and feminism, ecofeminism is seen as an approach that attracts
attention because ecological crises affect people's lives more and more every
day (Sturgeon, 2011: 238). Especially since the 1970s, there has been an increasing awareness and sensitivity about the environment. After the 1970s, the
years when the ecofeminism view emerged, there are some struggles against
the exploitation of the environment by women in various countries. While
ecofeminist struggles have occasionally been accused of elitism (the idea that
ecofeminists are a movement made up of priority/privileged Western women),

ecofeminism has highlighted links between environmental risks and the marginalization of precarious people (Delozière et al., 2023: 3). Therefore, it would not be wrong to interpret these struggles as the struggle of ecofeminism. Ecofeminist struggles should be evaluated as an indicator of how important the struggle of women in the environment is.

4.1.1 India

Vandana Shiva (Indian ecofeminist) is a pioneer who sees women as a key in solving social and environmental problems and lays the groundwork for ecofeminism dynamics. Shiva draws attention to not only the ideological but also the material connection of violence against nature and women. Especially Third World women are subject to nature in terms of providing for their families, themselves and the society. Therefore, the destruction of nature also means the destruction of women's life resources. According to Shiva, Third World women have a special bond and knowledge of nature. Shiva is also the person who brought the ecofeminism movement to the fore in India by actively participating in the Chipko Movement (Ojha, 2021; Agarwal, 1992: 124). "Chipko Movement" is one of the first examples that comes to mind when ecofeminist struggle is mentioned. It was formed in the 1970s to protect forests in the Garhwal hills of Northwest India. It is an event that sets an example for the struggle of the village women living in the region to protect the environment. The event in which women hugged the trees by opposing the cutting of trees by contractors has taken its place in history as an ecofeminist and ecological movement (Delozière, Gaborit and Kabbaj, 2023: 3; Rodriguez Stimson, 2016: 2; Agarwal, 1992: 124). Here, a new form of action has been adopted as a sign of personal commitment to the environment, not only the struggle to cut down trees, but also the embrace of trees. The Chipko movement is a symbol of women's spontaneous action against capitalist land usurpation (Delozière, Gaborit and Kabbaj, 2023: 3).

In the Chipko movement, women opposed projects that would bring short-term gains as well as high environmental costs and preferred to protect the environment. Another example of these struggles is a potato seed farm to be established in the village of Dongri Paintoli. The project, which will be realized by cutting down an oak forest, was supported by men as it would bring cash income, but women protested because local fuel and feed resources would be taken away. Here, it was thought that the money that men would earn would not benefit them and their children, and as a result, the protest was successful. Women have often been successful in their active struggles against illegal logging. The Chipko movement in India means more than an ecology movement and is an example of the struggle against gender inequalities. From the point of view of nature, women were aware of the importance of trees and that they were a part of the ecosystem and did not have commercial concerns (Agarwal, 1992: 147–148).

4.1.2   USA

Protests in Love Canal, a working-class neighbourhood on the outskirts of Niagara Falls in New York State, can also be considered within the scope of the ecofeminist struggle. In 1978, women took their place at the forefront of protests to dump toxic chemical wastes that negatively impacted residents' lives and polluted their lands. This struggle can be seen as an ecofeminist protest in terms of women's attitudes towards environmental inequalities (Delozière, Gaborit and Kabbaj, 2023: 3). The activists of the movements against toxic substances were mostly women, and they took action against the health problems caused by dangerous water sources. After the situation in Love Canal, Lois Gibbs, whose child had health problems, turned into an environmental warrior and led the Love Canal community. As a result, they were able to receive compensation from the State of New York for the effects of these health problems. However, in other local campaigns, women have been accused and mistreated as "hysterical wives". Both the experience of Gibbs and the negative situations caused the establishment of the "Hazardous Waste Network" in 1981(Salman and Iqbal, 2007: 858–859).

4.1.3   Kenya

In response to the constant pressure of development and progress by the Western capitalist logic, ecofeminism in Southern countries has led to an expansion of ecofeminist scope. An example of this is the Green Belt Movement (GBM) in Kenya in 1977. Here, women started a struggle against the privatization of communal lands, which is the source of local livelihood. This action aimed to combat deforestation due to timber and logging activities as well as opposition to privatisation. In this context, thousands of women took action and rebelled and started to plant trees again. After this event, it was seen as an inspiring experience for ecofeminists (Delozière et al., 2023: 3). GBM, which takes place in Kenya, has a different side to Chipko. GBM was not a spontaneous act, but took its inspiration from Professor Wangari Maathai's rural tree planting program in 1977. The aim here is to solve the fuel problem in rural areas, as well as to prevent soil erosion and desertification by surrounding nature with a green belt. In this way, an opportunity is created for women to be effective leaders. With the green belt, sensitivity to environmental problems has increased, the image of women has been improved, and basic links have been established between social needs and the improvement of women's conditions. The Green Belt movement thus became an important source of inspiration for ecofeminists (Salman and Iqbal, 2007: 859–860).

4.2 Can Ecofeminism Be the Solution to 21st Century Environmental and Ecological Problems? Lessons Learned

Chipko, the actions in the USA and Kenya point to the level of ecological awareness in women's daily lives and associate the improvement of women's conditions with the protection of the environment. With the development of ecofeminism in the 1980s, environmental awareness was created with some conferences and events (Women and Life on Earth: 80s Ecofeminism Conference, Women Pentagon Action and West Coast Eco Feminist Conference, USA Eco Feminist Conference) and its connection with women was tried to be revealed (Ling, 2014: 67–68).

It is both necessary and urgent that attitudes and actions towards the environment need to be changed. In the 21st century, it is seen that people are still not fully aware of the ecological damage. Under patriarchal domination, people's emotions become dull, and their perception of reality deteriorates. This results in ignoring activities that accelerate environmental destruction (Pompeo-Fargnoli, 2018: 8). In this case, as ecofeminism argues, the dissolution of the patriarchal system will also allow environmental activities to be sustainable. Ecofeminism connects women and nature in different ways. These are discrimination, reproductive roles and biological status. In this context, ecofeminism represents one of the philosophical and practical ways of solutions to environmental problems. Environmental degradation can be put to an end due to the behaviour patterns left to women and nature. Because the role of women's experience is at the forefront of the ecology movement, women's freedom is also linked to the regional/global women's freedom of the ecological movement. Ecofeminism attaches importance to difference and diversity; assimilates ecology in addition to feminist principles and blends it with regional/global ecological movements.

Since the 1970s, women have opposed the destruction of the environment, and various actions have been put forward against the forms of domination over both nature and women. Ecofeminism is not interested in establishing a natural bond between women and nature, but by critically evaluating women's gender roles determined by societies, they establish the woman-nature bond (Delozière, Gaborit and Kabbaj, 2023: 3). Establishing a new relationship between nature-human-society, ecofeminism is one of the most promising movements in environmental thinking despite all its weak points. Ecofeminism, which has the capacity to struggle in the face of difficulties, continues to be not only a criticism of domination but also a source of information by emphasizing the understanding of knowledge that values the world and prioritizes culture and creativity. Thus, despite its flaws, it makes a valuable contribution to the theory of feminism (Aziz, 2021: 26). Experiences such as GBM and Love Canal are examples that show successful results as a result of environmental actions. Ecofeminism cannot be defined singularly; it refers to a sense of unity between the natural environment, people and the planet. Therefore, although ecofeminism is correct as a philosophy in the face of environmental crises, it is still in a weak position in action (Salman and Iqbal, 2007: 861–862).

The current capitalist development paradigm has serious obstacles to the creation of sustainable environmental policies. Therefore, the mere acceptance of this inequality and destructiveness is not enough. While non-transformative measures only suppress symptoms for a period of time, they may not develop a therapeutic or preventive perspective. Alternative policies to be created with a feminist environmentalist understanding should be transformative rather than welfarist. It can be possible by changing the technologies used for production, the compositions of the products produced, the technology decision processes, the information systems on which the choices are based. For example, a change in decision-making processes may allow disadvantaged groups to switch to an approach that ensures democratic participation with a top-down approach. In this context, although the actions of women living in the local area are very valuable, there is a need for institutional arrangements that will allow rural poor women to be included in decision-making mechanisms for a transformational approach (Agarwal, 1992: 150–153). In this context, ecofeminism can also be considered a part of ecological and social transformation projects (Delozière et al., 2023: 12).

It can also be seen in protest movements where the thesis that women have a special relationship with nature is not true. Analysis of women's environmental reactions must be analyzed in terms of gender, class, race, property and power and placed within these realities. In this process, it should not be forgotten that women who are "victims" of environmental problems are also active elements in the protection and renewal of the environment. Environmental problems have negative effects on gender as they directly affect the livelihoods of poor and rural women. The differing effects of environmental degradation on processes such as property, gender-based division of labour and development are reflected in the resistance movements by creating opposition. In this context, short-term solutions offered to the problematics of the development paradigm are also questioned. Ecofeminism continues to be a source of hope for new social movements in order to achieve transformation, as it deals with environmental and gender issues together (Rao, 2012: 138–139).

Although it is criticized that there is too much diversity in the ecofeminist movement and that its main lines are not clearly defined, the existence of many ecofeminist movements has strengthened this critical access and contributed to the necessity of developing contemporary struggles against the climate crisis. In this sense, ecofeminism can be interpreted as a turning point in the face of climate crises. By drawing attention to the organizational and political innovations of ecofeminist struggles, ecofeminist thinking should be positioned to encourage strategic thinking in the face of global environmental threats (Delozière, Gaborit and Kabbaj, 2023: 3).

The use of ecofeminism as a tool against environmental threats should also bring about a gender-sensitive structure for participation processes. The active role of women in environmental decision-making processes, like all other decision-making processes, will lead to a more accurate determination of the problems as the party that is more negatively affected by the process. In order to realize a philosophy that blends women and nature, a magical and inclusive environmental approach needs to be developed. Because patriarchy is seen as responsible for environmental destruction and women's being secondary, and fighting against it can only be possible with a holistic approach. Ecology-oriented ecofeminism is an ecological movement led by women and argues that patriarchy is the source of nature and gender domination. In that case, the struggle against patriarchy will both lead to the emergence of an environmentally friendly approach and improve the conditions of women. Since women are the most affected by environmental destruction in the bond established between nature and women, an environmentally friendly approach will also allow for a development in favor of women (Ling, 2014: 67).

On the other hand, the adoption of the idea that women are seen closer to nature, which ecofeminism is most criticized for, may be a reason for the deepening of environmental problems in the 21st century. Because this bond established due to the biological roles of women can mean the reconstruction of gender norms, which is a phenomenon that feminism never wants. Here, the bond of women with nature should be based on the fact that women are affected by environmental changes much more than men. Women are in a close relationship with the world, not with nature, and this should pave the way for women to take an active part in sustainable policies. The fact that women are more affected by problems such as climate change, environmental pollution and deforestation should cause ecofeminism to develop more solutions for the needs in this regard. Sustainable environmental policies can also help achieve gender equality. Considering the role of women in the agricultural sector and their position as the primary food producer, ecofeminism can offer a perspective on sustainable and equitable policies. Women may be victims of environmental problems, but this does not mean that they cannot be effective architects of environmental regeneration. As can be seen from the Chipko movement, women should be conscious of the problems and listen to the voice of ecofeminism (Ojha, 2021). Ecofeminist actions are clear indicators of how women are active and effective actors in the face of environmental problems. Therefore, in the face of 21st-century environmental problems, ecofeminism offers a valuable framework in terms of lessons to be learned despite all its weak points, and complex and criticized sides.

5   Conclusion

Throughout history, the secondary and disadvantaged position of women in society has been questioned. In this context, the problem, which is discussed from various views, has the same philosophy in its essence, although it is divided into different branches from time to time. This philosophy is the fact that the conditions created by patriarchal domination put women at a disadvantage. The branch of feminism that places women on the basis of a relationship with the environment is called ecofeminism. Accordingly, the current patriarchal system is the cause of both environmental and women's problems. Therefore, the solution to both the environment and women's problems lies in the dissolution of the patriarchal system. According to ecofeminism, which is divided into some branches within itself, women and the environment have common points. Ecofeminism considers the domination of women and nature as interdependent approaches. In this sense, the ecological revolution is only possible with a struggle led by women. Because the attitude of societies towards nature is also a spread of the attitude towards women. Here, the solution lies in the implementation of egalitarian policies and the redesign of the distribution of social roles.

All humanity is responsible for the environment. Therefore, the choices made are of vital importance for the sustainability of the environment. Considering how much women are affected by environmental problems; it is obvious that they will play an active role in environmental justice. Therefore, it is necessary to raise awareness of women about the environment and patriarchy. Ecofeminism can be considered as an effective approach to better understand the current climate crisis. For a just and sustainable environment, the importance given to ecofeminist policies should increase. Ecofeminism sees the patriarchal mentality behind the exploitation of women and nature. Therefore, the patriarchal mentality is responsible for the way they treat both women and nature. In order to produce more effective solutions to environmental problems, the patriarchal system should be resolved, and a holistic perspective should be developed in the nature-society-woman triangle. Women are also more affected by environmental problems than men due to the gender roles imposed on them. In this context, women's voices should be at the forefront and their actions should be supported in order to create sustainable environmental policies. Of course, women's activities alone are insufficient to address environmental issues. It is necessary to develop a collaborative approach to this process. Because ecofeminism alone is not a magic wand in solving environmental problems. But in this process, it is clear that ecofeminism is a promising and stimulating approach. Involving all stakeholders in the process will be an effective way to solve environmental problems because not only women but also society is affected by the consequences arising from these problems. Despite all criticism, ecofeminism provides a strong theoretical foundation in the development of women's environmental movements. In this sense, transformative, holistic and non-short-term policies should be implemented., the patriarchal system should be fought, sustainable agricultural policies should be developed, women should be educated about the environment and patriarchy, and women should be involved in the participation processes. Based on all these factors, seeing ecofeminism as a solution to the environmental problems of the 21st century will be a very important approach to gender equality and environmental justice.

References

Agarwal, B. (1992). The gender and environment debate: Lessons from India. *Feminist Studies*, 18(1), 119–158.

Anjum, T. (2020). Ecofeminism: Exploitation of women and nature. *International Journal of English Literature and Social Sciences* (IJELS), 5(4). 846–848.

Archambault, A. (1993). A critique of ecofeminism. *Canadian Woman Studies*, 13(3), 19–22. https://cws.journals.yorku.ca/index.php/cws/article/view/10403/9492.

Aziz, A.A.A. (2021). Is ecofeminism a curse or a bliss? A critical study. *Arab Journal for Scientific Publishing* (AJSP), 20–29. https://www.ajsp.net/research/Is%20Ecofeminism%20a%20Curse%20or%20a%20Bliss.pdf.

Brough, A.R., Wilkie, J.E., Ma, J., Isaac, M.S., & Gal, D. (2016). Is eco-friendly unmanly? The green-feminine stereotype and its effect on sustainable consumption. *Journal of Consumer Research*, 43(4), 567–582.

Buckingham, S. (2004). Ecofeminism in the twenty-first century. *Geographical Journal*, 170(2), 146–154.

Canadian International Development Agency. (2002). Gender Equality and Climate Change. Why consider gender equality when taking action on climate change? https://www.oecd.org/dac/gender-development/44896501.pdf.

Carlassare, E. (2000). Socialist and cultural ecofeminism: Allies in resistance. *Ethics and the Environment*, 5(1), 89–106.

Çetin, O. (2005). Ekofeminizm: Kadın doğa ilişkisi ve ataerkillik. *Sosyoekonomi*, 1(1).

Cuomo, C. (2002). On ecofeminist philosophy. *Ethics and the Environment*, 7(2), 1–11.

Delozière, G., Gaborit, N., & Kabbaj, G. (2023). Ecofeminism. To Break Out of Strategic and Theoretical Impasses in the Face of the Climate Crisis.TransformNetwork. https://www.transform-network.net/fileadmin/user_upload/ecofeminism_en.pdf.

Estévez-Saá, M., & Lorenzo-Modia, M.J. (2018). The ethics and aesthetics of eco-caring: contemporary debates on ecofeminism (s). *Women's Studies*, 47(2), 123–146. https://www.tandfonline.com/doi/full/10.1080/00497878.2018.1425509.

Gaard, G. (2011). Ecofeminism revisited: Rejecting essentialism and re-placing species in a material feminist environmentalism. *Feminist Formations*, 23(2), 26–53. http://www.jstor.org/stable/41301655.

Heidegger,P., Nadège Lharaig, Katy Wiese, Anke Stock, Rose Heffernan. (2021). Why the European Green Deal needs ecofeminism: Moving from gender-blind to gender-transformative environmental policies. EEB&WECF. Report. https://eu.boell.org/sites/default/files/2021-07/Why%20the%20European%20Green%20Deal%20one eds%20ecofeminism.pdf.

Ling, C. (2014). Ecological criticism based on social gender: The basic principles of ecofeminism. *Higher Education of Social Science*, 7(1), 67–72.

Merchant, C. (1981). *The Death of Nature: Woman, Ecology, and the Scientific Revolution*. San Francisco: Harper and Row.

Ojha, S. (2021). Eco Feminism in Indian Context. Eduindex. https://eduindex.org/2021/11/12/eco-feminism-in-indian-context/.

Ottuh, P. (2020). A critique of eco-feminism: An attempt towards environmental solution. *International Journal of Environmental Pollution and Environmental Modelling*, 3(4), 167–179.

Plumwood, V. (2004). "Gender, Eco-Feminism and the Environment". In R. White (Ed.), *Controversies in Environmental Sociology* (pp. 43–60). Cambridge: Cambridge University Press.

Pompeo-Fargnoli, Alyson (2018). Ecofeminist therapy: From theory to practice. *Journal of International Women's Studies*, 19(6), 1–16. https://vc.bridgew.edu/cgi/viewcontent.cgi?article=2055&context=jiws.

Puleo, A.H. (2017). What is ecofeminism. *Quaderns de la Mediterrània*, 25, 27–34.

Rao, M. (2012). Ecofeminism at the crossroads in India: A review. *Dep*, 20(12), 124–142.

Regan, S. (2020). What Is Ecofeminism? Understanding the Intersection of Gender & the Environment. Mbgplanet. https://www.mindbodygreen.com/articles/ecofemin ism-history-and-principles.

Rodriguez Stimson, J.I. (2016). The Chipko movement: a pragmatic, material & spiritual reinterpretation. https://fid4sa-repository.ub.uni-heidelberg.de/3920/7/Rodriguez _Julio_Chipko_Movement_FINAL-1.pdf.

Salleh, A.K. (1984). Deeper than deep ecology: The eco-feminist connection. *Environmental Ethics*, 6(4), 339–345.

Salleh, A. (1992). The ecofeminism/deep ecology debate. *Environmental Ethics*, 14(3), 195–216. http://www.arielsalleh.info/theory/deep-ecology/debate/ee-debate-art.pdf.

Salleh, A. (1995). Nature, woman, labor, capital: living the deepest contradiction. *Capitalism Nature Socialism*, 6(1), 21–39.

Salman, A., & Iqbal, N. (2007). Ecofeminist movements – from the North to the South [with Comments]. *The Pakistan Development Review*, 46(4), 853–864. http://www .jstor.org/stable/41261200.

Sargisson, L. (2001). What's wrong with ecofeminism. *Environmental Politics*, 10(1), 52– 64. https://www.tandfonline.com/doi/pdf/10.1080/714000513.

Sturgeon, N. (2011). "Ecofeminist Movements". In *Ecology: Key Concepts in Critical Theory*, ed. by Carolyn Merchant, 2nd edition, pp. 237–249.

Unwomen. (2022). Explainer: How gender inequality and climate change are inter- connected. https://www.unwomen.org/en/news-stories/explainer/2022/02/explai ner-how-gender-inequality-and-climate-change-are-interconnected?gclid=Cjo KCQjwy9-kBhCHARIsAHpBjHiScKEjAJY_AjgPD84UagnWbrj64piwltoXDA3L2 Q9V5Jss436uGLAaAme6EALw_wcB.

Vural, E., Kantar, G. (2022). Feminist İdeoloji ve Söylem Karşısında Hukuk. *Namık Kemal Üniversitesi Sosyal Bilimler Meslek Yüksek Okulu Dergisi*, 4(2), 34–43.

Warren, K.J. (1990). The power and the promise of ecological feminism. *Environmental Ethics*, 12(2), 125–146.

CHAPTER 6

The Importance of Ecofeminism in Sustainable Development

Miray Özden

Environmental issues pose a serious threat to the sustainability of societies and global ecosystems. To address these problems, it is necessary to consider different perspectives and explain the subject in a multidimensional manner. In this context, ecofeminism has become an important approach. Ecofeminism highlights the connection between environmental issues and gender inequality, advocating that women can play a significant role in solving environmental problems. Ecofeminism emphasizes the interdependence between nature and human society. The fundamental goal of sustainable development is to prioritize actions that ensure the transfer of natural resources to future generations, and ecofeminism supports this idea by considering the interdependence between nature and humans and establishing connections between environmental sustainability and gender equality.

Ecofeminism argues that the relationship between nature and humans has been undermined by patriarchal systems and that this destruction also affects women. Women generally exhibit a stronger connection with nature and are more sensitive to environmental issues. The ecofeminist perspective suggests that women play a more active role in addressing environmental problems and hold great potential for achieving sustainable development goals. Ecofeminism also advocates for a greater representation of women in environmental policies and decision-making processes. By focusing on women's leadership roles and participation, a more inclusive and fair environmental policy can be established. Women's experiences and perspectives are valuable resources for understanding environmental issues and developing solutions. Furthermore, ecofeminism highlights the connection between gender equality and environmental sustainability, proposing that gender equality can become an essential element of environmental sustainability. This book chapter aims to define the relationship between ecofeminism and sustainable development, evaluate the impact of women on environmental policies, and emphasize the creation of policies and actions for a fair, sustainable, and inclusive future.

1   Introduction

As an ideology, feminism is inherently specific and politically autonomous. It originates from the standpoint that women are disadvantaged, unequal, and in a secondary position compared to men as they are oppressed and exploited. Unlike previous ideologies and social movements, feminism brings forth social gender hierarchy as a fundamental category. This hierarchy creates a foundational power relationship that shapes societies much like class contradictions. This reveals a social and political order in which men are dominant and women are dependent.

Feminism encompasses the liberation of women, preventing their subjugation, legitimizing their rights, and striving for equal rights in their public or private actions and activities. In other words, the concept of feminism includes activities related to women's legitimate rights, their subjugation, their status of being kept in equal standing or emancipation, and their demands for a different value. Feminism opposes gender discrimination and advocates various forms of economic, political, sociocultural, and societal equality between genders. It encompasses philosophy, sociology, politics and ethics. The primary objectives of feminism typically revolve around women's freedom and fundamental rights and address patriarchal structures and phenomena. The key issues addressed by feminism include equal rights and status with men in areas such as work, education, and childcare; reproductive rights such as the availability of safe abortion; advancements in women's health; prevention of violence against women; eradication of rape and sexual harassment; and the rights of lesbians, among other diverse areas.

It is widely recognized that there is no singular and fixed definition of feminism or feminist theory, and that there are different perspectives on how feminism has evolved throughout historical processes or how feminist movements have emerged. This can be attributed to different groups having varying viewpoints. The historical development of feminism manifests itself in different forms. Some categorize the development of feminism into one or two waves, whereas others divide it into three or four waves. However, the historical development of feminist movements is often considered to consist of three chronological waves, which are commonly referred to as the First, Second, and Third Waves of feminism. These three waves typically encompass the period from the 19th century to the 21st century. During these periods, women were influenced by different understandings, theories, and ideologies, and these influences have indirectly or directly affected the movements they have undertaken in pursuit of their rights or objectives in relation to women's rights.

The First Wave of feminism, which emerged towards the end of the 19th century and the beginning of the 20th century, was built upon the demands outlined by Wollstonecraft in her work *A Vindication of the Rights of Women*. In general, these demands include women's suffrage (the right to vote), equal opportunities in education, and women's property rights. The First Wave aimed to challenge traditional gender roles and patriarchal norms that limited women's rights and opportunities. It sought to achieve legal and political equality for women by focusing on issues such as suffrage, access to education, and property ownership. The efforts of the First Wave laid the foundation for subsequent feminist movements and paved the way for further advancement in women's rights.

Second Wave feminists no longer saw the inequalities created through socialization between genders as the sole cause of women's oppression. On the contrary, they believed that aspects that made women different from men contained the seeds of women's liberation. Instead of trying to diminish the polarization between masculinity and femininity, they sought to identify and define aspects of women's historical and psychological experiences that could serve as sources of power. Additionally, within the Second Wave feminist movement, there were radical, reformist, and comprehensive demands aimed at transforming the society. This idea, particularly embodied in Simone de Beauvoir's statement "One is not born, but rather becomes, a woman" and her declaration in *The Second Sex* that "Women's liberation will begin with their bodies," became a rallying cry.

The Third Wave of feminism emerged in the early 1990s as a response to the practices and misconceptions of second-wave feminism. This response primarily criticized the perspective that reduced feminism to the experiences of upper-middle-class white women and aimed to broaden the scope of women's movements. The Third Wave of feminism emphasizes the individual experiences and diverse perspectives of women, rejecting the notion of a universal, homogeneous understanding of womanhood prevalent in second-wave feminism. They highlight that women's issues are not solely the problems of white women and emphasize the need to address women's concerns at a universal level. Third-wave feminists have focused more on micro-politics, such as violence against women, sexuality, and women's empowerment. They also explored a wider range of topics than the previous two waves. Third Wave feminism addresses the issues that limit and oppress women and promotes increased awareness through activism and widespread education as catalysts for societal change. Additionally, the widespread use of digital technology has added a new dimension to feminist theories, leading to the emergence of the Fourth Wave of feminism. The Fourth Wave of feminism, which began in 2013, focuses on empowering women through the utilization of Internet tools and platforms. It harnesses the power of social media, online activism, and digital spaces to raise awareness, mobilize communities, and advocate for gender equality. The Fourth Wave of feminism recognizes the potential of digitalization to amplify marginalized voices, challenge traditional power structures, and facilitate global feminist solidarity. It embraces opportunities presented by the digital age to advance feminist causes and address contemporary issues facing women and gender minorities.

In the Fourth Wave stage, feminist discourses expanded to include women's resistance to male-dominated thinking in environmental issues as well. It has been recognized that departing from the prevailing mindset is crucial for taking more sustainable steps in the future. As a result, various movements, such as cyberfeminism, radical feminism, and ecofeminism, have gained prominence and have been incorporated into feminist discussions. These movements aimed to broaden the scope of feminist activism by addressing issues related to technology, the digital sphere, environmentalism, and the interconnectedness of gender, power, and ecology. They highlight the importance of challenging patriarchal norms and systems in all aspects of society, including the realms of technology and environment. By integrating these perspectives, the Fourth Wave of feminism seeks to create a more inclusive, intersectional, forward-thinking feminist movement.

The world is at a time when we have to sustain our dependence on resources that are vital to our planet's ecological balance and diversity. Human activities have led to problems that seriously affect the environment and endanger natural ecosystems. To overcome this challenge, concepts such as sustainable development and ecofeminism have become increasingly important.

Sustainable development is an approach that aims to ensure that future generations have the same opportunities by using existing resources in the most efficient way to meet people's needs. However, it is not only limited to economic growth and social development but also includes environmental sustainability. Therefore, sustainable development also involves environmental problems, such as preserving ecosystems, biodiversity, and climate change.

At this point, ecofeminism emerges. Ecofeminism seeks to build bridges between environmental sustainability and social gender equality by connecting nature and gender. This movement argues that women and nature are exploited and destroyed in similar ways. Ecofeminists argue that patriarchal social structures deepen environmental problems and inequalities and emphasize the unification of the power of nature and women to solve these problems.

In this chapter, we conduct an in-depth review to explore the relationship between sustainable development and ecofeminism and understand how these two concepts can work together. It will also assess the impact of ecofeminism on sustainable development policies and practices and discuss from what perspectives this approach will be used in future sustainability studies.

2   Sustainability and Sustainable Development: a Conceptual Perspective

The concept of sustainability has become significant in making decisions regarding not only environmental issues such as climate change and biodiversity loss, but also social issues that concern different levels of society, such as poverty and health problems. Owing to the importance of the concept of sustainable development, or perhaps as a result of it, it is challenging to interpret and operationalize it in various ways, making its implementation and utilization in, for example, planning processes difficult. The source of these different interpretations lies in sustainability discourses that reflect different perspectives on human relationships with nature as well as varying assessments of justice and different evaluations of what is defined as a problem and what is seen as a solution.

Sustainability, defined as "the ability to maintain the continuity of diversity, productivity, and development while preserving the ability to endure," was introduced to the literature in a report titled "Our Common Future" published by the World Commission on Environment and Development, operating within the United Nations (UN) in 1987. Sustainability is widely used in various fields. It constitutes the fundamental starting point of development, allowing the current generation to meet their needs by benefiting from the natural resources that the Earth possesses without compromising the rights of future generations to meet their needs from these resources (Keleş, 2017). Sustainability refers to the concept of using resources and engaging in practices that meet present needs without compromising the ability of future generations to meet their needs. This involves balancing economic, environmental, and social factors to ensure long-term viability and well-being. Sustainability aims to promote responsible consumption, resource conservation, environmental protection, and social equity. It emphasizes finding solutions that can support and maintain a healthy and prosperous society while also preserving the natural environment for future generations. The goal is to create a harmonious balance among economic development, social progress, and environmental protection.

The Brundtland Report stated that the emergence of sustainable development was influenced by poverty in developing countries and by unsustainable consumption and production patterns in developed countries. This called for the creation of the concept of sustainable development to address critical environmental issues and socioeconomic problems in society by integrating development and environmental concerns and developing common solutions. The report defined sustainable development as "development that meets the needs of the present without compromising the ability of future generations to meet their own needs" (UN, 1987). It also highlighted the rapid increase in poverty, the limitations imposed on people's lives by technology and social development and stated that sustainable development would provide an opportunity to meet everyone's basic needs and fulfill desires for a better life as a proposed solution.

Sustainable development, despite being defined in various ways, is essentially regarded as an approach that increases awareness of the environmental, social, and economic constraints we face in society and balances the fulfillment of potential needs that may arise in this regard. Sustainable development goes beyond a predetermined outcome and encompasses a continuous journey that requires multiple steps, involving methods of experimentation and diffusion as well as elements of transparency and learning (Sustainable Development Commission, 2011). Therefore, this approach involves taking steps to select the best available path that benefits everyone. The metaphor of sustainable development as a journey entails the adoption and implementation of sustainable development principles in all areas by different organizations, policies, operations, and individuals.

The central concept in sustainable development is the need for intergenerational equity. This is because future generations have the same rights as present ones. More precisely, this establishes the concept of intergenerational equity. Intergenerational equity means that people from different political, economic, social and geographical contexts have the same rights (SDC, 2011).

The understanding of sustainable development determines the common denominator in the economic and social development goals of countries as "sustainability". This common goal, which also embraces the future, aims to enable everyone to meet their basic needs and expectations for a better life (Sustainable Development, 2022).

The success of the concept of sustainable development, which is mainly a resource for environmental issues and ecology, is that it has served as a source of inspiration for international debates and has inspired a great deal of in-depth research, thus helping to answer the question of what the dimensions of sustainable development are over time. In this respect, development should not be perceived as a permanent state or a static construct but rather as a continuous process that refers to the integration of three fundamental and integral aspects of development: environmental, economic, and social. The definition of "sustainability" is the study of how natural systems work, how they maintain their diversity, and how they produce all that the ecology needs to balance. Therefore, it is a broad definition that includes more than one dimension.

The three main dimensions that form the backbone of sustainable development and are included in many national standards and certifications are defined as follows (Environmental Science, 2018):

– *Economic sustainability:* Economic sustainability can be defined as the capacity of an economic system's indicators to grow in a sustained and progressive manner (in particular, the capacity to generate income and employment to sustain the population). In a regional system, economic sustainability means having the ability to generate and sustain the highest value-added, with the most efficient mix of resources, to increase the specificity of regional products and services.

– *Environmental sustainability:* Environmental sustainability can be defined as the capacity to maintain the three basic functions of the environment over time: resource supply, waste, and direct usefulness. In other words, within a territory (region), environmental sustainability helps preserve and regenerate the environment and its features, as well as natural resources and environmental heritage. It also focuses on helping us identify the elements that emphasize the environment and how to protect our environment from the damaging aspects of technology.

– *Social sustainability:* Social sustainability can be defined as the ability to guarantee well-being (security, health, and education) that is equally distributed across social classes and genders. Social sustainability means increasing the capacity of different stakeholders and institutions at all levels to interact effectively and improve the dialogue between them towards the same goals and objectives.

Sustainable development is founded upon political and ethical principles, positing that the social and economic dynamics of contemporary economies can harmoniously align with enhancing living conditions while indefinitely replenishing natural resources. It is therefore necessary to guarantee economic development that is truly compatible with social equity and ecosystems that can act in environmental balance and respect the so-called "Rule of Balance of the Three E's: Environment, Equity, Economy" (SOGESID, n.d.). Nevertheless, it is important to highlight the close interconnections shared by these dimensions. These interconnections are concepts of "livability, fairness, sustainability, and achievability", which constitute common areas for all three dimensions. These concepts are illustrated in Figure 6.1.

When considering the dimensions of sustainable development depicted in the above figure, they should be perceived as a framework of system components that contribute equally to achieving the same goal rather than being independent. Consequently, every plan or activity should consider these relationships. A plan or program that supports only one or two dimensions does not contribute to sustainable development. The assessment of sustainable development depends on the effective integration of all dimensions into the process and structuring them in accordance with the shared goals of being livable, fair, achievable, and sustainable.

Sustainable development, in addition to the belief that it requires significant individual behavioral changes in the mentioned dimensions (environmental, social, and economic), also demands a high level of commitment from political administrations and governance at all levels (international, national, and regional) in decision-making. In 2005, the Labour Party in the United Kingdom launched a renewed strategic plan to secure a sustainable future. Within the framework of this commitment, a plan titled "Common Future: Different Paths" was created, outlining specific principles for sustainable development. This document aimed to institutionalize sustainable development as a central organizing principle for governance and implemented the following five

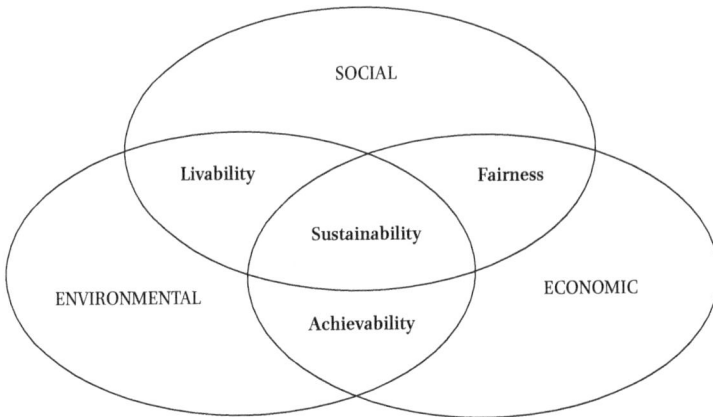

FIGURE 6.1   The relationship between the three dimensions of sustainable
             development and the three E's rule of balance
             SOURCE: SUSTAINABLE DEVELOPMENT (2018), *THE EVOLUTION
             OF THE "SUSTAINABLE DEVELOPMENT" CONCEPT,* HTTP://WWW
             .SOGESID.IT/ENGLISH_SITE/SUSTAINABLE_DEVELOPMENT.HTML,
             (21.10.2018).

principles: "living within environmental limits; ensuring a strong, healthy, and just society; achieving a sustainable economy; promoting good governance; and using sound science responsibly." These principles were adopted for sustainable development and should be considered in all plans, as stated by the Sustainable Development Commission (2011):

- *Living within environmental limits:* Respecting the boundaries of the planet, the environment, resources, and biodiversity; improving our surroundings; and ensuring the preservation of natural resources necessary for life without compromising their availability for future generations.
- *Ensuring a strong, healthy, and just society:* The objective is to fulfil the varied requirements of present and future communities, foster individual welfare, encourage social unity, instill a sense of belonging, and establish equitable prospects.
- *Achieving a sustainable economy:* Establishing a strong and stable sustainable economy that provides a prosperous environment for everyone, offering opportunities, and promoting the efficient and effective use of resources.
- *Using evidence-based practices effectively:* Encouraging the creation and improvement of robust scientific evidence by considering policy making, and eliminating scientific uncertainty while also taking into account public attitudes and behaviors.
- *Promoting good governance:* Encouraging effective and participatory governance systems for all sections of society, multiplying platforms that enhance individuals' creativity, reflecting their energy, and providing a pluralistic understanding of sustainable practices.

This strategic text in the UK emphasizes the importance of state support in achieving sustainable development and setting common goals. When sustainable development is expressed as a process, it necessitates the inclusion of various actors in the process and suggests that the opinions, recommendations, and criticisms put forward by decision-makers should be secured within the framework of legal texts and that the determination of common goals can be made in this direction.

3   The Relationship between Women and Nature in Ecological
       Approach: Ecofeminism

Murray Bookchin is a prominent figure in defining the relationship between nature and humans. He is an American scientist recognized as the founder of the social ecology movement, which aligns with libertarian, socialist, and

ecological thought. Bookchin gained attention by synthesizing anarchist traditions with contemporary ecological consciousness. Starting in the 1960s,
he directed criticism of modern social structures from a radical ecological
perspective, conducting extensive research and examination on the social
and political origins of the ecological crisis. According to Bookchin, ecological movements that prioritize the preservation of natural resources while
disregarding the social causes of ecological problems (such as deep ecology,
green politics, eco-feminism, and other radical ecological movements) are not
genuinely humanistic and possess a distorted understanding that serves the
destruction of the environment. It is a futile expectation to believe that such
ecological movements can provide solutions to ecological crises and lead to
societal change (İnce, 2020).

The fundamental starting point of social ecology is the idea that problems between society and nature do not arise from conflicts between society
and nature themselves, but rather from social development (Önder, 2002).
According to Bookchin, the perceived dichotomy and division between society
and nature today stems from divisions within the social realm and from conflicts among individuals (Bookchin, 1994). Therefore, the ecological problems
witnessed today must be attributed to the "irrational" and "anti-ecological"
nature of the society in which they occur. The root of the problem lies in the
conception that humanity must exploit and dominate nature, a conception
that ultimately originates from the domination and exploitation of humans
over each other. According to Bookchin, this understanding, which can be
traced back to primitive times when men began to exploit and subjugate
women within patriarchal families, fundamentally found its initial form in
gerontocratic structures (rule by the elderly). Since then, humans have increasingly been seen not as subjects, but as objects and mere resources. Hierarchies,
classes, forms of property, and statist institutions that emerge from social
domination have been conceptually transferred to humanity's relationship
with nature. Nature, in turn, has come to be viewed as a mercilessly exploit-
able resource, an object, and a raw material, much like slaves on a latifundium
(Bookchin, 1994). The ecological problems faced today are the result of this
understanding.

Ecofeminism is a conceptual movement that identifies the behaviors towards
nature with women and explores environmental issues and climate change
from a feminist perspective. Emerging as an intellectual field and social movement after the 1970s, the ecofeminist approach seeks to establish a connection
between gender inequality and ecological destruction to provide a comprehensive response to contemporary problems. According to this perspective,
there exists a systematic relationship between the oppression of women and

the exploitation of nature, as well as between the patriarchal system, its extension of capitalism, and the exploitation of women and nature. Ecofeminists argue that colonialism, the global ecological crisis, the exploitation of labor, racism, and the subjugation of women are interconnected and share a common pattern in the historical process in which we exist (Demir, 2018).

The concept of ecofeminism was first used by feminist activist 'Françoise d'Eaubonne' in her book *La Féminisme ou la Mort* (*Feminism or Death*), published in 1974 (Ferry, 2000). Throughout her book, d'Eaubonne discussed a new ideology that combined feminism and ecological approaches, which she referred to as "ecofeminism." In this work, she established a connection between the oppression of women and nature, asserting that the freedom of both women and nature would be intertwined (Tong, 2006).

Ecofeminism emerged in the 1970s and gained prominence as a highly debated topic during the 1980s. Ecofeminism is a movement that recognizes the connection between the exploitation of the natural world and the oppression of women. It emerged in the mid-1970s, fueled by the forces of the second and third waves of feminism as well as the environmentalist movement. Ecofeminism seeks to address both the gendered understanding that feminism challenges and solutions to environmental issues by combining feminist and environmentalist perspectives (Mellor, 1997). It aims to fight against the existing worldview while striving to resolve nature and environmental problems.

Ecofeminism has emerged as a result of the intersection between feminist research and various social justice and environmental movements. This exploration highlighted the interconnected oppressions experienced in relation to gender, ecology, race, species, and nation. Key foundational texts, such as Susan Griffin's *Woman and Nature* (1978) and Carolyn Merchant's *The Death of Nature* (1980), played a significant role in uncovering these connections. Mary Daly's *Gyn/Ecology* (1978), another impactful piece, exposed the historical and cross-cultural mistreatment of women, which received validation from male-dominated establishments such as religion, culture, and medical science. Daly's research established a link between women's physical well-being and the environment, highlighting the significance of reclaiming a language and mindset that revolves around women.

In the 1980s, feminist activism took an ecological and feminist perspective that emphasized the interconnectedness of militarism, corporatism, and unsustainable energy production. This perspective was exemplified by the alliance formed between antinuclear protests and the peace movement. At Greenham Common in England, the women's peace camp, known as "Women for Life on Earth," began in 1981 and lasted until 2000. The camp pressured the Royal Air Force to halt the operation and testing of nuclear cruise missiles, expressing concerns about the future of children and the living world as the foundation of life. The early years of this movement were documented in Alice Cook and Gwyn Kirk's book *Greenham Women Everywhere* (1983), which featured photographs and interviews. Another anthology, *Reclaim the Earth* (1983) by Leonie Caldecott and Stephanie Leland, presents international feminist perspectives on the intersection of women and ecology. It established a connection between the "Women's Pentagon Action" and the women's peace camp, encompassing a wide range of concerns such as women's health, poverty, food security, forestry, urban ecology, indigenous communities and their environments, technology, animal rights, childbirth, female infanticide, labor, recreation, militarism, philosophy, and spirituality. This anthology bridged the gap between theory and activism, offering not only scholarly work but also poetry, and featuring a diverse range of feminists including Wangari Maathai, Rosalie Bertell, Wilmette Brown, Marta Zabaleta, the Manushi Collective, and Anita Anand, who contributed insights on topics such as the Green Belt Movement, nuclear power and health, black ghetto ecology, the Mothers of the Plaza de Mayo, female infanticide, and the Chipko Andolan (Gaard, 2011).

When it comes to the ecofeminist ideology, three main paths of development can be identified. The first path revolves around examining ideas regarding domination in history and political theory. Feminists who study Marxist theories have rejected claims that sovereignty is only analyzed within the context of capital accumulation and production relations, pointing out the deficiencies of theories that ignore both nature and women. The second path relates to feminist research on history, which argues that women are not subordinate to men, and focuses on discussions about the liberation of both the world and women. The third path is through environmentalism. According to Schmonsky (2012), many women with careers in public policy, technology, science, and environmental studies are connected to feminism. Particularly, women are becoming interested in issues that hinder their careers and are directing their efforts towards ecofeminism, which provides new meaning to their work (Schmonsky, 2012).

Feminist and environmentalist women who come together to discuss the intersections of feminism and environmentalism emphasize the necessity of respecting women and nature, highlighting that throughout human history, women and nature have been associated and both have been oppressed (Plumwood, 2004). Women and nature have often been portrayed under the male-dominant understanding as chaotic, irrational, and objects to be controlled, whereas men have been depicted as rational and controlling beings.

While trying to make the destructive effects of patriarchy and capitalism on nature and women more visible and provide solutions to them, it also addresses the contradictions between production and reproduction. Because "changes in production relations and social and biological reproduction ... are the basis of social change" (Carlassare, 2000). For example, when radioactivity, toxic chemicals, and hazardous waste threaten the biological reproduction of human species, ecofeminists perceive these threats as attacks on women's bodies and children, and they rise against them. Household products, industrial pollutants, plastics, and packaging waste are elements that invade women's homes and jeopardize their lives. Such chemicals pollute the water and food systems, leading to diseases and birth defects, posing a threat to women's lives. The ecofeminist agenda focuses on interconnected and sustained contextual processes that bind all beings together rather than addressing short-sighted and one-sided production.

Ecofeminism combines environmental justice and gender equality. The fundamental principles of ecofeminism are as follows (Warren, 1987; Warren, 1997, Hawkins, 1998):

- *Ecological consciousness:* Ecofeminism emphasizes the sacredness of nature and the need for humans to live in harmony. It strives to protect the integrity of nature and to promote environmental sustainability.
- *Social gender equality:* Ecofeminism approaches gender equality from the perspective of advocating for the rights of women to live in society with equality, freedom, and justice. Ecofeminists have argued that gender discrimination in society is closely related to environmental issues.
- *Mutual interdependence:* Ecofeminism highlights the importance of mutual interdependence between humans and nature. The destruction of nature and increase in environmental problems also harm humans. Ecofeminists contend that an exploitative and controlling mindset towards nature hinders a sustainable future.
- *Rejection of violence:* Ecofeminism criticizes the negative effects of violence on nature and women. Ecofeminists argue that the devastation of nature and gender-based violence has the same roots and reinforces each other. Therefore, ecofeminism aims to end the violence against nature and women.
- *Partnership and cooperation:* Ecofeminism encourages collaboration and a spirit of solidarity. By uniting the power of women and nature, it advocates collective action to create a sustainable future. Ecofeminists emphasize that we are interconnected and dependent on each other to ensure the well-being of both humans and nature.

While these principles form a general framework for ecofeminism, ecofeminist thought may encompass various sub-movements and interpretations. The connection between ecology and feminism also encompasses both emotional and environmental elements and ecofeminism results from this dualistic relationship. Ecofeminism asserts that nature and women are exploited and harmed similarly. This movement opposed the tendency of a male-dominated culture to control and exploit both nature and women. Ecofeminists argue that the degradation of nature and gender-based violence stems from a shared root and reinforces each other (Ağkurt, 2023).

This emotional connection enables ecofeminism to stand against discrimination and violence towards women and nature, relying on sensitivity and empathy. Women, traditionally perceived as having a close relationship with nature and playing a significant role in the sustainable use of natural resources, represent a group in which ecofeminism seeks to protect and strengthen the relationship between women and nature.

This environmental connection allows ecofeminism to emphasize the sacredness of nature and the importance of environmental justice. Ecofeminism advocates living in harmony with nature and striving to achieve environmental sustainability. The degradation of nature, environmental issues, and climate change are focal points of ecofeminism. This can also be explained with the help of Table 6.1 (Ağkurt, 2023).

Ecofeminism argues that patriarchal understanding that oppresses women also leads to ecological problems by constantly seeking to control and transform nature according to its own desires. At this point, ecofeminism asserts that addressing both women's issues and ecological issues together by

TABLE 6.1   Elements of ecofeminism

Spiritual vision	Environmental vision
The Earth and all life forms are sacred and should be protected.	The world is an ecosystem where all species are interconnected.
Humans exist in a community with the Earth.	Humanity should live in harmony with nature.
The most important value is spirituality.	Nature should be the primary value.
Change should be made to reclaim the past.	Change should be made to build the future.
Explorations should be made to understand Mother Nature and live in harmony with her.	One should live in harmony with nature.

liberating them from patriarchal understanding will lead to the resolution of
these issues. Ecofeminists envision a world without domination over nature
and women, blending feminist ideology and ecological elements in the same
context and demanding an equal, just, and oppression-free world.

4   Can Ecofeminism Be a Solution to Achieving Sustainable Development Goals?

The emergence of the concept of sustainable development was driven by concerns for the well-being of humanity and the planet (Hopwood et al., 2005).
However, recent studies suggest that the vague and subjective nature of this
concept has allowed corporate narratives to shape its interpretation (Jacobs,
1999). While the original aim of sustainable development was to offer an alternative to the prevailing economic paradigm, it has instead been absorbed into
the same model, where economic growth takes precedence over ecological
and social welfare (Banerjee, 2003). It has also been observed that within the
framework of sustainable development, nature is often treated as a commodity
to be controlled (Tregidga et al., 2013). However, little attention has been paid
to understanding the structural connections between gender and nature in
corporate discourse. This raises the following question: How can we gain a better understanding of the interplay between gender and nature in the current
conceptualizations of sustainable development? If sustainable development
continues to be employed within corporate narratives, it is crucial to conduct
research to uncover the intertwined systems of dominance exerted on gender
and nature within these discourses.

Sustainability and sustainable development focus on balancing the delicate
line between technological and economic progress among competitive needs,
and the necessity to protect the environment in which we and others live.
Sustainability is not only about the environment, but also about examining
the long-term effects of our actions on societal health and how they can be
improved to ensure that individuals or their living spaces are not harmed as a
result of environmental legislation (Environmental Science, 2018). Therefore,
when defining sustainable development, it is important to emphasize and
articulate the goals it aims to achieve and express as a process that contributes
to the creation of common international texts related to this process.

The Millennium Development Goals, adopted in September 2000 at the
United Nations Millennium Summit in New York, represent the development
goals outlined in the Millennium Declaration. The Millennium Development
Goals consist of eight main objectives that were planned to be achieved by

2015 by 192 member countries of the United Nations. These eight Millennium Development Goals were developed to measure and monitor progress in sustainable development and poverty reduction by 2015 in a measurable and trackable manner (UN, 2023).[1]

The third goal of the Millennium Development Goals focuses on "Promoting gender equality and empowering women". This goal aims to empower women and promote gender equality in society. It seeks to ensure that women have increased access to opportunities in areas such as education, health, employment, and political participation.

This goal encompasses various sub-goals, including increasing women's access to education and healthcare services, enhancing their employability and economic empowerment, promoting women's participation in political decision-making, and preventing gender-based violence.

The Millennium Development Goals were replaced by Sustainable Development Goals (SDGs) in 2015. The Sustainable Development Goals (SDGs), also known as the Global Goals, are a universal call for action that includes targets to be achieved by United Nations member countries by the end of 2030. They focus on resolving social, cultural, and ecological issues in 17 main areas, such as eradicating hunger and poverty worldwide, fighting against climate change, ensuring gender equality, promoting quality education, and fostering responsible production and consumption. This came into effect in January of 2016. Each goal consists of specific targets and indicators to monitor progress towards achieving them (UN, 2013).

At least 7 of the sustainable development goals include provisions related to women. Goal 5 of the SDGs specifically focuses on "Gender Equality". It aims to achieve gender equality and empower both women and girls. This goal addresses issues such as eliminating discrimination, ending violence, and harmful practices against women and girls; ensuring equal rights and opportunities; promoting women's leadership and participation; and ensuring universal access to sexual and reproductive health and rights. The nine aims within the main theme of gender equality can be prioritized and summarized as follows (UNSDG, 2018):

---

1   The eight main components of the Millennium Development Goals are as follows: "– Goal 1: Eradicate extreme poverty and hunger. – Goal 2: Achieving Universal Primary Education. – Goal 3: Promote gender equality and empower women. – Goal 4: Reduces child mortality. – Goal 5: Improving maternal health. – Goal 6: Combat HIV/AIDS, malaria, and other diseases. – Goal 7: Ensure environmental sustainability. – Goal 8: Develop a global partnership for development".

- *Aim 7:* Reforms should be implemented to ensure equal rights for women in accordance with national laws, specifically in accessing economic resources, land, and other forms of property, having control over them, accessing financial services, inheritance, and natural resources.
- *Aim 8:* The development and utilization of enabling technologies, particularly information and communication technologies, should be enhanced to empower women and advance their empowerment.
- *Aim 9:* Robust policies and legally enforceable legislation should be adopted and strengthened to promote gender equality and empower women and girls at all levels.

These summaries capture the essence of goals within the context of gender equality and their connections to ecofeminism's network of relationships. Ecofeminists argue that the prevailing global economy is characterized by a value system that subjugates both women and nature, considering itself superior to traditional subsistence economies. The modern economic system is based on a hierarchical structure of values, primarily driven by monetary profit and prestige. However, it overlooks or undervalues certain elements, such as the resilience of ecosystems, the unpaid domestic labor performed by women, and the social reciprocity found in non-market economies of communal societies.

One core principle of ecofeminism asserts that male control of land has resulted in a dominant culture known as patriarchy, which manifests in practices such as food exports, overgrazing, the tragedy of the commons, exploitation of people, and an exploitative approach to land and animals, valuing them solely as economic resources. Additionally, some ecofeminists have argued that the degradation of nature directly contributes to the degradation of women.

The connection between women's subordination and the degradation of the natural world is rooted in the central role of women in the support economies of reproduction, unpaid domestic work, and social reciprocity within the realms of home and community. These aspects form an unvalued economy, representing women's experiences – a "WE-economy". Conversely, the valued economy is male-dominated, reflecting men's experiences a "ME-economy". (Linnik, 2008).

The ecosystem explains the construction of destructive economic systems and views the WE economy as the foundation for an alternative, non-exploitative, and sustainable economy. As the ME economy has largely marginalized women, the lives and experiences of women hold the potential for an alternative path. Throughout history, women have been the backbone of economic and social systems, despite their work often being unrecognized (Linnik, 2008).

Therefore, within the dynamics of sustainable development, the main arguments encompassed by ecofeminist economics are outlined as follows (Tisdell, 2005):

- *Critique of Dualistic Value Systems:* Ecofeminist economics challenges dualistic value systems that prioritize profit and monetary measures while disregarding unvalued or undervalued aspects, such as the resilience of eco-systems, unpaid domestic work, and social reciprocity.
- *Subordination of Women and Nature:* Ecofeminist economics highlights the interconnectedness between the subordination of women and degradation of the natural world. It emphasizes how women's roles in support econo-mies, reproductive labor, and community-based activities have been under-valued and exploited within dominant economic systems.
- *Alternative Pathways:* Ecofeminist economics proposes alternative pathways to address the shortcomings of mainstream economic models. It advocates an economy that values and incorporates the perspectives and experiences of women, emphasizing sustainability, non-exploitation, and the well-being of both humans and the environment.
- *Recognition of Unacknowledged Labor:* Ecofeminist economics seeks to rec-ognize and value the labor performed by women that has historically been overlooked or undervalued, such as unpaid domestic work and community care work. It aims to challenge and transform the existing power structures that perpetuate gender inequalities within economic systems.
- *Sustainability and Environmental Justice:* Ecofeminist economics empha-sizes the importance of environmental sustainability and the pursuit of jus-tice for both women and the natural world. It critiques the exploitation of nature for profit and advocates a more harmonious relationship between humans and the environment.

Overall, ecofeminist economics provides a framework that critiques existing economic paradigms, identifies the intersections between gender and the envi-ronment, and advocates alternative economic models that prioritize equality, sustainability, and well-being. In addition, the following statements can be added for further elaboration (Weiss and Moskop, 2020; McMahon, 1997):

- *Intersectionality:* Ecofeminist economics recognizes the intersectionality of oppression, understanding that the subordination of women is experienced differently based on factors such as race, class, and other social identities. It emphasizes the need to address these intersecting forms of discrimination and advocate inclusive and equitable economic systems.
- *Care Ethics:* Ecofeminist economics highlights the importance of care ethics in economic decision-making. It emphasizes the value of caregiving, both within the domestic sphere and in broader societal contexts, and argues

for policies that prioritize social well-being and the quality of relationships over economic considerations.

- *Ecological Wisdom:* Ecofeminist economics emphasizes the need for ecological wisdom in economic systems. It recognizes the intrinsic value of nature and advocates for sustainable practices that respect Earth's ecosystems, promote biodiversity, and ensure the long-term well-being of both humans and the natural world.
- *Grassroots Movement:* Ecofeminist economics acknowledges the significance of grassroots movements and community-based initiatives in challenging dominant economic structures. It supports the empowerment of local communities, alternative economic practices, such as cooperatives and community-supported agriculture, and the democratization of economic decision-making processes.
- *Global Solidarity:* Ecofeminist economics recognizes the importance of global solidarity in addressing economic and environmental challenges. This calls for collaboration and cooperation among diverse groups, acknowledging that issues of gender equality and environmental sustainability are global concerns that require collective action and shared responsibility.

By incorporating these additional statements, a more comprehensive understanding of ecofeminist economics and its perspective on sustainable development can be achieved (Linnik, 2008).

1. There would be a shift in focus from detached and disembodied structures to work and consumption patterns that prioritize the human life cycle and ecological sustainability.
2. Local production would be oriented towards meeting local needs and utilizing sustainable local resources while minimizing waste.
3. Essential food provision is local and seasonal, with an emphasis on locally grown produce. Direct purchasing arrangements with local farmers and promotion of farmers' markets are encouraged.
4. The main focus of economic systems is the provision of necessary goods and services, rather than prioritizing profit generation. Individuals should be able to live and work within a provisioning system without the need for harmful or exploitative work.
5. The emphasis is on meaningful work rather than employment for the sake of financial gain. Individuals are not required to engage in harmful work to sustain their livelihoods. Any additional profit-oriented economic activity is subject to strict regulations regarding resource usage, pollution, and labor exploitation.
6. Work and life can be integrated into interactive workplaces and living environments. Activities would be shared among people of all ages and

abilities, and households would vary in size from single persons to multiple persons.

7. Fulfilling necessary work would be a shared responsibility between genders, with work and leisure activities intertwined. Festivals and celebratory events would regularly punctuate productive work.

8. Inter-regional and international trade are viewed as cultural exchanges as well as economic transactions. Travel is undertaken primarily for educational and communication purposes rather than excessive consumption.

9. Personal security is rooted in the social reciprocity of a provisioning WE-economy economy rather than relying on wealth accumulation systems, particularly in old age.

Building an economic system that genuinely values women and nature requires a clear vision, understanding, and significant political effort, beginning at the local community level where everyone resides.

Ecofeminism plays a crucial role in advancing sustainable development by highlighting the interconnectedness among gender equality, environmental sustainability, and social justice. Overall, ecofeminism provides a critical lens through which to analyze and transform systems of oppression, inequality, and environmental degradation. By integrating gender equality, social justice, and environmental sustainability, ecofeminism contributes a more inclusive, equitable, and ecologically balanced approach to sustainable development (Julian and Molina, 2013).

Ecofeminism questions the adoption of an individual-centered neoclassical economic model as a basis for ecological economic theory. It argues that this model is detrimental to the environment and is biased in terms of gender. Instead, ecofeminism advocates a bottom-up approach to tackling environmental degradation, which considers lived experiences rather than relying on abstract theoretical constructs. Within the context of existing systemic inequalities, ecofeminism asserts that relying on the concept of the 'invisible hand' is inadequate in attaining efficiency, equity, and sustainability. By centering on marginalized voices and perspectives, ecofeminism offers a unique approach to conceptualizing the social world and prioritizing bottom-up analysis instead of top-down approaches.

The issue at hand extends beyond the concept of an economic man or market alone. The concern lies in the potential monopoly of value by the economic man and market. Ecofeminists caution that if this were to occur, not only would the entire world be perceived and treated as a mere instrument, but it would also be entirely instrumentalized.

From the perspective of ecofeminism, the current economic theory fails to fully acknowledge the diverse array of values present in both social and natural realms. Additionally, it falls short of adequately addressing the intricate web of relationships among individuals and between humans and the natural world. Therefore, ecofeminism argues that economic men provide an insufficient foundation to build ecological economics.

Sustainability encompasses the durability of systems and processes. In the field of ecology, this pertains to the extent of diversity and productivity within biological systems. Similarly, in environmental science, sustainability refers to the quality of not causing harm to the environment or depleting natural resources, thereby promoting a long-term ecological balance. The ecological foundations for sustainable development include addressing fundamental human needs, such as access to and quality of air, water, food, and shelter. From the perspective of feminist critical analysis, feminist sustainability necessitates ethical principles, such as solidarity, reciprocity, and non-hierarchical, non-violent relationships among human societies, as well as between humans, non-human entities, and ecosystems.

To achieve sustainability, ecofeminists emphasize the importance of various actions. One key aspect is the reduction of waste in production processes. This involves minimizing the generation of waste materials and implementing efficient waste management strategies. Additionally, ecofeminists advocate reducing reliance on fossil fuels, which contribute to environmental degradation and instead promote the use of renewable energy sources, such as solar, wind, rain, tides, and waves. Emphasizing the importance of recycling, ecofeminists encourage the reuse of materials to minimize waste generation (Weiss and Moskop, 2020).

Furthermore, ecofeminists have stressed the need to address air and water pollution by implementing measures that reduce emissions and contaminants. By adopting sustainable practices and technologies, such as improved industrial processes and stricter environmental regulations, it is possible to mitigate negative impacts on the environment. Ultimately, the goal is to lower greenhouse gas emissions, which play a significant role in mitigating climate change.

Overall, ecofeminists recognize the urgent need to shift towards a sustainable way of life. By taking steps such as waste reduction, transitioning to renewable energy sources, recycling, and reducing pollution, individuals can contribute to creating a more sustainable and ecologically balanced future (Merchant, 1996).

The role of women as advocates for environmental sustainability, emphasizing their cultural and symbolic connection to nature, and the disproportionate impact of environmental degradation on them and their children. Ecofeminists argue that by recognizing and addressing these issues, women can play a crucial role in promoting a sustainable future.

These concerns include damaging rainforests and woodlands, polluting and over-fishing oceans and lakes, polluting the atmosphere through burning fossil fuels, and damaging agricultural land through unsustainable farming practices, which are indeed important areas of environmental focus. These issues have wide-ranging impacts on ecosystems, biodiversity, climate change, and human wellbeing (Gaard, 2011).

By advocating sustainability, women can contribute to the preservation and conservation of their natural resources. They can engage in various activities, such as promoting renewable energy, supporting conservation efforts, encouraging sustainable agricultural practices, and raising awareness about the importance of protecting the environment. Women's involvement can lead to the development of equitable and inclusive environmental policies and practices.

It is important to note that while women have a significant role to play in environmental sustainability, it is essential to engage all members of society, including men and governments, in these efforts. Achieving sustainable development requires collective action, where individuals, communities, and institutions work together to mitigate environmental damage and promote a long-term ecological balance. Collaboration between stakeholders is crucial for achieving meaningful and lasting changes.

5   Conclusion

Traditional theories have assumed that natural resource supply is unlimited and that these resources have infinite potential for transformation into products within the production process. Traditional development theories based on the assumption of unlimited natural resource supply have not taken into account the limits, depletes, long-term problems, and negative impacts on the natural environment. At the core of this misconception lies the perception of natural resources as capital, as a revenue-generating commodity. However, the majority of capital is derived from the resources provided by nature. Understanding and resolving ecological problems require recognizing nature as an economic factor as well. The convergence of labour, capital, and technological change toward harmony with nature has led to the emergence of a new approach to development. This new approach, known as sustainable development, is based on the principle that economic and technological activities should in no way endanger the natural resources necessary for the continued existence of life worldwide.

The fundamental goal of sustainable development is to integrate the economic, ecological, and social dimensions in decision-making. This understanding highlights the necessity of supporting new conceptual steps in the implementation of decisions at both the central and local levels within a holistic approach. The concept of sustainability emphasizes the need for a participatory framework. It refers to the process being carried out in a participatory structure where all stakeholders affected by the decisions embrace the process and comply with the decisions made.

In the preservation of ecological balance, various concepts and ideological currents accompany sustainability, some of which are traditionally recognized while others are considered modern approaches. The widespread use of the internet and the awareness brought about by globalization regarding "basic rights and freedoms" have also updated traditional ways of thinking in the conservation of nature and the environment. Ecofeminism is one of these ideological currents that started to be discussed, particularly in the 2000s, and it has become part of the feminist waves (the end of the third wave, the fourth wave). Feminism, with its different approaches and theories, attempts to define the oppression imposed on women, explain its causes and consequences, and present strategies and policies for women's liberation. As part of the fourth wave of feminism, "hashtag activism" establishes connections among women, creates mutual support networks, and strengthens awareness of social and legal rights. Online social networks enable women to transcend national, cultural, class, and religious boundaries and recognize shared conditions, issues, and emotions.

Ecofeminism establishes a relationship between nature and women while also referring to the male-dominated aspects of production processes. It associates the stages of environmental degradation with women and criticizes the oppressive aspects of men that subjugate women. By addressing respect for nature and its preservation through the lens of women, ecofeminism emphasizes the need to recognize women's labor in economic processes. With these aspects, ecofeminism aligns with the goals of gender equality within the framework of sustainable development and continues its work towards achieving these goals, raising awareness through activist movements.

Ecofeminist women combat these hazards by changing family consumption patterns, recycling household waste, and protesting methods of waste disposal. They strive to preserve traditional ways of life and act to reverse the ecological damage caused by irresponsible companies and exploitative industries. Ecofeminists closely monitor issues related to gender inequality, employment, workforce participation, and the design and implementation of political practices, challenging the methods through which traditional society reproduces itself.

The contributions of ecofeminism to sustainable development goals are diverse. Firstly, ecofeminism highlights the close relationship between women and nature, emphasizing that women can play a significant role in the sustainable use and conservation of natural resources. Women can promote sustainable agricultural practices within their communities, take leadership in environmental conservation projects, and actively participate in ensuring environmental justice.

Secondly, ecofeminism advocates for the integration of fundamental values such as gender equality and women's rights at the core of sustainable development. Women's access to education and healthcare, participation in economic opportunities, and involvement in political decision-making processes are crucial for the success of sustainable development. Ecofeminism underscores the relationship between gender equality and sustainable development, demonstrating that progress in these areas mutually reinforces each other.

Lastly, ecofeminism offers a different and inclusive perspective on environmental issues and sustainability. This approach provides a framework that includes traditionally marginalized or overlooked communities and considers their perspectives. As a result, sustainability efforts become more equitable, inclusive, and effective.

However, for ecofeminism to contribute to sustainable development goals, more awareness and collaboration are needed. This requires raising awareness and mobilizing action from all segments of society. In summary, the contributions of ecofeminist thought within the framework of sustainable development can be summarized as follows:

1. *Sustainable use of nature and resources:* Ecofeminism focuses on women's close relationship with nature and emphasises that they can play an important role in the sustainable use and conservation of natural resources. Women's promotion of sustainable agricultural practices in their communities, their leadership of environmental protection projects and their active role in ensuring environmental justice contribute to the sustainable use of natural resources.

2. *Gender equality and women's rights:* Ecofeminism argues that gender equality and women's rights should be among the core values of sustainable development. Women's access to education and health services, participation in economic opportunities and participation in political decision-making processes are important for the success of sustainable development. Ecofeminism emphasises the relationship between gender

equality and sustainable development and demonstrates that progress in these areas is mutually reinforcing.

3. *Inclusiveness and consideration of different perspectives:* Ecofeminism offers a diverse and inclusive perspective on environmental and sustainability issues. It provides a framework that includes traditionally excluded or ignored communities and considers their perspectives. This enables sustainability efforts to become more equitable, inclusive and effective.

4. *Balancing the relationship between nature and humans:* Ecofeminism emphasises the balancing of the relationship between nature and humans. It emphasises the importance of living with and respecting nature, rather than seeing it only as a resource or a tool. This approach emphasises the need to protect the natural environment, which is at the heart of sustainable development, and to pass it on to future generations.

5. *Social transformation and raising awareness of sustainability:* Ecofeminism can contribute to raising awareness on social transformation and expanding the educational pillar of development. This is because the active awareness of women will contribute to the education of other segments of society on sustainability.

References

Ağkurt, G. (2023). Doğa-Kadın Dayanışması: Ekofeminizm. https://atauni.edu.tr/yuk lemeler/5aa74ad99d41bd5a499babbbaa139179.pdf.

Banerjee, S.B. (2003) Who sustains shose development? Sustainable development and the reinvention of nature. *Organization Studies,* 1(24), 143–80.

Bookchin, M. (1994). *Özgürlüğün Ekolojisi: Hiyerarşinin Ortaya Çıkışı ve Çözülüşü.* İstanbul: Ayrıntı Yayınları.

Caldecott, L. & Leland, S. (1983). *Reclaim the Earth: Women Speak Out for Life on Earth.* London: Women's Press.

Carlassare, E. (2000). Socialist and cultural ecofeminizm: Allies in resistance. *Ethics & Environment,* 5 (January), 89–106.

Cook, A. (1983). Greenham Women Everywhere: Dreams, Ideas and Actions from the Women's Peace Movement. Pluto Press.

Daly, M. (1978). Gyn/Ecology: *The Metaethics of Radical Feminism.* Boston, MA: Beacon Press.

Demir, M. (2018). Kadını ve Doğayı Birlikte Düşünmek. Doğu-Batı Dergisi. https://yav uzyilmazbiz.blogspot.com/2018/01/ekofeminizm.html.

Environmental Science, (2018). What Is Sustainability and Why Is It Important? https://www.environmentalscience.org/sustainability.

Ferry, L. (2000). *Ekolojik yeni düzen*. İstanbul: Y.K.Y.

Gaard, G. (2011). Ecofeminism revisited: Rejecting essentialism and re-placing species in a material feminist environmentalism. *Feminist Formations*, 23(2), 26–53.

Griffin, S. (1978). *Women and Nature*. London: The Women's Press.

Hawkins, R.Z. (1998). Ecofeminism and nonhumans: Continuity, difference, dualism, and domination. *Hypatia*, 13(1), 158–97.

Hopwood, B., Mellor, M. & O'Brien, G. (2005). Sustainable development: Mapping different approaches. *Sustainable Development*, 13, 38–52.

İnce, M. (2020). A critical review of Murray Bookchin's *Understanding of Social Ecology*. *Amme İdaresi Dergisi* 53(4): 49–75.

Jacobs, M. (1999). "Sustainable Development as a Contested Concept". In Dobson, A. (ed.) *Fairness and Futurity: Essays on Environmental Sustainability and Social Justice*, pp. 21–45. New York, NY: Oxford University Press.

Julian, İ. & Molina, S.G. (2013). Towards an integrative approach to sustainability: Exploring potential synergies between gender and environment. *Cepal Review* 110, 49–65.

Keleş, R. (2017). Kentleşme Politikası, İmge Kitabevi, Ankara.

Linnik, J. (2008). Ecofeminism: A New Concept of Sustainable Development. https://essuir.sumdu.edu.ua/bitstream/123456789/8189/1/10.pdf.

McMahon, M. (1997). From the ground up: Ecofeminism and ecological economics. *Ecological Economics*, 20(2), 163–173.

Mellor, M. (1997). *Feminism and Ecology*. New York: New York University Press.

Merchant, C. (1980). *The Death of Nature: Women, Ecology and the Scientific Revolution*. New York: Harper & Row.

Merchant, C. (1996). *Earthcare: Women and the Environment*. New York. Routledge.

Önder, T. (2002). "Toplumsal Ekoloji Üzerine Bir İnceleme". Türkiye Günlüğü, 70.

Plumwood, V. (2004). *Feminizm ve Doğaya Hükmetmek* (çev. B. Ertür). İstanbul: Metis.

Schmonsky, J. (2012). The growing importance of ecofeminism. https://www.magzter.com/stories/Education/Eternal-Bhoomi/The-Growing-Importance-Of-Eco-Feminism.

SOGESID. (n.d.). *Sustainable Development*. Retrieved from http://www.sogesid.it/english_site/Sustainable_Development.html.

Sustainable Development Commission, (2011). Governing for The Future: The Opportunities for Mainstreaming Sustainable Development. https://www.sdcommission.org.uk/data/files/publications/SDC_SD_Guide_2011_2.pdf.

Sustainable Development, (2022). What is Sustainable Development. https://sustainabledevelopment.gov.mt/what-is-sustainable-development/.

Tisdell, A. (2005). *Economics of Environmental Conservation*, Second Edition. Cheltenham, UK/Northampton, MA, USA: Edward Elgar Publishing.

Tong, P.R. (2006). *Feminist Düşünce* (çev. Z. Cirhinoğlu). İstanbul: Gündoğan.

Tregidga, H., Kearins, K. & Milne, M. (2013) The politics of knowing "organizational sustainable development". *Organization & Environment*, 1(26), 102–29.

United Nation, (1987). Report of the World Commission on Environment and Development: Our Common Future, https://sustainabledevelopment.un.org/mil estones/wced.

UNSDG. (2018). *Gender equality: A key SGD accelerator*. A case study from the Republic of Moldova

United Nations. (2023). The 17 Goals. https://sdgs.un.org/goals.

Warren, J.K. (1987). Feminism and ecology: Making connections. *Environmental Ethics*, 1(9), 320.

Warren, J.K. (1997). *Ecofeminism: Women, Culture, Nature*. Bloomington and Indiana-polis, IN: Indiana University Press.

Weiss, P. & Moskop, W. (2020). Ecofeminist manifestos: Resources for feminist per-spectives on the environment. *Women's Studies International Forum*, 83, 102418.

CHAPTER 7

The Politics of Cyberfeminism

Gökmen Kantar

Feminism, which emerged theoretically in the 18th century, is an ideology based on expanding the social position and rights of women. Increasing technological innovations in the world with globalization have made feminism debatable within the digital new media order. These discussions, based on the role, rights and problems of women, led to the emergence of a new wave of feminism. This new wave of digital-centred feminism has shaken the supremacy of the masculine culture that dominates technology. Shaking the technologically masculine dominance of women led to the emergence of a new feminist understanding in Haraway's work. Emphasizing that women should come to the forefront in the technological world, Haraway claimed that the new media order connected to the internet also affects political systems. Technological developments that emancipated women and liberated them from restrictions with social networks led to the birth of cyberfeminism, the last wave of feminist thought. Cyberfeminism, which believes that the empowerment of women in all areas of society can only be achieved by taking more part in the new media order, emphasized that technology affects the power and authority centre in terms of political discourse. This study, which is qualitative research, will focus on the effect of feminism on political decision-makers in the global world system in terms of economic, social and political aspects. For this reason, the United Nations positioning of women in social terms, which is the decision maker in the international community, will be interpreted through recent feminist movements.

1   Introduction

From the past to the present, the struggle for women's identity has continued with the strength and determination of women to overcome the difficulties they face in all areas of life. In this struggle, the woman, who has overcome all difficulties despite all obstacles, has achieved many successes in the social field, although she has not yet achieved the great victory she wants or desires. Although the intellectual basis of the problems faced by women is philosophical, historical, economic and social, the decision-making mechanism in the solution process is politics. This seemingly incomprehensible intellectual complexity led to the theoretical emergence of feminism as a concept that focuses on women and discusses women's identity within the scope of social sciences.

Feminism, which emerged as a view against the oppression and difficulties faced by women in the social sphere, is a system of thought based on the role, rights and problems of women. In the historical process, until the development of the idea of feminism in Europe in the 19th century, women's economic, social and political participation in social life with their identity was not possible. This social inequality against women's identity formed the basis of a masculine identity in shaping power and authority. These non-modern systems of governance prevented the advancement of women's rights, starting from the democracy of antiquity until the mid-20th century. In the recent period, the problems faced by women in the social sphere could only be solved with the level of development of countries and the suitability of their governance systems. From this point of view, it is not really possible to provide the definition and development of feminist thought in a general framework when we consider the cultural and social differences between countries. However, by putting Europe, the center of enlightenment and modern thought, at the center of feminist thought, a theoretical development process can be expressed scientifically.

In this study, which adheres to the qualitative research method, the chronological development of feminist thought will be discussed through a literature review. For this reason, in the first part of the study, the First Wave Feminist Movement, in which feminist thought emerged theoretically and women's struggle turned into a social movement, will be examined first. Then, the Second Wave Feminist Movement, in which women's gains in citizenship rights and their demands for equality were legalized, will be explained. Immediately afterwards, Wave III of the Feminist Movement, which includes postmodern and poststructuralist debates that examine women's sexual, racial, political and economic struggles in terms of identity, will be emphasized. Finally, the first part will be completed by evaluating the IVth Wave Feminist Movement of the idea of feminism, which has been re-discussed and redefined due to technological developments today. In the second part of the study, Haraway's cyberfeminist thoughts will be examined in relation to the feminist debates against the increasing use of the internet and the masculine domination in the digital sphere with technological developments. Then, cyberfeminist thought will be defined and its development and current debates on social networks connected to the internet will be emphasized. From this point of view, the reflections of gender-based inequalities in cyberfeminist culture in the formation of gender-neutral cyber identity will be discussed and the links between concepts will be explored.

In the third part of the study, the impact of cyberfeminist discussions over social networks on the internet on decision-makers on a global scale will be evaluated and its reflection on cyberfeminist policies will be examined in the example of the United Nations (UN). In the concluding part of the study, the impact of cyberfeminist discourses on UN policies, which are international decision-makers, will be interpreted and a current evaluation of feminist thought will be made. In this way, the current state of feminism and the women's movement in the historical process will be revealed and the gains or improvements in material conditions will be determined. In addition, with these evaluations, it will be examined to what extent cyberfeminist discourses are at the centre or at a distance from the current problems of women.

2   Feminist Movements from Past to Present

Feminism, which puts women's struggle for equality, rights and problems at the centre of the movement, emerged in 18th-century Europe and gained economic, social and political character. From a theoretical point of view, feminism constructed itself both theoretically and practically in the field of social sciences and regained its reality in different cultures and societies. In this respect, instead of making a general definition of feminism, its developmental stages in the historical process will be evaluated with its main lines. In this way, by avoiding the mistake of stereotyping feminism or defining it; the discursive opposition of feminist thought will be analyzed based on the equation of time, ground and mind. In this part of the study, let us first take a look at the difficulties faced by women before feminism at every stage of social life in the historical process.

Although the history of humanity dates back millions of years, our knowledge about these ancient periods is quite limited. However, scientific knowledge about human life dates back to the Neolithic Period, 10,000 years BC. In this period, which was the beginning of the transition to agriculture as well as hunter-gatherer, women participated in social life equally with men and there was superiority and equality between the sexes. Towards the middle of the Neolithic Period (6000–3000 B.C.), agriculture became richer with technical advances and private property begins to develop. The proprietorial approach due to technical advancements led to the second position of women in this period and instead of the egalitarian approach between men and women in the field of gender, the dominance shifted in favour of men

(Michel, 1993: pp. 11–23). On the other hand, humanity's struggle for life was divided into various institutions of life with these developments. This division of labour in social life directly affected women's social status and directed women to domestic life (childcare, housework, food gathering, etc.) that concerned the family. In this period, while women became prominent in the private sphere of family life in private life, men became active in the public sphere of life where power and authority were shaped (Mazoyer and Roudart, 2009: pp. 54–55). This new social life brought about administrative and economic differences among people. With the transition of people to settled life, classes emerged in society; the foundation of economic and administrative forms was laid. Thus, the concept of property found its counterpart in society over time and gained commercial meaning. This new period brought about a form of civilization and a form of government that divided society into classes as opposed to society as a whole (Wolf, 2000: 18–19). This form of civilization legitimized the social sphere with urban-rural, rich-poor, male-female, and later citizenship-based slave classes. The settlements where those who produced and those who owned production were separated and where social life continued were called "Polis". While the Polis shaped the way of governance and life in ancient times, it also had a profound impact on the lives of women. In the Greek democracy of Antiquity, women living in urban polis were left far away from gender equality in political administration; they had similar rights to slaves and foreigners (Karakoç and Özden, 2020: 585). This inequality in the field of gender pushed women away from power and brought them closer to a second position on an economic basis (Pelizzon, 2009: 31). With the emergence of economically based classes, women were pushed out of the public sphere of life through the profession of motherhood and into the private sphere of home and domestic life. This historical process of women continued unchanged in monotheistic religions and philosophical thoughts, leading to the emergence of a patriarchal cultural system in the medieval world. Cultural, political and religious institutions were designed according to this patriarchal understanding and the social system found its masculine character. This social system emphasized male hegemony in the public sphere: politics, education, law, religion, health, art and culture, while women were active in the domestic sphere: elderly and childcare, cleaning, cooking, housework, etc. The general character of medieval society was a feudal masculine period in which reason, logic and critical approach to human life were weak and scholastic thought was active (Roberts, 2010: 231). These inequalities against women in the social sphere turned into an objection after the *Enlightenment Period*. Capital accumulation and the Industrial Revolution, which began with the impact of Geographical Discoveries, reshaped the balance of classes in social life. The bourgeois class, which came to the forefront with the Industrial Revolution, began to voice the position and rights of women in society. Especially after the French Revolution of 1789, ideas emphasizing human rights developed. In this period, the British writer and philosopher Mary Wollstonecraft published her book *A Vindication of the Rights of Woman*; published in 1792, it emphasized the human rights of women. This book, which has a special place for feminist thought based on the struggle for women's rights, emphasized that women should not only have domestic duties but should also have all the rights of men, especially the right to education (Arat, 1991: 16). The intellectual foundations of the First Wave Feminist movement started in the 18th century and turned into a social movement towards the middle of the 20th century. Feminism, which advocates equality in terms of gender in the social sphere, gained a different quality in the social sphere with the liberal thought that emerged due to the Industrial Revolution (Şeren, 2018: 95). With the idea of liberalism, the redefinition of concepts such as individualism, equality, freedom and property influenced the realization of women's rights and problems. The idea of feminism developed under the influence of the liberal enlightenment thought of the First Wave Movement and put masculine domination at the centre of discussions on citizenship, political participation and the individual. These debates targeted the existence of policies and laws that encouraged all kinds of prohibitive prohibitions in women's social life and defended women's right to be human. The famous English woman philosopher Wollstonecraft's statement in her book published in 1792, *"Truth for man and woman, if I understand the meaning of the word correctly, should be the same" is the main focus of this struggle* (Wollstonecraft, 2012: 78). During this period, women's rights defenders publicly voiced demands for education, the right to work and political participation. The target of feminists' criticism of existing policies during this period was masculine powers and their dominant policies. The thinkers of the period, who criticized the fact that natural rights only covered men, argued that women's rights were suppressed by male domination (Donovan, 2016: 33–34). The first wave of the feminist movement, which started in Europe and centred in England and France, affected countries such as Germany and the United States of America (USA) and had legal consequences on equal citizenship rights. With the legal arrangements made, women gained political, social and economic rights in social life. The first wave feminist movement, which started with limited opportunities, broke male domination in all areas of life within a period of 200 years; and women's rights were legally guaranteed with the concept of equal citizenship (Çakır, 1996: 19). Thus, with the first wave of feminist thought, the principled and legal foundations of women's rights in the social sphere were laid.

After the mid-20th century, the Second Wave Feminist movement carried forward the First Wave Feminist movements and brought egalitarian demands concerning gender through the female body to its agenda. Emphasizing that legal regulations on women's rights should not be limited, the feminists of this period gave a new impetus to the Second Wave movement on equality with their public debates. Emphasizing that the achievements of women in the social sphere should be internalized, feminists put the gender phenomenon and political norms in their targets in the United States and in many European countries such as the United Kingdom and France towards the end of the 1960s (Michel, 1993: 106). Wave II feminists criticized the policies of masculine power in favour of men, which considered women's biological sex difference as the second sex, and criticized the inequality between men and women in society. The feminist thought of this period, which asserted that women's existence in social life is a right to life, stated that the woman's body belongs to her; they expressed women's rights for the first time in a radical way on issues such as fertility and abortion. Simone de Beauvoir, one of the thinkers of the period who struggled with external criticisms against the female identity, brought a new criticism to the innate sexual identity and masculine policies with her words "One is not born a woman, one becomes a woman" (Beauvoir, 1993: 231). The Second Wave Feminist movement, which developed during the Cold War period, also gained social ground under the influence of modernity and liberal policies. In this socialization process, the characteristics of the male and female sexes were politicized from an individual perspective. Radical feminism, which emerged in the US during this period, focused on the male-dominated mentality as the political and social source of women's problems. Radical feminists emphasized that women who tried to be imprisoned in patriarchal lifestyles were subjected to the social imprisonment of their bodies and biological sex. In order to end this imprisonment, radical feminists argued that women's sexual identities should be liberated, and women should have the right to bodily sovereignty. With these ideas, the social role of women and their analytical status within the concept of the family were reshaped (Yıldırım and İşler: 2022: 7). Criticizing the existence of patriarchal structure and gender inequality within the family institution, this approach argued that men have equal responsibilities with women in the family (Millett, 2018: 64). In addition to liberal and radical feminism, policies based on cultural, Marxist and socialist feminist ideas developed during this period.

Disagreeing with the classical approach of liberal thought, cultural feminists adopt to locate the equal nature of women and men directly on feminine pride in institutions instead of socio-political institutions. Taking a more radical stance than liberal feminism with this way of thinking, cultural feminists emphasize the superiority of women over men, as opposed to equal position-ing vis-à-vis men, and therefore emphasize the need to focus on the cultural reality of women. In this respect, cultural feminism, also known as women's nationalism, has been on the agenda of debates with this idea. Uniting femi-nist movements that disagreed among themselves, cultural feminism not only criticized masculine identity but also managed to emphasize feminine bonds instead of lesbianism (Echols, 1989: 244). Cultural feminism, which brought women's identity to the forefront in a process in which women were requested to withdraw into their own shells, did not adopt women's military service like liberal feminists because it was contrary to women's peaceful character. This peaceful character of cultural feminism was seen as a subversive attitude and weakened cultural feminist thought. Another criticism of cultural feminism is that it is biologically based and that it is based on the idea of female superiority rather than equality between men and women. The reality that cultural ideas are not always in favour of women has always kept cultural feminism at the centre of debates. In addition, its leftist tendencies and the universal sister-hood model, which inhibits women's voices, have left cultural feminism at the centre of criticism in terms of other feminist movements (Narayan, 1998: 86–106). For this reason, left-wing feminists left cultural feminism and entered into new feminist approaches.

In place of Karl Marx, who did not pay special attention to women's rights and problems, Marxism allocated a place for the feminist movement within itself. Friederich Engels criticized the position of women in the family institu-tion in his work The German Ideology, which he wrote by paying attention to Marx's advice; he stated that the division of labour enslaved women in the ser-vice of men. Asserting that women's labour is their own free property, Engels claimed that the maternity law enslaves women (Engels, 2011: 27). Seeing monogamous marriage as progress in the historical process, Engels criticizes the contradiction between men and women and the domination of men over women. Marxist feminism is disturbed by the position of women in the family and the dominance of men. Thus, it criticizes liberal feminism on the grounds that gender equality cannot be achieved in the capitalist order.

According to feminist thinkers, it is necessary to separate Marxist feminism from socialist feminism due to political concerns. Rosemarie Putnam Tong, who criticizes Marxist feminists for not including women due to their class distinction, emphasizes that the Marxist thought that does not see gender has led to socialist feminism (Tong, 2006: 271). While socialist feminist thought accepts the class doctrine and materialist understanding of history, which are linked to the economic ideas of Marxism, she emphasizes that the patri-archal family structure obscures these titles of Marxist thought. Accordingly,

she specifically reconsiders the problems caused by the patriarchal family system within socialist feminist thought. While emphasizing that the obstacles
women face in social life can be psychological, theoretical and economically
based, she looks for the oppression of women within the family in hierarchical
structures. For this reason, according to socialist feminism, women's problems
should be sought not only in the spheres of production but also in the socio-
economic-based spheres of production where society is institutionalized.
Socialist feminism, which sees reproduction in social life as a factor that eliminates class differences and gender inequality, rejects the sexist understanding and positioning of women trapped in the narrow patterns of economic
relations (Ferguson, 2013: 235–255). As a result, socialist feminism, like Marxist
feminism, argues that inequality between men and women will end with the
collapse of the capitalist order.

Feminism, which is women's struggle for existence against all masculine
dominance and power relations in social life, is a political concept with historical continuity after modern thought. The third wave of feminist movements
emerged in the early 1990s. Feminists of this period, who analyzed women's
existence from sexual, racial, political and economic perspectives based on
class differences within social structures and women's identity, started a new
global feminist movement with the influence of poststructuralist and postmodernist movements. Although it did not have a wide and innovative impact on
a global scale like other feminist movements before it (Waves I and II), it contributed to the redefinition of feminist ideas and debates centred on women.
According to Josephine Donovan, this theoretical renewal pushed the feminist
movements, which were divided in large numbers, towards an anti-capitalist
and ecofeminist orientation with globalization (Donovan, 2016: 33–34). The
Third Wave Feminism movement, which was more individualistic than other
feminist wave movements, addressed women's identity from a postmodernist
perspective. Criticizing that feminism, which fought against masculine domination in social life, *created a common female figure* against men, the postmodern feminist approach argued that the common female identity imprisoned
women under a single identity. Fatmagül Berktay, addressing the concept of
woman from a holistic perspective, emphasized in her postmodern critique
that a single concept of woman does not represent all women, that woman
discursively contains more than one reality (Berktay, 2013: 17). In line with
the continuity and intensity of feminist thought, the feminist thought of this
period differed from other feminist thoughts; beyond the difference between
men and women, it developed a new theoretical definition by discursively con-
structing the difference between women themselves. These different realities
among women's identities gave new meaning to the perception of gender in

the light of poststructuralist and postmodern feminist thought. In this way, the Third Wave Feminist movement, which reconsidered power, identity and differences, broke down the concepts attributed to women such as mother, wife and sister, and opened a new window to feminist thought.

3   Cyberfeminism

In this section, we will try to explain the concept of Cyberfeminism, which started with the Third Wave Feminist movement and continued by covering the Fourth Wave Feminist movement. During the dizzying pace of technological developments in the global world, internet-based communication and interactions have reached an important point in people's daily lives. Digital technology encompasses human life; the fact that it has turned the world into a global village has increased intercultural communication as well as societies. While individuals, societies and cultures changed in interaction; digital culture rebuilt modern capitalist life in the last quarter of the 20th century. The new media order also introduced the terminology of digital culture in terms of identity with concepts such as digital culture, network society, user or profile. In addition, the new media order based on digital technology was influenced by offline cultural, political and economic structures and transformed new cultural, political and economic models online (Güzel, 2016: 85–86). Feminist thinkers, influenced by the cyberculture that developed in the 1980s due to technological developments and entered human life, opened a new window within the systematic of feminist thought. The concept of cyber (to direct, control, manage), which appears before the compound concept of cyberfeminism, was first used in Norbert Wiener's work *Cybernetics*, written in 1948 (Varol, 2014: 224). The concept of cyber, which has a managerial meaning, was added to feminism by thinkers, aiming to direct and manage the feminist movement in social networks in the digital environment. Cyberfeminism, which is used to define sexist movements in the digital universe, has tried to put forward a virtual feminist terminology by referring to the internet world and the social networks that have developed in relation to it. Cyberfeminism, which is the aspect of feminist thought that looks at the internet, tried to reshape norms, traditions, institutions and human actions in the cyber environment with the cyberculture it created. Cyberfeminism, which embodies all waves of feminism, can be defined as an answer to the question of how it is rather than what it is. It would not be correct to explain cyberfeminism within a general feminist framework or to include it in a single group. Cyberfeminism, which does not have a precise definition, was defined by Faith Wilding as "an attractive and anti-identity method beyond hierarchy" as a female rebellion against the masculinely constructed and dominating cyberspace (Wilding, 1998: 10). Women's struggle for existence in cyberspace, which is a male space according to the patriarchal system, is an important focus and political method of cyberfeminist thought. From this point of view, cyberfeminism is based on the interactions between women and cyberspace and is carried out on both a theoretical and discursive relationship of action. Although the origins of cyberfeminist thought can be traced back to the invention of the computer, the practice of cyberfeminist thought in action gained momentum in the early 1990s. In this period, names, groups and projects that can be considered pioneers in cyberfeminist thought emerged and contributed to the development of cyberfeminist theory. Donna Haraway and the Cyborg Manifesto can be considered as the starting point of cyberfeminism. In this work, Haraway saw the cyborg, the combination of machine and organism, as a problem that changes what is considered the female experience; she stated the diversity of feminism and that it is not possible to be named with a single adjective. Haraway argued that the cyborg, which she sees as a post-gender problem, is neither male nor female; it is genderless. Considering the human as a bodied subject, Haraway argued that a bodied subject has a historical, class and social positioning and emphasized that the body can change without being fixed in the light of technology (Haraway, 2006: 16, Haraway, 2015). Feminists, who brought the relationship between women and technology into the field of technological gender, initiated a new debate and overthrew the masculine domination in cyberspace on the basis of genderlessness. While cyberfeminism, which emerged from cyberculture, was viewed pessimistically by some feminists and optimistically by others; it revealed a new perspective on the relationship between subject and power. In this respect, feminists established a network with women in the new media order that developed depending on technology with the cyberfeminism they developed. In a process where the gender inequality of individuals in cyberculture continues, cyberfeminism stipulated that a solution to this situation must be brought; tried to examine the digital environment in this sense. This approach, which emerged with the technology and cyber connection of gender, drew attention to the transformative power of the virtual world and the gender, race and class distinctions of women. According to Kember, who sees the representation of women in the historical process as incomplete and inaccurate, cyberfeminism aims to create an anarchic attitude in the virtual world (Kember, 2002: 627). Cyberfeminism, which sees women's participation in cyberspace as incomplete and opposes masculine dominance, tried to achieve gender equality by supporting women's participation. Aiming to eliminate inequalities in cyberculture, this movement prioritized domestic violence, pornography and women's rights, empowering women in the virtual world. Considering the diversity of information in cyberspace, she argued that information, which has no specific position and is multifaceted, is influenced by many cultures and this creates new areas of oppression for women. For this reason, the representation of women was redefined in cyberculture, revealing different representations of women instead of single woman. Cyberfeminism, which calls women in different directions rather than through restrictive roles, sees the virtual world as a public space and socialized its actions on people. Cyberfeminists, who became public on social networks, organized politically and socially and managed to create platforms on the internet. Through these newly created platforms on the Internet, feminists tried to determine policies that affect social life. In addition, according to Standish, who refers to the Internet, which makes the theoretical and practical education of cyberfeminism accessible to people, as a super library, cyberspace has facilitated access to information with the unlimited information content it provides (Standish, 1999: 418). Identities that formalize or emphasize the sense of belonging have been reconstructed in cyberspace with the addition of much information such as picture, age, gender, race, religion, education and profession. Cyber identity, one of the actors of cyberculture, is a concept based on the practices developed by the individual online. Cyber identity, which defines the individual through the Internet, can also be expressed as digital identity, virtual identity, online identity. The cyberfeminist movement, like other feminist movements, is a rebellion movement based on gender equality, eliminating discrimination and fighting against masculine domination. Criticizing the oppressive and exploitative structure of men in cyberspace, cyberfeminism invited society to confront its own identity politics against sexist masculine power. In this way, she tried to create a freer public space in the virtual environment by cyberidentifying her identity as an excluded, marginalized and disenfranchised woman. On the other hand, while the distinction between public and private spheres of the new media order has become more ambiguous with media tools; the participatory structure of the internet has further publicized people's private life. The virtual world is a cyber culture that presents the public appearance and representation of human beings as a show of power. In this culture, the individual enters into a cyber publicity by sending messages all over the world about his/her representation and appearance. The cyberspace, which offers the opportunity for human desires and wishes in terms of the self, intertwines public and private life. Thus, the woman transcends her borders online from anywhere in the world with internet access and enters into a cyber public space. In terms of identity, the woman thus achieves the position she cannot achieve in real life with her cyber identity. With this unlimited right to public space offered to women by the Internet, patriarchal practices are controlled and transformed into a more democratic discourse. While the relationship between cyberfeminism and cyber identity therefore reveals a multidimensional relationship; the cyber environment offers individuals opportunities that they cannot have in the real world (Brophy, 2010: 930–931). The concept of *freedom* finds its new meaning in the virtual normal order as behaviours that are not considered normal in social life and theoretically explained as *disinhibition* are easily accepted in online virtual environments. Although cyber identity is under the control of the individual, the construction of the virtual reality of this identity in the cyber environment can gain different meanings. Because the individual in social life gains a new body and meaning through his/her cyber identity. In this respect, cyber identity has a discursive structure in which not only what it says but also how it says it gains importance. With this variable identity structure, cyber identity is redefined according to the desires and wishes of the individual in the form of identity tourism. For this reason, cyber identity multiplies the female identity in the public sphere by defining different women instead of defining a single woman against men. This approach has led to a social redefinition of gender between men and women in terms of family, body and power.

Cyberfeminism, which argues that information technologies are gendered, developed against gender inequality and masculine domination in the virtual environment. Arguing that technology and digital development are male-influenced, feminists proposed the de-gendering of the internet and called for a redefinition of gender in this sense. The force that drives cyberfeminists to this idea is the desire to establish a structure based on equality in terms of gender identities by destroying the masculine dominance in technology with a genderless approach. Beyond the problem of men's monopolization of technology, this idea is the one-way power of the masculine gender over technology. For this reason, cyberfeminism, which seeks to de-gender technological institutions and technology education, aimed to break the virtual practices, masculine oppression and single-sexist approach of patriarchal thought. Cyberfeminists claimed that even robots, which are technological productions, are produced according to gender. In this respect, according to Søraa, the fact that robots are designed according to male and female genders complicates this genderless policy. For example, the term android (with the suffix and meaning "man or male") is also used for robots produced according to the female gender. We can also liken this masculine signification to patriarchal practices in social life that try to characterize all people with the word "man". As can be seen from this example, real-life designations and definitions are discursively reconstructed within technology in relation to culture

(Søraa, 2017: 99–105). This technological gendering identifies the production of the robot with a human-like interaction. In Eyssel and Hegel's study, participants associated short-haired masculine robots with managing the house and long-haired feminine robots with cleaning and caring for the house. Eyssel and Hegel argue that the perception of the long-haired robots close to women in the physical characteristics of the robots produced is due to gender stereotypes and that this interaction finds its counterpart in virtual reality as in social life (Eyssel and Hegel, 2012: 2214–2216). Similarly, Apple's Siri, Samsung's Bixby, and Microsoft's Cortana, which provide services with artificial intelligence software, are servant applications that have a female voice and help men. The use of women's voices in advertising, marketing and service purposes in accordance with gender inequality is a sexist approach to technological masculine domination. For this reason, feminist thought, which wants technological learning and development to be shaped on the basis of gender equality in intelligence, has called for the implementation of artificial intelligence software programs in cyberspace that give women equal representation.

Moving away from social reality; the individual who enters the virtual environment turns into a cyborg with the combination of man and machine. Manfred E. Clynes and Nathan S. Kline, who first introduced the concept of cyborg in 1960, used it to describe the merging of a human with a machine on a space voyage and the realization of bodily functions. Today, however, the theoretical discussion of the term cyborg began with Haraway's Cyborg Manifesto. In this work, Haraway analyzed the term cyborg in terms of gender, leading to the beginning of cyberfeminism. She argued that the term cyborg, the reality of the body in cyberspace, is a discursive construction of power centred on information and power. The concept of femininity, where gender does not constitute an innate identity, is a social phenomenon in the cultural sphere.

According to cyberfeminists, the female identity that exists in patriarchal societies is in a state of exploitation in cyberspace as in real life. For this reason, the Cyborg liberates the woman and her body because it does not carry socially sexist concerns; it positions the woman without making a distinction between private and public spheres. The term "cyborg", coined by Haraway, constructs a new reality for women discursively in the virtual environment by getting rid of gender inequalities. On the other hand, the cyborg redefines the institutions of race, class and sexuality constructed by social culture by getting rid of masculine domination in the cyber environment (Fernandez, 2003: 37).

The idea of cyberfeminism, an idea of the postmodern era, of moving identity from a single whole to a structured, fragmented whole is closer to anonymity than identity. From the point of view of feminism, Cyborg defines identity as a variable in a fluid structure and does not see classification in terms of gender as appropriate. This ambiguity adopted by Haraway in terms of gender and identity has been obscured by cyberfeminists in the 2000s. Wave I of the cyberfeminist movement established a close relationship between women and machines and supported the development of genderless identities in the digital world. The Second Wave of the cyberfeminist movement, on the other hand, was uncomfortable with subjecting the concept of feminism to a definition or limitation (Haraway, 2006: 13–22). One of the main criticisms of cyberfeminist thought is that it does not pay attention to social differences when addressing women's identities. Again, cyberfeminism, which ignores the limited participation of women in the digital environment, is criticized for desexualizing social identity. In addition, cyberfeminist sexuality in the discourses of de-gendering has initiated transgender or post-gender debates and transformed them into new mass movements. For this reason, those who argue that an identity cannot be formed independent of a social gender have claimed that cyberfeminism ignores the material causes and social dimensions of gender.

4   The Impact of the Cyberfeminist Movement and Feminist Policies on International Decision Makers

Decision-making is an activity carried out nationally or internationally through all kinds of individual, social and institutional structures. From a social perspective, decision-making processes are the production of policies in accordance with the nature of politics. In this respect, feminist thought, as a social actor, wants to have a political impact on national and international decision-makers by bringing women's issues and women's rights to the public agenda. In this section, which is the last part of our study, the political impact of feminist thought on decision-makers will be interpreted by evaluating women's conferences, which have political binding worldwide, within the scope of the UN's work. In addition, in this section, we will make a comparison between the institutional structure of the UN, its emergence, the issues it focuses on women's issues and the political discourse of feminist thought and the political production of the UN as a decision maker. From this point of view, the extent to which the UN has globalized women's rights and women's issues in the world and turned them into a universal policy and the latest situation of the UN on women's issues from the past to the present will be discussed.

In the 18th century, during the era dominated by modern thought, a widely accepted movement known as the Doctrine of Human Rights asserted that individuals inherently possess inalienable and inviolable rights. This idea became widespread in Europe and gained a legal character with the French Revolution of 1789 and the Universal Declaration of the Rights of Man and Citizen. The UN was founded in 1945 by 51 countries as an international decision-making organization to ensure international peace, security, social progress and human rights in the world. The UN, which is the continuation of the League of Nations in legal and political terms, is an international organization established by the victorious states as a result of the World Wars that took place in the 20th century. From a theoretical point of view, the concept of human rights gained international status with the UN Charter at the end of World War II (1945) and a concrete character with the European Convention on Human Rights in 1950. Since these legal arrangements for humanity with an egalitarian understanding were made by masculine decision-makers, they were not of a nature that valued women's problems and women's positions. Feminist movements criticized these documents, which were politically produced by male-dominated decision-makers, for ignoring women's issues. The UN, which put women's rights, women's issues and equality between women and men on its agenda in its founding charter, is a 78-year-old international decision-making institution based on gender equality. Thus, the Commission on the Status of Women (45 member states) was established within the UN in 1946 to grant equal rights to women, and social policies based on gender equality and solving women's problems were developed (The Advancement of Women, pp. 3–4). The first period of the UN (1945–1962) focused on women's rights and policies to solve women's problems, with a focus on policies to secure women's legal rights. These steps to solve the problems women face in education, work, political participation and family life are policies aimed at eliminating gender inequalities. In 1952, the UN adopted the Convention on the Political Rights of Women, which regulates women's political participation. With this convention, women were given the right to vote and be elected on equal terms in the social sphere (Hevener, 1983: 28). This text, which was legally binding on the member states that signed the convention, coincided with the mass popularization of feminist thought in the 20th century through the use of media and communication tools. This can be seen as a reflection of the political pressure of feminist movements on decision-makers.

As the most important international decision-making institution for the development of women's rights and the solution of their problems, the UN has also pioneered the organization of World Women's Conferences attended by women from all nations, cultures and non-governmental organizations around the world. The first World Conference on Women, held in Mexico City in 1975, addressed the issues of equality, development and peace under three main headings: International cooperation, peace, political participation, education, employment, health, nutrition, family, population, housing and other social problems. With the action plan prepared after the conference (1975–1985 Decade Plan), all member states of the UN were offered political solutions to women's problems. It was also during this period that the UN General Assembly adopted the legal Convention on the Elimination of All Forms of Discrimination against Women (CEDAW) in 1979 (The Advancement of Women, p. 5). In the midst of the Ten Year Action Plan, the Second World Conference on Women was convened in Copenhagen in 1980. Although it was seen that political progress had been made with the resolutions adopted at the UN General Assembly on the current position of women, it was observed that progress on women's issues in the international community was slow. For this reason, a second action plan was prepared at the conference in Copenhagen in addition to the Ten Year Plan. This second plan, which centred on domestic violence, sought solutions to the special situations of groups such as refugee women, young women and women with disabilities, which required urgent solutions. When the action plan adopted by the UN in 1975 came to an end, women's organizations convened at the Third World Conference on Women in 1985 in Nairobi, Kenya, to review achievements and set goals for the year 2000. At the Conference, the increasing arms race between the two blocs during the Cold War, the widening income gap between countries and economic crises were observed as hindrances to the agenda of policies on women's issues. The Nairobi Strategies were adopted by the representatives of 157 countries partic- ipating in the Conference. The strategy, which brought a new approach to the solution of women's problems, emphasized that women's participation in all areas of social life is not only a right but also a social obligation. The IV World Conference on Women, planned as a "Conference of Commitments" under the leadership of the UN, convened in Beijing, the capital of China, in 1995 with 17,000 participants representing 189 countries. The Beijing Conference, the largest women's conference ever held, discussed 12 topics and adopted the Beijing Declaration and Platform for Action. With this declaration, member states committed to implementing gender equality in all their institutions, policies and decision-making mechanisms and to enter into a restructuring process.

At a special session of the UN General Assembly in 2000 (Beijing+5), gen- der equality, development and peace were discussed and the UN Millennium Declaration, a plan of action for the future (until 2015) on achievements and challenges, was announced. The UN decided to merge the four different wom- en's offices it had established within its organization and announced the establishment of the UN Entity for Gender Equality and the Empowerment of Women (UN Women) in 2010. The main principle of this unit is to ensure women's empowerment and gender equality: Advancement of Women (DAW), the International Institute for Research and Training for the Advancement of Women (INSTRAW), the Office of the Special Adviser on Gender Affairs and the Advancement of Women (OSAGI) and the UN Development Fund for Women (UNIFEM). This unifying unit (UN Women) worked on more concrete projects and training under the UN umbrella, while at the same time supporting UN member states to realize their national development goals (The Advancement of Women, pp. 50–61).

As a result of the efforts of feminist movements and women's groups, the UN Security Council (UNSC) adopted Resolution 1325, laying a foundation that women can be the spokespersons and agents of change in the world's political problem-solving and peace processes (Heathcote, 2018, 375). Resolution 2467, also adopted by the UNSC in 2019, was a legal instrument to prevent sexual violence in acts of war and terrorism and to support families, including children born of sexual violence in conflict (Jansson and Eduards, 2016: 590).

Adopting gender equality and the empowerment of women in all areas as its founding principle, UN Women has attributed a special meaning to women and the principle of gender equality in its *Strategic Plan* (2022–2025), including girls in global development. According to the principle of gender equality, it was aimed to empower all women and girls and support them in terms of education, health, employment, political representation and finance. In the aftermath of the COVID-19 pandemic worldwide, this strategy prioritized women in sustainable development, aiming to eliminate women's economic, social and political backwardness in the social sphere (UN-Women-Strategic Plan, 2022: 3). The concept of women's empowerment envisioned by the UN and promoted by member states as international decision-makers has generated an in-depth debate among contemporary feminist groups. In particular, some cyberfeminist groups, who believed that the concept of gender could be achieved through *de-gendering*, put pressure on international decision-makers beyond the identity of women on a global scale. This gender-neutral approach led to controversy in the measurement and evaluation of empowerment (Stromquist, 1955: 13). This new feminist debate naturally led to new uncertainties and differences in discourse among political actors according to the different cultural characteristics and beliefs of the international community worldwide. While these gender debates over women's issues continue in the world, the issue of women's rights and gender equality will of course be on the agenda of the UN, an international decision-making organization, and efforts will continue to be made to solve women's problems in the international system.

5   Conclusion

Focusing on women's problems, rights and the struggle for equality, feminism emerged in 18th-century Europe. Gaining new meaning in different cultures and societies, feminism gained an economic, social and political character. In the historical process, from antiquity to the present day, women have been pushed out of the public sphere and into a private life tied to the home through the profession of motherhood. The patriarchal structure in cultural, political and religious institutions in the social system caused power and authority to assume a masculine identity. Feminism, which emerged due to the Industrial Revolution, showed its influence on political thought systems, and developed as Liberal, Cultural, Marxist, Socialist and Radical Feminism. The transformation of feminist thought into a mass movement around the world happened with liberalism. The First Wave Feminist Movement (18th-20th century), which put the masculine domination of the individual at the center of the discussions, put the concept of political participation and citizenship at the center of the discussions. The Second Wave Feminist Movement (mid-20th century), which brought gender-related egalitarian demands on women's bodies to the agenda, took women's rights and problems to a higher level and made political sanctions on the UN, an international decision-making institution. The UN, the leading institution of the women's struggle, encouraged the organization of World Women's Conferences with its member states. By announcing the decisions taken at the conference to the international community, the UN gave Women's Rights a legal character. In response to the women's struggle, which became massive and legalized on a global scale, the Third Wave Feminist Movement (1990s) emerged based on class differences within society and women's identity.

The feminist movement, which has a political impact on international decision-makers, started to discuss the concept of Cyberfeminism in its third and fourth waves. Influenced by the cyber culture that developed due to technological developments on a global scale, feminism opened a new window for itself with the cyberfeminist concept. The concept of cyber, which has a theoretically managerial meaning, became the feminist movement's new way of thinking on digital media and social networks. Cyberfeminism, which is a revolt against masculine domination in the digital universe, tried to reshape norms, traditions, institutions and human actions in the cyber environment with the cyberculture it put forward. The development of Cyberfeminist Theory emerged with Donna Haraway's Cyborg Manifesto, which challenged masculine dominance in cyberspace. By supporting women's participation in cyberspace; cyberfeminism, which tries to achieve gender equality, put forward different representations of women instead of a single woman in cyberculture. Cyber identity, one of the actors of cyberculture, is a concept based on the individual's online actions. Cyber identity, which defines the individual through the Internet, can also be explained as digital identity, virtual identity, online identity. Cyberfeminism, which wanted to de-gender technological institutions and technology education, wanted to break the virtual practices, masculine dominance and mono-sexist approach of patriarchal thinking. For this reason, cyberfeminists, who argue that technology and digital developments are male-dominated, aim to redefine gender in this sense by proposing the de-gendering of the internet. Influenced by postmodern thought, cyberfeminism, which sees identity as fragmented rather than a singular whole, is more inclined towards the concept of social disidentification. With this system of thought, cyberfeminist thought has been criticized for not paying attention to social differences in terms of identity. In addition, the cyberfeminist concept of sexuality in the discourses of desexualization has brought the transgender or post-gender debates to a new dimension. In this respect, those who argued that an identity independent of gender could not be formed claimed that cyberfeminism ignored the material and social dimension of gender. This genderless approach led to measurement and evaluation in relation to the feminist movement. As these gender debates continue through feminist discussions, women's rights and gender equality will of course continue to be on the UN agenda.

References

Arat, N. (1991). Feminizmin ABC'si. Simavi Yayınları, İstanbul.

Beauvoir, S. (1993). Kadın "İkinci Cins" 1 Genç Kızlık Çağı [Female "Second Sex" Adolescence]. Çeviren: Bertan Onaran, 7. Baskı, Payel Yayınları, İstanbul.

Berktay F. (2013). Toplumsal Cinsiyet Çalışmaları [Gender Studies]. 2. Baskı, Eskişehir, T.C. Anadolu Üniversitesi Açık Öğretim Fakültesi Yayınları.

UN Women Strategic Plan (2022–2025). Building a World of Gender Equality, file:/// C:/Users/DELL/Downloads/UN-Women-Strategic-Plan-2022-2025-brochure-tr%20 (1).pdf.

Brophy, J.E. (2010). Developing a corporeal cyberfeminism: Beyond cyberutopia. *New Media & Society*, 12(6), 929–945.

Çakır, S. (1996). Osmanlı Kadın Hareketi [Ottoman Women's Movement]. Metis Yayınları, 2. Basım, İstanbul.

Donovan, J. (2016). Feminist Teori [Feminist Theory].Çeviren: Aksu Bora, Meltem Ağduk Gevrek, Fevziye Sayılan, 11. Baskı, İletişim Yayınları, İstanbul.

Echols, A. (1989). *Daring to Be Bad: Radical Feminism in America 1967–1975*. Minneapolis: University of Minnesota Press.

Engels, F. & Marx, K. (2011). Alman İdeolojisi [German Ideology], Çeviren: Emir Aktan, Alter Yayıncılık, Ankara.

Eyssel, F. & Hegel, F. (2012). (S)he's got the look: Gender stereotyping of robots. *Journal of Applied Social Psychology*, 42(9), 2213–2230.

Ferguson, S. (2013). Sosyalist Feminist Geleneğin Güçlü Yanlarını Geliştirmek [Developing the Strengths of the Socialist Feminist Tradition], Çeviren: Oya Gözel Durmaz, Özuğurlu, Aynur (Ed.), 21. Yüzyıl Feminizmine Doğru, NotaBene Yayınları, Ankara.

Fernandez, M. (2003). "Cyberfeminism, racism, embodiment". In M. Fernandez, F. Wilding, and M.M. Wright (eds.). *Cyberfeminist Practices*. Brooklyn, New York: Autonomedia.

Güzel, E. (2016). Dijital Kültür ve Çevrimiçi Sosyal Ağlarda Rekabetin Aktörü: "Dijital Habitus". [Digital Culture and the Actor of Competition in Online Social Networks: "Digital Habitus"].Gümüşhane Üniversitesi İletişim Fakültesi Elektronik Dergisi. 4(1).

Haraway, D. (2006). *Siborg Manifestosu, Geç Yirminci Yüzyılda Bilim, Teknoloji ve Sosyalist-Feminizm [Cyborg Manifesto, Science, Technology and Socialist-Feminism in the Late Twentieth Century]*. Osman Akınhay (Ed.). Istanbul: Agora Kitaplığı.

Haraway, D. (2015). Anthropocene, Capitalocene, Plantationocene, Chthulucene: Making Kin. *Enironmantal Humanities*, 6.

Heathcote, G. (2018). Security Council Resolution 2242 on women, peace and security: Progressive gains or dangerous development? *Global Society*, 32 (4): 374–394.

Hevener K. N. (1983). *International Law and the Status of Woman*. Boulder, CO: Westviev.

Jansson, M. & Eduards, M. (2016). The politics of gender in the UN Security Council Resolutions on women, peace and security. *International Feminist Journal of Politics*, 18(4): 590–604.

Karakoç, R. & Özden, M. (2020). Demokrasi Anlayışında Yeni Bir Yaklaşım: Müzakereci Demokrasi [A New Approach to Democracy: Deliberative Democracy], Trakya University. *Journal of Social Science*, 22(1): 579 – 598. https://doi.org/10.26468/trakyasobed.726760.

Kember, S. (2002). Reinventing cyberfeminism: Cyberfeminism and the new biology. *Economy and Society*, 31(4), 626–641.

Mazoyer, M. & Roudart, L. (2009). Dünya Tarım Tarihi – Neolitik Çağdan Günümüzdeki Krize [World Agricultural History – From the Neolithic Age to the Present Crisis], Çeviren: Güle Ünsaldı, Epos Yayınları, Ankara.

Michel, A. (1993). Feminizm [Feminism]. Çeviren: Şirin Tekeli. İletişim Yayınları, İstanbul.

Millett, K. (2018). Cinsel Politika [Sexual Politics]. Çeviren: Seçkin Selvi, 4. Baskı, Payel Yayınları, İstanbul.

Narayan, U. (1998). "Essence of Culture and a Sense of History: A Feminist Critique of Cultural Essentialism" [Kültürün Özü ve Bir Tarih Anlayışı: Kültürel Özcülüğün Feminist Bir Eleştirisi], *Hypatia*, 13(2), 86–106.

Pelizzon, S.M. (2009). Kadının Konumu Nasıl Değişti? Feodalizmden Kapitalizme [How has the Position of Women Changed? From Feudalism to Capitalism], Çeviren: İhsan Ercan Sadi ve Cem Somel, İmge Kitabevi, Ankara.

Roberts, J.M. (2010). Avrupa Tarihi [History of Europe]. Çeviren: Fethi Aytuna, İnkılap Yayınları, İstanbul.

Şeren, G.Y. (2018). Toplumsal Cinsiyete Duyarlı Bütçe Politikalarının Feminist Kökenleri [Feminist Origins of Gender Sensitive Budget Policies], Fe Dergi, Feminist Eleştiri 10, Sayı 1, Ankara, DOI: 10.1501/Fe0001_0000000199.

Søraa, R.A. (2017). Mechanical genders: How do humans gender robots? *Gender, Technology and Development*, 21(1–2), 99–115.

Standish, P. (1999). Only connect: computer literacy from Heidegger to cyberfeminism. *Educational Theory*, 49(4), 417–435.

Stromquist, N.P. (1995). Women, education and empowerment: Pathways towards autonomy. In C.M. Afionuev (Eds.), *The Theoretical and Practical Bases for Empowerment*. Hamburg: UNESCO Institute for Education.

The United Nations and The Advancement of Women: 1945–1996, The United Nations Blue Book Series, Volume VI, revised edition.

Tong R.P. (2006). Feminist Düşünce [Feminist Thought], Çeviren: Zafer Cirhinlioğlu, Gündoğan Yayınları, İstanbul.

Varol, S.F. (2014). Kadınların Dijital Teknolojiyle İlişkisine Ütopik Bir Yaklaşım: Siberfeminizm [A Utopian Approach to Women's Relationship with Digital Technology: Cyberfeminism]. *International Journal of Social Science*, 1(27).

Wilding, F. (1998). Where is feminism in cyberfeminism? *N.paradoxa*, 2, 6–12.

Wolf, Eric R. (2000). Köylüler [Villagers]. Çeviren: Abdulkerim Sönmez, İmge Yayınevi, Ankara.

Wollstonecraft, M. (2012). Kadın Haklarının Gerekçelendirilmesi [The Justification of Women's Rights] Çeviren: Deniz Hakyemez, 11. Baskı, Türkiye İş Bankası Kültür Yayınları, İstanbul.

Yıldırım, Ş. & İşler, A.M. (2022). Kronik Hastalıklar ve Aile İşlevselliği: Yapısal Aile Terapisi Yaklaşımı Çerçevesinde Bir Değerlendirme [Chronic Diseases and Family Functioning: An Evaluation within the Framework of Structural Family Therapy Approach]. H. Küçükkaragöz ve E. Kocayörük içinde, Aile Terapisinde Yaklaşımlar, Eğiten Yayıncılık, Ankara.

CHAPTER 8

Social Policy and Cyberfeminism

Ayşe Mine İşler

Today, women face problems such as violence, abuse, inability to work and access to education. Women's inclusion in social life, protection from all kinds of violence and discrimination, and access to basic rights such as education and health are realized through social policies. From the past to the present, a patriarchal perspective has dominated social policies and women have been relegated to a secondary role. Women's struggle to gain rights and to exist in social life has been achieved through feminist movements. With the feminist waves that developed due to social and political changes, social policies gradually became gender sensitive. Today, with the development of technology and the widespread use of the Internet, cyberfeminism, which is called the fourth-wave feminist movement, has emerged. With cyberfeminism, women's struggle has moved to the digital sphere. In this study, the relationship between social policy and feminism is discussed and the impact of cyberfeminism on social policy is mentioned.

1   Introduction

When the position of women in the historical process is analyzed, it is seen that women have generally remained in second place and have been in a constant struggle to gain rights. The ideology that accompanies this struggle of women is feminism. Feminism is an ideology and an activist movement that focuses on the struggle of women against the patriarchal system, who are subjected to discrimination and oppression solely because of their gender. Feminism desires women to exist in the social sphere with legal rights. The position of women in society is determined by the social policies in a country. With gender-sensitive social policies, women can exist in all areas of life. Feminist movements are effective in making policies gender sensitive in patriarchal life order. Therefore, the relationship between social policy and feminism is important.

In this study, the impact of feminist movements in general and cyberfeminism in particular on social policy will be analyzed. Therefore, in the first part of the study, the relationship between social policy and women will be discussed. In this section, firstly, the concept of social policy will be explained and a theoretical basis will be provided. Then, the relationship between women, gender and social policy will be discussed and the transition process from social policies in which women are secondary to gender-sensitive policies will be explained.

In the second section, feminist movements and women's achievements from the past to the present will be presented within the scope of the reflection of feminist movements on social policy. Firstly, the First Wave Feminist Movement and women's demands for citizenship and suffrage in this process will be analyzed. Then, Second Wave Feminism, in which birth control, abortion and social rights demands are effective, and Third Wave Feminism, which focuses on micro social policies by emphasizing women's differences with the influence of postmodern theories, will be discussed.

In the third section, "cyberfeminism", which emerged with the development of technology and social media networks and opened a new field of struggle for women's movements, will be evaluated within the Fourth Wave Feminist Movement (to be consistent with others). In this context, firstly, the philosophy of cyberfeminism will be explained from Haraway's perspective. Then, the reflection of feminist movements in cyberspace on today's social policies will be evaluated.

In the conclusion part of the study, feminist movements will be evaluated by revealing the changing position of women in social policies from past to present. At the same time, the achievements of the cyberfeminist movement will be interpreted in the context of its impact on social policies. In the following process, inferences will be made on the status of cyberfeminism.

2   Social Policy and Women

This section will provide a theoretical foundation by explaining the concept of social policy. Then, gender and the changing perception of women in social policy will be discussed.

2.1   *Social Policy*

Social policy is a term formed by the combination of the Latin concept of policy, which means "a collection of measures taken for a specific purpose", and the word socius, which means "partner, friend, companion" (Andaç, 2014). It is used to express the regulations and practices of states in line with certain objectives. The concept of social policy, which was first used by Professor Wilhelm Heinrich in the 19th century, was put into practice by Bismarck in

Germany in the 1870s. Theoretically, it came to the agenda in 1911 with Ottovan Zwideneck Südenhorst's work *Sozialpolitik* (Şahin, 2018).

The biggest factor in the emergence of the concept of social policy has been the social problems experienced after the industrial revolution and the concept of social policy has gained strength with the development of the concept of social policy. With the industrial revolution in Western Europe in the 19th century, women and children in particular were exposed to long hours of work, working conditions unworthy of human dignity emerged, intense workloads and wages too low to sustain a minimum life constituted the social face of the new factory order.

In the new social structure that emerged after the Industrial Revolution, as a result of the relations of production and distribution, the wealth of the owners of capital increased while the owners of labour, the workers, have become poorer and poorer (Serdar, 2014). In this period, the unfair distribution of income led to a struggle between labour and capital. At this point, social policy has emerged as policies produced to peacefully end the injustice between labour and capital within the capitalist social structure, to produce reasonable solutions, and to build a more livable social order in the face of existing social imbalances (Danış, 2007). The problems created by the Industrial Revolution and the currents of thought that emerged after the French Revolution eliminated the possibility of the state remaining neutral in economic and social life and enabled social policies to become a necessity for states (Özaydın, 2012).

When the origins of the concept of social policy are examined, it is seen that there are narrow and broad definitions. In the narrow sense, social policy is defined as a branch of science aimed at eliminating conflicts and imbalances between workers and employers in the capitalist economic order and ensuring harmony between classes in connection with the way social policy emerged. The scope of social policy in the narrow sense is the protection of the labour force, the institutionalization of industrial relations, the fair distribution of income and the minimization of tensions between workers and employers (Koray, 2011). In this context, the regulations called "Factory Laws" constitute examples of social policy. The first one, enacted in England in 1802, limited the working hours of child labourers and introduced a narrow social policy approach. The protection of women and children and their inclusion in social policy was realized with the Ten-Hour Law enacted in 1847, and the working hours of children and women were reduced. During the period, many laws regulating working conditions continued to be enacted. In 1942, the Beveridge Report, the first institutional social policy implementation, has been published. Then, the International Labor Organization's Philadelphia Declaration, which included regulations on the protection of women and motherhood, had been published in 1944. With these regulations, the state increased its interventions in social and economic life and the social state emerged (Davutoğlu, 2015; Özaydın, 2012). With the development of the social state understanding, the scope of social policy has also expanded.

A social state is a state that identifies the needs of its citizens and takes it upon itself to provide them with a standard of living and a level of welfare befitting human dignity. The social state provides basic rights and services to every citizen based on equality of opportunity and aims to ensure social justice and social peace in society. In this respect, a social state is characterized as a state understanding that legitimizes the state's intervention in social and economic life (Özbudun, 2010).

The social state has duties such as reducing and eliminating unemployment, ensuring social security, eliminating social inequalities, providing education, health and social services to all its citizens, and ensuring social cohesion. The state fulfils this duty through the social policies that it puts forward and carries out. In this context, social policy in a broad sense is not limited to the solution of problems between workers and employers but covers all individuals and social groups in need of protection as a requirement of the social state and regulates their relations with the state.

Today, social policy has assumed the identity of a policy directed towards combating all kinds of problems that negatively affect social life. Especially in developed Western societies, the increasing differentiation of problems and needs has led to the expansion of the scope of social policy and the enrichment of social policy practices. Issues such as social exclusion, discrimination, and protection of the rights of women, youth, children, the elderly, ex-convicts, immigrants, disabled people, the environment and consumers have become the subject of social policy and gained importance as third generation social policies (Tokol and Alper, 2011).

2.2   Social Policy, Gender and Women

The aim of social policy is to ensure social welfare and social justice in a society. In connection with this aim, social policy also has objectives such as social integration, social peace, social cohesion and social development. In order to achieve the stated objectives and ensure social justice, social policy refers to the arrangements made by the state for individuals and groups that are characterized as disadvantaged in society and need to be protected through policies. Social policy is the protection of individuals against various risks, injustices and inequalities as a requirement of the social state approach (İçağasıoğlu and Özbesler, 2009).

Today, women face problems such as violence, abuse, exclusion from working life/lower wages compared to men, maternity leave, care responsibilities in a patriarchal society, and lack of access to education. In the face of these problems, it is a necessity for the social state to support women, to improve and secure their rights, to apply positive discrimination against women and to protect women through social policies. Women's inclusion in working life and social life, protection from all forms of violence and discrimination, and access to basic rights such as education and health are realized through social policies.

Previously, only protection-oriented social policies were implemented for women, who were seen as economically dependent, whereas today there is a social policy approach that prioritizes women's rights, secures women's rights and freedoms, and aims to ensure women's presence in all areas of social life. However, this change in the social policies developed for women is shaped according to the level of development and gender perception of countries. In countries where gender perception is intense, women face many obstacles in all areas of life and their integration into society is hindered due to gender-insensitive social policies. At this point, it would be useful to talk about gender and gender-sensitive social policies.

Gender is a concept that differs from biological sex and is interpreted through social and cultural elements (Altınova and Duyan, 2013). Gender is defined as the social roles, responsibilities, power and social position, demands and expectations, rights and opportunities that are determined for women and men in society by traditions and social institutions. The attribution of these to women and men by society is defined as a social construction (Oakley, 1972). Gender is reproduced through socialization and social institutions (Connell, 1998). Due to these constructed roles, inequality between women and men is created in social, political, economic, cultural, educational, decision-making mechanisms, etc. areas of life, women's place in society is questioned and women are put in the second plan (Durgun and Gök, 2017; Ridgeway, 2011). In societies where this understanding prevails, social policies based on inequalities and limiting women to the private sphere and removing them from the public sphere are observed. The public sphere is where laws are made, social policies are formulated and citizens participate in this process through political participation. The private sphere is defined as the space within the household where the needs of family life are met. While men, who are seen as the head of the family, participate in politics and business life in the public sphere, women are restricted to the private sphere. Women in the private sphere cannot participate in the public sphere and are engaged in household chores such as caring for children/elderly family members, cooking and cleaning (Ecevit, 2011).

Gender equality is defined by the Council of Europe (2004) as the recognition of the differences between men and women, the acceptance of women and men as equal and the same value in social life. The first step towards gender equality was taken by the United Nations Commission on the Status of Women in 1946. In 1948, the Universal Declaration of Human Rights, which was signed in 1948, emphasizing only being a "human being" without discriminating between men and women was also a very important turning point (Yumuş, 2012). In the following period, various studies on women's rights were carried out. In 1975, the World Conference on Women was organized and at the end of the conference, the United Nations General Assembly declared the "Decade of Women". The most important development regarding gender equality during the Women's Decade was the adoption of the "Convention on the Elimination of All Forms of Discrimination against Women" (CEDAW) in 1979. CEDAW is a convention that eliminates discrimination based on gender and aims to ensure that women and men enjoy fundamental rights and freedoms equally. (Bener, 2011; İçli, 2017).

The "Beijing Declaration", which emerged as a result of the Fourth World Conference on Women held in Beijing in 1995, is also very important in terms of imposing responsibility on states for gender equality. With the Declaration, states are held responsible for ensuring gender equality, women's empowerment and the reflection of gender approach to social policies (İleri, 2016). With these developments in gender and women's rights, gender equality policies have gained importance for states. Policies that aim to eliminate gender inequality are called gender equality policies, and these policies ensure women's empowerment and equal participation in economic and social life.

The embedding of gender equality policies in state policies is referred to as "mainstreaming". All over the world, gender mainstreaming has enabled countries to redevelop their programs in the political, economic and social spheres (Sumbas, 2020).

The development of the idea of human rights and women's movements have been influential in these advances in gender equality in social policies. In 1789, First Wave Feminism emerged with the currents of thought created by the French Revolution and with this movement, women's political rights were emphasized. Second Wave Feminism, which developed in the 1960s, put gender on the agenda and fought for issues such as abortion, birth control and domestic care (Donovan, 2015). In the 1990s, third-wave feminism created a wider field by focusing on different women's issues. After the 1990s, with the widespread use of the internet, the fourth-wave feminist movement began to be mentioned (Kolay, 2015). With feminist movements, women have raised awareness about gender equality, opposed rights violations through various actions and created pressure on states, enabling social policies to prioritize women's rights. Feminist movements, which have been effective in the development of social policies in favour of women, will be discussed in the second section in connection with the subject.

3 Feminist Movements from Past to Present and Their Reflections on Social Policy

3.1 *Feminism and Social Policy*

The emergence of feminism has been related to the social position of women throughout human history. The first information about human history coincides with the First Neolithic Period. In this period when hunting and gathering were dominant, a peaceful social structure was observed and men and women participated in life equally. No superiority or dominance between the sexes is observed. In the Middle Neolithic Period (6000–3000 BC), settled life began and private property began to develop. From this period onwards, the foundation was laid for social institutionalizations that led to the subordinate position of women. From this period onwards, monotheistic religions and philosophical schools of thought emphasized the difference between men and women, myths about women's subordination were created and the groundwork was laid for the representation of humanity in the male gender. Cultural, political, religious and social institutions were built in accordance with the patriarchal system (Kolay, 2015). The subordination of women has led women to seek their rights over time. The basis of women's demands for rights dates back to the Renaissance. Christine de Pisan was the pioneer of women's movements during the Renaissance. Pisan opposed the oppression of women by the church and the kingdom and fought for women's access to education (Michel, 1997). Women's struggle for gains continued over time and throughout the late 18th and 19th centuries, the women's movement defined its ideology as feminism. Feminism is derived from the Latin word "feminine" meaning woman and was first used in France in 1837. The currents of thought that emerged with the French Revolution and the openings regarding women's rights constitute the basis of feminism. Feminism, which requires action to ensure and expand women's rights, is also defined as a doctrine of action (Vural and Kantar, 2022). Feminism has an understanding that rejects women facing oppression and hardship, exclusion from social life and marginalization only because they are women. In this context, feminism is defined as a movement that aims to end sexism and the oppression associated with sexism.

Feminism has developed in different ways from the moment it emerged until today. Feminist movements that started with the right to vote have continued to progress by focusing on issues such as sexual freedom, childbirth, gender, and specific problems of women. With the spread of the feminist movement, the idea of feminism has sought solutions to universal problems and in this process, women have made significant gains in societies where feminist thought has become widespread (Taş, 2016). Making the achievements of feminist movements visible and putting them into practice is possible through the social policies established by countries while making existing social policies more women-oriented is possible through feminist criticism and feminist actions. In other words, feminism can change the agenda of social policy. Therefore, feminism and social policy are closely interrelated.

Wilding (1998) states that the feminist perspective has expanded the field of social policy, the position of women has changed through feminist analyses, and the idea of equal opportunities has become embedded in social policies. Feminists, who see the basis of women's problems in gender equality, focus on the position of women in social policy, especially in the family and employment. The feminist movement opposes the system in welfare states that sees women as the main caregiver, confining them to the private sphere and focusing on protecting the family in this way. In this context, feminism brought a breath of fresh air to the approach of welfare states to the family. In the second wave of feminism, social policy was given more importance both academically and in terms of action, and feminism's sphere of influence on social policy expanded. In this period, studies were conducted on issues such as immigrant women, reproduction and abortion, sexual abuse, elderly and child care, parental leave (Lewis, 2011).

Feminist ideas differ among themselves due to the issues they focus on and their perspectives. Therefore, there are different feminist approaches to social policy. Liberal feminism, Marxist feminism, socialist feminism and radical feminism are prominent in the analysis of social policy. While liberal feminism formed the basis of wave I feminism, radical, Marxist and socialist theories came to the fore in wave II feminism (Lewis, 2011). Liberal feminism was shaped around the idea that women and men should have the same rights, arguing that women and men are not ontologically different, and influenced social policy in terms of women's access to citizenship rights. Radical feminism addresses its views on oppression and the oppressed and states that the oppression against women is universal. It defines the reason for this oppression as the patriarchal social structure. According to radical feminists, women's common problems are sexual exploitation, violence, birth control and abortion. They try to influence social policy through these problems (Atan,

2015). The socialist and Marxist view of feminism, on the other hand, links the experiences of women to capitalism and analyzes them through class and gender distinctions. Within the capitalist structure, while women are subjected to class-based exploitation, they are simultaneously oppressed by the patriarchal structure (Pelizzon, 2009). For this reason, socialist feminists try to influence social policies on employment and education in order to empower women and free them from oppression (Lewis, 2011).

When we look at feminist movements, it is seen that they have been shaped in different periods. These periods are generally referred to as the I. II. III. and IV. Feminist Waves cover a wide period of time from the 19th century to the 21st century. Women have been influenced by different ideologies and their demands have been shaped by the changing social structure and globalization. The impact of feminist movements on social policy in line with rights and demands has therefore varied in each period.

3.2 First-Wave Feminism

Although First-Wave Feminism became evident at the end of the 19th century, feminist ideas on women's rights to political participation and education can be found in *The Book of The City of Ladies* written by Christine de Pisan in 1405 (Heywood, 2013). The first feminist text in the modern sense was Mary Wollstonecraft's *Vindication of the Rights of Women* in 1792. Mary Wollstonecraft, who was influenced by the Enlightenment period's thoughts, aimed to change the social structure by questioning the relationship between men and women from a broad perspective, including family, politics and economy (Başak, 2013). The first wave of feminism was shaped by the demands for women's suffrage, property rights and education in this work. In the 1776 American Declaration of Independence and the 1789 French Declaration of the Rights of Man, feminists, who thought that women's rights were not sufficiently addressed, started to make demands in social and political areas with the influence of the *Vindication of the Rights of Women*.

Against this background, the first wave of feminism began in 1848 with the Seneca Falls Congress organized by Lucretia Mott and Elizabeth Cady Stanton. At the end of the Congress, women announced a 12-point list of demands. These included the right to vote, which drew the reaction of the male-dominated society, as well as equal opportunities in education and labour, and the right to own property. The decisions taken at this congress paved the way for women's struggle for suffrage (Grady, 2018).

In this period, liberal feminists wanted to obtain the right to vote in order to have equal rights in the political sphere dominated by men and to benefit equally from the right to an education that would enable them to acquire the qualifications for the political sphere (Dinçer, 2021). The struggle for women's suffrage, which is identified with the first wave of feminism, started in the 19th century and intensified in the 20th century. During this period, among women living in Europe, only women whose husbands held important positions and were hierarchically in a higher class could vote, while other women did not have the right to vote. Therefore, the right to vote remained an important problem (Bensadon, 1994). The main aim of the feminist movement centred around the right to vote was to enjoy all the rights of being a citizen and to be equal to men in the public sphere. This first feminist wave, which aimed to end the dominance of men over social institutions, began to develop in the USA in 1840, in England in 1850, in Germany and France in 1860 and in the Scandinavian countries in the 1870s (Çaha, 1994).

Women's suffrage struggles, which spread rapidly in Europe and America, varied in each country depending on factors such as culture, constitution and patriarchy (Bock, 2004). In America, the suffrage struggles that started after the War of Independence were combined with the anti-slavery movement in 1840. During this period, women fought for social and political rights and against racism. As a result of this struggle, suffrage associations were established in 36 states in America at the end of the 19th century. All women, regardless of ethnic origin, were able to vote in 1920 with an amendment to the Constitution. In England, women were granted the right to vote in 1918, but this right did not extend to all women. In order for women to vote, they had to be at least 30 years old and own property. By 1928, these conditions were abolished and all women in England gained the right to vote (Holborn, 2018). At the end of the First World War, 21 countries, including the United States and England, as well as Russia, Germany and 21 other countries, recognized women's suffrage unconditionally. Among the 21 countries was the Republic of Turkey, which recognized women's suffrage earlier than many European countries. In Turkey, women were granted the right to vote in local elections on March 20, 1930, and on December 5, 1934, with an amendment to the constitution, they gained the right to vote and be elected in parliamentary elections. In France, women gained the right to vote at the end of the Second World War (Badinter, 1992).

After the industrial revolution, women's participation in social life as workers and the changes in the position of women led to the expansion of the limits of women's demands for public rights (Şeren, 2018). Women workers organized and reacted to the fact that they were paid less than men, and as a result of their ongoing struggle, feminists succeeded in establishing the principle of "equal pay for equal work" in the League of Nations with the Treaty of Versailles in 1918. In addition to the right to vote, the first-wave feminist movement was accompanied by demands for rights such as equal opportunity in education, the right to be equal before the law, the right to take part in governance, and the right to property.

In the first wave of feminism, the most important result of the feminist movement was to lay the foundation for steps to change the male-dominated mental structure and to gain rights in the political and social spheres by resisting the patriarchal social structure. After this period, feminists continued to demand social, political, economic and legal rights. However, by the 1960s, women focused on the psychological and sexual reflection of patriarchy and gender beyond the political and public sphere. Thus, second-wave feminism began with the idea of women's emancipation.

3.3   Second-Wave Feminism

With the achievement of basic rights such as the right to vote and the right to work in the first wave of feminism, the women's movement was interpreted as having achieved its goals and a period of stagnation was experienced. Although feminism was thought to have come to an end in this period, the infrastructure of feminist theories was created. By the 1960s, a new questioning of the body, sexuality and gender had begun and the feminist movement took off and the second wave of feminism began. The women's movements of this period differ from the first wave of women's movements in their ideology, organizational forms and activism (Berktay, 2013).

The second wave feminist women's movement aimed to bring women into public life with their own unique identities in all institutions dominated by patriarchal cultures, such as the family, school, church and the state, and wanted to 'create a female public life space' (Çaha et al., 2016). For this reason, the discourse of "the personal is political" became the slogan of second-wave feminism and criticized the exclusion of the private sphere from social policy in policy making. The slogan "the personal is political" has many meanings. First of all, women's experiences started to be seen as scientific data for the first time. On the other hand, with this discourse, women demanded a transformation in the gender-based division of labour in both the public and private spheres. It was emphasized that this transformation would only be possible through "sisterhood". Sisterhood implies that all women are subjected to common oppression and oppression and therefore have common interests. From the 1960s onwards, women began to support each other against male domination and to use the term sisterhood (Atan, 2015; Berktay, 2013).

In this period, which is referred to in the literature as the second wave of feminism, women's demands became widespread all over the world due to the acceleration of intellectual developments and academic developments. In this period, the study of women's history gained importance and feminist theory and practice emerged as a transformative vision. The feminist movement tried to see beyond the economic, legal and political structures of society in order to improve the position of women. Accordingly, issues such as gaining social rights, women's right to abortion and contraception, violence against women, illness, unemployment, and the right to have sole say over their own bodies came to the fore.

Women have organized awareness-raising meetings and organized themselves in different countries and geographies to share their experiences and have taken actions to influence social policies in these areas. The National Organization of Women (NOW), one of the most important organizations established by women to seek rights, was founded by Betty Friedan in the USA in 1966. This organization emphasized women's human rights and continued to work on demands such as women's participation in working life, the right to equal pay, the examination of family law in the context of gender equality, and an end to sexist representations in the media. NOW, whose number of members reached 10,000 in 1971, gained an important place in social policy on women's rights (Michel, 1997).

The period of the rise of second wave feminism was also a period of technological advances, and the 1960s was a period of technological advances that enabled women to give birth safely. However, women had difficulties in accessing these advances in women's health and reproduction, as well as contraceptive drugs. The feminist movement fought for alternatives to sexual health and childbirth for all women and for an end to oppressive laws and patriarchal norms. Stating that they were the only ones who could decide on their bodies and that sexuality and reproduction were different things, feminists demanded the widespread use of birth control (Demirağ, 2020). As a result of women's struggles in this field, contraception was legally accepted in the UK in 1967 and reflected in social policy. As women continued to organize on this issue, the right to abortion was legalized in the USA in 1973, France in 1975, Italy in 1978, and Turkey in 1983 (Kolay, 2015).

During this period, women gained rights such as the right to abortion, as well as the right to take part in politics, the right to employment, the right to education and the right to develop themselves in the field of fine arts. However, these rights provided by law were not fully reflected in life practices due to traditions and sexist approaches (Donovan, 2015). For this reason, the second wave of feminism focused on gender and the patriarchal system.

Simone de Beauvoir's words "One does not become a woman, one is born a woman" and her words in her book *The Second Sex* that "the liberation of women will start from their bellies" became the starting point of gender struggles. In this period, radical feminists introduced the concept of gender by linking the oppression of women to the patriarchal system. They addressed issues such as pornography, abortion, contraception and violence theoretically for the first time and fought for their rights on these issues. Women have stated that patriarchal structures perpetuate unequal roles and that the institution of the family, being based on a patriarchal structure, increases sexist exploitation (Taş, 2016). The patriarchal orders placing the family at the centre and imposing the role of motherhood and home-maker on women, and seeing the man as the person who provides economic gain and controls expenditures, has confined women to the home and removed them from work life, that is, from the public sphere (Demir and Kantar, 2023). Marxist feminists, who argued that this situation devalued women's domestic labour over time and created a kind of slavery relationship between men and women, put women's employment in the public sphere at the centre of their struggle (Ecevit, 2011).

The most important achievement of the Second Wave feminist movement and the struggle was the signing of international agreements for the legal status of women and the provision of social rights. The prioritization of women's rights by the United Nations, which is based on equality between men and women and influences social policies in this regard, has been a turning point. In the process leading to international agreements, as mentioned earlier, the First World Conference on Women was convened in Mexico in 1975. This conference raised awareness that discrimination against women was an important problem and the years 1976–1985 were declared as the "Women's Decade". In 1979, the Convention on the Elimination of All Forms of Discrimination Against Women (CEDAW), which has more comprehensive powers, was adopted. With this convention, discrimination against women was defined and national and international policies were made to eliminate this situation.

CEDAW is a treaty for the protection of women's human rights, the equal recognition and protection of all human rights for women and the prevention of violations. With CEDAW, violence against women is opposed and discrimination against women in economic, social and political spheres is prevented. Responsibility for achieving these goals was assigned to states, non-governmental organizations and the private sector.

To summarize, in the second wave of feminism, women have struggled against the patriarchal system and gender stereotypes in politics, culture, social life, science and social policy and have achieved many gains in the context of women's rights. Despite these gains, second-wave feminism was criticized for including only upper and middle-class women and white women, and third-wave feminism emerged in the 1990s.

3.4   Third-Wave Feminism

Third-wave feminism emerged in the 1990s as a reaction to the ideology of second-wave feminism and its reflection on life practices. Third-wave feminism criticized the focus of previous waves of feminism on the upper and middle classes and its focus only on white women. By rejecting a uniform universal perception of femininity, they aimed to leave behind the reductionist perspective and to address women's movements on a more inclusive and broader plane. With the influence of multiculturalist and postmodernist theories, the differences between women were addressed and it was emphasized that differences are valuable (Arat, 2017). In this context, it is seen that the aim of the third-wave feminist movement was to bring together all women, old and young, from different ethnic origins, classes and cultures (Taş, 2016). The concept of the Third Wave was born when young people who wanted to protest against the US Supreme Court decisions came together and called themselves "Third Wave Feminists" for the first time (Türkoğlu, 2015).

Third-wave feminism differs significantly from first and second-wave feminism, which are considered as continuations of each other. It rejects some of the stereotypes of second-wave feminism or accepts some of the things that the second-wave rejected, such as makeup. It argues that it is possible for women to be both smart and beautiful (Gaag, 2018). At the same time, third-wave feminists, who rejected the " personal is political" approach identified with second-wave feminism, emphasized women's identity rather than generalizing women's problems and emphasized influencing policies through individual women's problems (Türkoğlu, 2015).

The third wave of feminism, which is concerned with micro-social policies, has dealt with more diverse issues than the second wave, such as gender, violence, abuse, sexuality, women's empowerment, war, justice and equality, and environmental issues. Aiming for social change, third-wave feminists supported activism that raised awareness to achieve this goal (Özveri, 2009).

Third-wave feminists have attached great importance to the fight against violence against women, and at the end of their long years of struggle, they have achieved important gains that have influenced social policies in the international arena. After the 1993 World Conference on Human Rights in Vienna, women's rights were addressed separately for the first time in the United Nations' human rights documents. The Conference declared that "women and girls are an integral, indivisible and indispensable part of universal human rights". With the declaration signed as a result of the conference, the measures to be taken by states to prevent violence against women were explained (Karal and Aydemir, 2012). On the same date, the United Nations General Assembly signed the Declaration on the Elimination of Violence against Women. The

Declaration on the Prevention of Violence against Women was adopted on December 20, 1993, without a vote. In the Declaration, the responsibilities of states for the prevention of violence and the protection of the victims of violence were discussed in detail and it was decided that states should make regulations in their domestic laws for the protection of women. Following the Declaration, which was a driving force for states to make regulations in their domestic laws, anti-violence laws were enacted in Austria in 1997 and in Germany in 2002. In Turkey, the "Law on the Protection of the Family" entered into force in 1998 (Moroğlu, 2005). Another important development was the Beijing Declaration and Platform for Action that emerged as a result of the Beijing Conference held in 1995 with the participation of 189 countries. The Beijing Declaration recognized violence against women as an act against human rights and emphasized that states should take responsibility for preventing violence against women (Karal and Aydemir, 2012).

With the development of technology and the internet after the 1990s, women have created electronic spaces, websites, discussion platforms and blogs to convey their ideas to the masses, announce their problems and continue their struggles. With the transfer of these women's struggles to digital life, cyberspace was opened to feminism and a new wave of cyberfeminism emerged. The fourth wave of cyberfeminism, which has similar demands to the third wave of feminism, creates a difference due to its form of struggle (Akan, 2020). In this context, in the next section, cyberfeminism, which is considered within the Fourth-Wave Feminism, will be discussed and the development and philosophy of cyberfeminism will be mentioned. Then, the link between cyberfeminism and social policy will be examined.

4 Fourth-Wave Feminism: Cyberfeminism

4.1 Cyberfeminism

With the development of digital technologies in today's world, the internet and social media have become a part of our lives and the spread of the internet has created network societies. The network society consists of social networks and the networks spread through social media are constantly expanding their sphere of influence and determining the technology that creates them. With the networks created, governments can manage perceptions and construct their own realities. Therefore, today the internet has become a space used to defend the agendas and policies of states. However, thanks to the internet, people from different social classes, races, ethnic origins and educational levels can come together and challenge the problems in the world order. They

can do this through social media, transcending temporal and spatial boundaries (Castells, 2008). With these digital developments, different groups can
be represented on the Internet and people can see the internet as a means of
expanding the public sphere (Dahlberg, 2001).

According to feminist thinkers, internet technologies are shaped by masculine gender ideology and hegemonic patterns. Masculine dominance in technology is seen as a situation that needs to be fought. On the other hand, the
fact that the internet contributes to women's ability to make their voices heard,
to organize, and to convey their demands to policymakers more easily makes
the internet, that is, cyberspace, important for women's movements. The focus
of cyberfeminism is women's use of cyberspace. Although the foundation of
cyberfeminism was formed in the third feminist wave, with the development
of the internet, its theoretical basis and practical practice took shape in the
fourth wave.

Cyberfeminism, which focuses on the relationship between network technology and women, has a perspective that adds feminist theory to technology,
the Internet and social media (Aydemir and Genç, 2022). While the suffix feminism in the concept refers to the movement that defends women's rights and
freedom; the prefix cyber refers to the internet through the meaning of "directing, controlling, managing" (Wilding, 1998) Cyberfeminism creates an impact
on the body and technology by countering the cyberspace, which is thought to
be the domain of men and gendered in a masculine way. In doing so, it aims to
reorganize cyberspace within the feminist movement, adapt feminist practices
to the digital age, and to raise awareness by criticizing sexist discourse and
political views. The common point of cyberfeminists is that women should use
internet technologies for empowerment and take control in this field (Aydemir
and Genç, 2022).

Donna Haraway and Sadie Plant have been prominent figures in the emergence of cyberfeminism and are considered the mothers of cyberfeminism.
Donna Haraway's "A Cyborg Manifesto" and Sadie Plant's *Zeros + Ones* are
considered the founding texts of cyberfeminism. Haraway's article "A Cyborg
Manifesto", which forms part of her book *Simians, Cyborgs and Women*, has
been an important source for the philosophy and practice of cyberfeminism
(Gillis, 2004).

Haraway created a new feminism by stating that the blurring of the boundaries between man and machine would gradually disable the categories of
men and women. Imagining a world without male or female gender, Haraway
demanded feminists to abandon icons emphasizing the female gender and
adopt a genderless approach. Haraway emphasized genderlessness by saying
"I would rather be a cyborg than a goddess". Haraway's approach to sex and

gender has been called cyborg feminism (Hall, 1996). Haraway's cyborg is a "post-gender" hybrid, fictional creature. Haraway constructed the image of the cyborg as a breaking of the flesh/metal opposition, and as a result, allowed for the "transgender". Haraway (2006) stated that by the end of the twentieth century, everyone had become a cyborg, that is, the boundaries between organism and machine had blurred, and this situation was pleasing for women. However, despite this development, she stated that women continue to be exploited due to the relations of domination reconstructed through communication technologies and defined this exploitation as "informatic domination". In order to utilize the emancipatory possibilities of science and technology for cyberfeminist purposes, it is important to understand the new forms of power and oppression shaped by the informatics of domination.

Cyberfeminists believe that a masculine identity dominates the design of internet technologies and that it is possible to see this through robots. Robots are designed as male or female and feminine robots are produced in the context of gender schemas. Masculine robots, on the other hand, strengthen the masculine structure and legitimize male domination (Søraa, 2017). In this context, Haraway states that new technology, engineering and virtual technologies can change the understanding of gender identity, thus ending the masculine dominance in the technological field and transforming the relationship between women and technology (Haraway, 2006).

Sadie Plant, another important figure in cyberfeminism, addresses the relationship between technology and women in a similar way to Haraway. Saying "As machines get smarter, women get freer", Plant argues that contrary to popular belief, technology is not masculine but feminine. In her book *Zeros + Ones*, Plant metaphorizes the numbers 0 and 1 used in computer programs, describing zeros as feminine and ones as masculine. She mentioned that zeros will replace ones in the digital future and that internet technologies will transform women's lives (Daniels, 2009).

As seen in Haraway and Plant's arguments, the philosophy of cyberfeminism is generally shaped by technology, body and identity. According to cyberfeminists, digital technologies based on the brain, not brawn, and built through social networks enable a new relationship between women and machines. Thanks to this new relationship, there will be no distinction between men and women in virtual networks, class, ethnicity and other forms of identity will be transcended and an environment of equality for women will be created in the virtual public sphere (Wajcman, 2006). At the same time, the body is abandoned through technology and the internet is defined by cyberfeminists as a disembodied cyberspace. Internet users leave their bodies behind when they enter the virtual environment and are liberated by interacting through new identities (Paasonen, 2011).

Cyberfeminism, in which women aim to end masculine domination by gaining control over the internet and at the same time sustaining women's movements through the internet and social networks, can influence social policies as an important power today. In the following section, the relationship between cyberfeminism and social policy will be discussed in this context.

4.2 Reflections of Cyberfeminism on Social Policy

The first examples of cyberfeminism in action are seen in blogs called "Web Logs" in the 1990s. Through blogs, women all over the world started to interact with each other and create an online culture. Later, with the establishment of social networks such as Facebook (2004), YouTube (2005) and Twitter (2006), online culture became widespread, women took their struggles to cyberspace and a new public space was created for social movements (Henry, 2015). With the use of social networks, women can organize regardless of education level, race, ethnicity and location. Women continue to struggle with many of the problems they face, including gender, in online networks. As a result of a problem experienced by any woman, unity is created on social media and awareness is raised on that issue, women can stand against injustices and influence the powers and decisions made through online activism. Thus, the internet and social media become active tools for raising consciousness, raising awareness and influencing social policies (Kaya, 2018).

When we look at the current practice of cyberfeminism, we see that activist movements are generally realized by using hashtags on Twitter. Women who organize through hashtags can announce their problems to the whole world in a short time, become visible in the public and political sphere, and form public opinion and influence policies for the solution of the problem. In addition, civil society organizations also advocate for women's rights through their websites and create pressure on governments to demand women's empowerment. In this context, it can be said that one of the important functions of the cyberfeminist movement is to mobilize policymakers to create change in the political sphere. Brimacombe et al. (2018) argue that through social media, cyberfeminists put pressure on policymakers both through "bottom up" public mobilization efforts and "top down" international media attention.

Violence against women, abuse, mobbing in the workplace, motherhood discourses and gender issues are frequently addressed in cyberfeminism. In the United States, hashtag campaigns such as #YesAllWomen, #SafetyTipsForLadies and #StopStreetHarassment initiated by women to fight rape and rape supporters have been very effective and have raised awareness and advocacy efforts in other countries in a short time (Clark, 2016). In Fiji, street harassment became an important agenda on International Women's Day in 2012 and the Secretary General of the Fiji Taxi Association made a statement blaming women for street harassment. In response, women organized with the hashtag #TakeBackTheStreets and expressed their reactions on social networks such as Twitter and Facebook. As a result, the general secretary who made the statement had to resign (Brimacombe et al., 2018). On October 24, 2017, #MeToo, a cyberfeminist movement that has been influential all over the world, began. In response to actress Alyssa Milano's allegations of sexual harassment by Hollywood producer Harvey Weinstein, women organized and started the #MeToo movement. With 12 million tweets in the first 24 hours, it became a movement against sexual harassment and sexual assault, with women all over the world sharing their experiences of sexual harassment. Due to its huge impact, this movement has become a priority agenda of the media and governments and has been effective in prosecuting and punishing perpetrators of sexual harassment (Mendes et al., 2018).

At a point where cyberfeminism is gaining momentum, it is seen that important national and international organizations are also addressing women's issues through their social media accounts. United Nations Women (UN-Women) continues to share posts on issues such as violence against women, economy and working life, and gender equality through its @unwomen social media account.

As can be seen, cyberfeminism enabled women to organize quickly against many problems experienced by women in social environments without cleaning time and space. The result between social policy and cyberfeminism is that what is happening is made visible, information about the problem is developed and explanations are developed, and cyberfeminist movements ultimately influence policy advocates and result in gaining rights.

5   Conclusion

From the past to the present, women have always remained secondary in social life and have been excluded from the public sphere due to patriarchal social structures and restricted to the private sphere, that is, the domestic sphere. The subordination of women has led to women's search for rights over time. Women's movements that emerged with the search for rights took their ideology from feminism. At this point, feminism and social policy have always been in a relationship. While women have revealed the shortcomings of social policy with feminist movements, they have shaped social policies for women to exist in social life. In each period of feminism, gains have been made in different social policy areas and have been effective in the creation of gender-sensitive social policies.

With the first wave feminist movement, women fought for access to basic citizenship rights with the understanding of liberal feminism and made significant gains in this regard. After the first wave of the feminist movement, there was a period of stagnation and the second wave of feminism began with women's sexual health, birth control and abortion. Radical, Marxist and socialist theories were influential in this process. In the third feminist wave, micro-social policies were emphasized by focusing on women's differences and the values of difference. With the development of the internet at the end of the third-wave movement, women's movements gradually moved to the digital environment and cyberfeminism, which is expressed as the fourth feminist wave, emerged.

Cyberfeminism, shaped by the ideas of Haraway and Plant, reacts to the masculine dominance of technology and proposes the de-gendering of technology and cyberspace. However, it emphasizes the use of technology and social networks in favor of women. Cyberfeminists have brought the issues addressed by third-wave feminism into cyberspace and changed the shape of the struggle. Using social media effectively, cyberfeminism makes the problems visible by organizing on social networks such as Twitter, Facebook, Youtube and blogs. Cyberfeminism, due to its ability to reach a large number of people in a short period of time, creates pressure on states and can transform social policies. With the active use of social media by national and international organizations and non-governmental organizations, cyberfeminism has become more important in today's world. With the development of technology, the internet and social networks, it is thought that cyberfeminist movements will maintain their effectiveness in the coming years.

References

Akan, E. (2020). Sosyal medyada feminist söylem: Dijital feminizm, [Digital feminism: Feminist discourse in social media]. Unpublished Master's Thesis, Mardin Artuklu University, Institute of Social Sciences.

Altınova, H.H. & Duyan, V. (2013). Toplumsal cinsiyet algısı ölçeğinin geçerlik güvenirlik çalışması [Reliability and validity study of gender perception scale]. *Toplum ve Sosyal Hizmet*, 24(2), 9–22.

Andaç, F. (2014). İş hukuku: Sosyal politika bakımından türk çalışma hukuku uygulaması [Labor law: Turkish labor law practice in terms of social policy]. Detay Yayıncılık, Ankara.

Arat, N. (2017). *Feminizmin ABC'si*. Say Yayınları, İstanbul.

Atan, M. (2015). Radikal feminizm: "kişisel olan politiktir" söyleminde aile [Radical feminism: family in the discourse of "the personal is political"]. *The Journal of Europe – Middle East Social Science Studies* 1(2), 1–21.

Badinter, E. (1992). Biri ötekidir kadınla erkek arasındaki yeni ilişki ya da androjin devrim [One is the other, the new relationship between men and women or the androgyny revolution]. İstanbul: AFA Kadın Yayınları.

Başak, S. (2013). "Toplumsal cinsiyet". In İ Beşirli, Ed. *Soyoloji'ye Giriş*, pp. 211–243. Ankara: Grafiker Yayınları.

Bener. Ö.G. (2011). Kadınların toplumsal cinsiyet rolleri çerçevesinde aile içi yaşamı algılama biçimleri [Women's perceptions of family life within the framework of gender roles.]. *Türkiye Sosyal Araştırmalar Dergisi* 15(3),157–171.

Bensadon, N. (1994). Başlangıçtan günümüze kadın hakları [Women's rights from the beginning to today] (Ş. Tekeli, 2. Basım, Çev.). İstanbul: İletişim Yayınları.

Berktay, F. (2013). Feminist teoride yeni açılımlar.[New openings in feminist theory]. Y. Ecevit, & N. Karkıner içinde, Toplumsal cinsiyet sosyolojisi. Eskişehir: Anadolu Üniversitesi Yayını.

Bock, G. (2004). Avrupa tarihinde kadınlar. [Women in European history]. (Z Yılmazer, 1.Basım, Çev.). İstanbul: Literatür Yayıncılık.

Brimacombe, T., R. Kant, G. Finau, J. Tarai & J. Titifanue (2018). A new frontier in digital activism: An exploration of digital feminism in Fiji. *Asia Pac Policy Stud,* 5(3), 508–521.

Castells, M (2008). *Enformasyon Çağı: Ekonomi, Toplum ve Kültür* [The Information Age: Economy, Society and Culture]. (E Kılıç, Çev.). İstanbul Bilgi Üniversitesi Yayınları.

Clark, R (2016). Hope in a hashtag: The discursive activism of "#WhyIStayed". *Feminist Media Studies,* 16(5), 788–804.

Connell, R.W. (1998). *Toplumsal cinsiyet ve iktidar – toplum, kişi ve politika.*[Gender and Power – Society, Person and Politics]. İstanbul: Ayrıntı.

Council of Europe. (2004). *Gender Mainstreaming*. Strasbourg: Council of Europe Press.

Çaha, Ö. (1994). *Feminizm ve Sivil Toplum* [Feminism and Civil Society]. Birikim, İstanbul.

Çaha, Ö., Yılmaz, S.A. & Çahan, H. (2016). *Türkiye'de Cam Tavan Sendromu: Hizmet Sektöründe Kadın* (3. Basım). İstanbul: KADEM.

Dahlberg, L(2001). The internet and democratic discourse, information. *Communication & Society,* 4(4), 615–633.

Daniels, J (2009). Rethinking cyberfeminism(s): Race, gender, and embodiment. *Women's Studies Quarterly,* 37(2), 101–124.

Danış, Z. (2007). Sosyal hizmet mesleği ve disiplininde sosyal politikanın yeri ve önemi [The place and importance of social policy in social work profession and discipline]. *Toplum ve Sosyal Hizmet,* 2, 51–64.

Davutoğlu, A. (2015). Türkiye"de Refah Rejiminin Cinsiyeti: Feminist Eleştirel Bir Bakış, Yayımlanmamış Doktora Tezi, Kocaeli Üniversitesi Sosyal Bilimler Enstitüsü.

Demir, B. & Kantar, G. (2023). Sosyal hizmetin kurumsallaşmasında kadın kimliği bağlamında ideolojik semboller [Ideological symbols in the context of women's identity in the institutionalization of social work]. *Stratejik ve Sosyal Araştırmalar Dergisi*, 7(1), 201–212.

Demirağ, H. (2020). Dış politikada toplumsal cinsiyet. (Yüksek lisans tezi). Karabük Üniversitesi.

Dinçer, Ç.D. (2021). Post-kolonyal kadın yurttaşlığının liberal feminizme eleştirisi [A critique of post-colonial women's citizenship to liberal feminism]. *Uluslararası Anadolu Sosyal Bilimler Dergisi*, 5(1), 215–228.

Donovan, J. (2015). *Feminist Teori*. (Çev. A. Bora, M.A. Gevrek, & F. Sayılan), İstanbul: İletişim.

Durgun, C. & Gök, G.O. (2017). Toplumsal cinsiyet eşitsizliği bağlamında BRICS & G7 ülkelerinin karşılaştırmalı analizi [A comparative analysis of BRICS & G7 countries in the context of gender inequality.] *BUJSS*, 10(2), 20–32.

Ecevit, M. (2011). "Epistemoloji". In Y. Ecevit, & N. Karkıner, Toplumsal Cinsiyet Sosyolojisi (pp. 32–64). Eskişehir: Anadolu Üniversitesi Yayını.

Gaag, N. (2018). Feminizm, dünyanın neden hala bu kelimeye ihtiyacı var [Feminism, why the world still needs the word]. (B Aydaş, Çev.). Sel Yayıncılık, İstanbul.

Gillis, S. (2004). "Neither cyborg nor goddess:The (im)possibilities of cyberfeminism". In Gillis, S., G. Howie and R. Munford (Ed.) *Third Wave Feminism A Critical Exploration*. Basingstoke/ NewYork: Palgrave MacMillan, pp. 185–196.

Grady, C. (2018). The waves of feminism, and why people keep fighting over them, explained. https://www.vox.com/2018/3/20/16955588/feminism-waves-explained -first second-third-fourth Erişim tarihi: 20.06.2023.

Hall, K. (1996). "Cyberfeminism." In Herring, S.C. (Ed.) *Computer-Mediated Communication: Linguistic, Soial and Cross-Cultural Perspectives*. Amsterdam:John Benjamins Publishing Company, pp. 147–170.

Haraway, D. (2006). *Siborg manifestosu: Geç yirminci yüzyılda bilim, teknoloji ve sosyalist feminizm [The Cyborg Manifesto: Science, Technology and Socialist Feminism in the Late Twentieth Century]*. O Akınhay (Ed.). İstanbul: Agora Kitaplığı.

Henry, A (2015). *Feminism Unfinished: A Short, Surprising History of American Women's Movements*. New York: w.w. Norton & Campany Ltd.

Heywood, A. (2013). *Siyasi ideolojiler [Political ideologies]*. Adres yayınları, Ankara.

Holborn, M. (2018). Women's suffrage - February 1918, first women gain right to vote in parliamentary elections. Retrieved from: https://www.theguardian.com/gnmeduc ationcentre/2018/feb/05/womens-suffrage-february-1918-first-women-gain-right-to -vote-in-parliamentary-elections.

İçağasıoğlu, A & Özbesler, C. (2009). Türkiye'de aileye yönelik sosyal politika ve hizmetler [Social policies and services for the family in Turkey]. *Aile ve Toplum,* 5, 18.

İçli, G. (2017). Toplumsal cinsiyet eşitliği politikaları ve küreselleşme [Gender equality policies and globalization]. *Pamukkale Üniversitesi Sosyal Bilimler Enstitüsü Dergisi,* 133–143.

İleri, Ü. (2016). Sosyal politikalarda kadın ve cinsiyet ayrımcılığı ile ilgili başlıca uluslararası ve ulusal hukuki düzenlemeler. [Major international and national legal regulations on women and gender discrimination in social policies]. *HAK-İŞ Uluslararası Emek ve Toplum Dergisi,* 5(12), 128–153.

Karal, D & Aydemir, E. (2012). Türkiye'de kadına yönelik şiddet.[Violence against women in Turkey]. *Uluslararası Stratejik Araştırmalar Kurumu,* 55–56.

Kaya, Ş. (2018). Kadın ve sosyal medya [Women and social media]. *Gaziantep University Journal of Social Sciences,* 17(2), 563–576.

Kolay, H. (2015). Kadın hareketlerinin süreçleri, talepleri ve kazanımları [Processes, demands and achievements of women's movements]. *EMO Kadın Bülteni,* 3, 5–11.

Koray, M. (2011). Avrupa Birliği ve Türkiye'de "cinsiyet" eşitliği politikaları: Sol feminist bir eleştiri. ["Gender" equality policies in the European Union and Turkey: A left feminist critique]. *Çalışma ve Toplum,* 2, 13–5.

Küçüköz, A.D. & Genç, H.N. (2022). Siberfeminizm: Cinsiyetlendirilmiş teknolojinin ötesi. [Cyberfeminism: Beyond gendered technology.]. *Kesit Akademi Dergisi,* 8(32), 290–310.

Lewis, J. (2011), Feminist yaklaşım [Feminist approach] Ş Gökbayrak, içinde, Sosyal Politika: Kuramlar ve Uygulamalar. Siyasal Kitabevi Yayınları, Ankara.

Mendes, K., J. Ringrose, J. & J. Keller. (2018). #MeToo and the promise and pitfalls of challenging rape culture through digital feminist activism. *European Journal of Women's Studies,* 25, 236.

Michel, A. (1997). Feminizm. [Feminism]. (Ş. Tekeli, Dü.) İstanbul: İletişim Yayınları Andree.

Moroğlu, N. (2005). Uluslararası belgelerde kadın erkek eşitliği. [Equality between women and men in international documents]. İstanbul Barosu Yayını.

Oakley, A. (1972). *Sex, Gender and Society.* Harper & Row, New York.

Özaydın, M.M. (2012). "Sosyal politikanın tarihsel gelişimi" ["Historical development of social policy"]. In Oral A.G & Şişman Y. Eds., *Sosyal Politika.* Eskişehir: Anadolu Üniversitesi Yayınları.

Özbudun, E. (2010). *Türk Anayasa Hukuku.[Turkish Constitutional Law].* Yetkin Yayınları: Ankara.

Özveri, D. (2009). Feminist teorinin gelişim sürecinde uluslararası ilişkilere bakışı üzerine kısa bir değerlendirme [A brief evaluation of feminist theory's perspective on international relations in the development process]. In H. Çomak, Uluslararası İlişkilere Giriş: Teorik Bakış. 1. Basım. Kocaeli: Umuttepe Yayınları.

Paasonen, S (2011). Revisiting cyberfeminism. *Communications,* 36(3), 335–352.

Pelizzon, S.M. (2009). *Kadının konumu nasıl değişti feodalizmden kapitalizme* [*How the position of women has changed from feudalism to capitalism*]. Eds. İhsan Ercan Sadi, Cem Somel, İmge Kitapevi, Ankara.

Ridgeway, C.L. (2011). *Framed by Gender.* Oxford: Oxford University Press.

Şahin, M. (2018). Sosyal politika bağlamında düzgün iş ve Türkiye'deki performansına ilişkin bir alan araştırması 'Çorum İli İmalat Sanayi Örneği' [A field research on decent work in the context of social policy and its performance in Turkey 'The Case of Manufacturing Industry in Çorum Province']. Ankara: Türk Metal Sendikası Araǥtırma ve Eğitim Merkezi Yayınları.

Serdar, A.B. (2014). *Sosyal politika kavramı* [*The concept of social policy*]. Dora Yayınları, Bursa.

Şeren, G.Y. (2018). Toplumsal cinsiyete duyarlı bütçe politikalarının feminist kökenleri [Feminist roots of gender responsive budget policies]. *Fe Dergi,* 10(1), 94–108.

Søraa, R.A. (2017). Mechanical genders: how do humans gender robots? *Gender, Technology and Development,* 21/1–2, 99–115.

Sumbas, A (2020)., Kadın ve siyaset [Women and policy]. KA-DER Yayınları.

Taş, G. (2016). Feminizm üzerine genel bir değerlendirme: kavramsal analizi, tarihsel süreçleri ve dönüşümleri [An overview of feminism: its conceptual analysis, historical processes and transformations]. *Akademik Hassasiyetler,* 3(5), 163–175.

Tokol, A. & Alper, Y. (2011). *Sosyal politika* [*Social Policy*]. Dora Yayıncılık: Bursa.

Türkoğlu, E. (2015). Emine; Uluslararası İlişkiler Kuramında Feminizm. (Yayımlanmamış yüksek lisans tezi). Selçuk Üniversitesi, Konya.

Vural, E. & Kantar, G. (2022). Feminist ideoloji ve söylem karşısında hukuk [Law in the face of feminist ideology and discourse]. *Namık Kemal Üniversitesi Sosyal Bilimler Meslek Yüksek Okulu Dergisi,* 4(2), 34–43.

Wajcman, J (2006). Technocapitalism meets technofeminism: Women and technology in a wireless world. *Labour and Industry: a Journal of the Social and Economic Relations of Work,* 16(3), 7–20.

Wilding, F. (1998). Where is feminism in cyberfeminism? *N.paradoxa,* 2, 6–12.

Yumuş, A. (2012). Kalkınma Planları Çerçevesinde Toplumsal Cinsiyet Eşitliği Anlayışını Ekonomik, Toplumsal ve Siyasal Boyutları (Uzmanlık Tezi). T.C. Başbakanlık Kadının Statüsü Genel Müdürlüğü.

CHAPTER 9

Cyberfeminism Shapes the Future of Marketing

Fatma Pelin Erel

This chapter explores the intersection of feminism, cyberfeminism, and marketing in the context of the digital era. It emphasizes the need for companies to understand and cater to the specific needs and preferences of female consumers while avoiding gender stereotypes. By acknowledging the power imbalances between women and men in the digital realm, cyberfeminism seeks to effect meaningful change and empower women. The study highlights the role of marketing communications in reinforcing stereotypes and objectifying women but also recognizes the evolving landscape of marketing, which now focuses on building enduring relationships. Women's inherent strengths in relationship-building position them as valuable contributors in this field. Furthermore, the paper examines the effects of the internet and social media on marketing practices, emphasizing the need for companies to be aware of the positive and negative impacts and adapt their strategies accordingly. Through responsible social media engagement and challenging traditional stereotypes, companies can attract a wider customer base, enhance their reputation, and contribute to a more equitable society. The paper concludes by stressing the importance of continued exploration of strategies that challenge gender stereotypes and promote gender equality in marketing, ultimately striving for a society with equal opportunities and choices regardless of gender.

1 Introduction

Feminism, as a social and political movement, advocates for gender equality and the empowerment of women, shedding light on the discrimination they face while emphasizing the neglect or unfulfilled nature of their specific needs, asserting that substantial transformations in social, economic, and political structures are required to address them (Delmar, 1986). Cyberfeminism, born in the 1990s, is a philosophical perspective that acknowledges the presence of power imbalances between women and men in the digital realm, while also encompassing the proactive efforts of cyberfeminists to effect meaningful change in this dynamic (Hawthorne and Klein, 1999).

In the digital era, companies aiming to take part in the market should be aware of the needs and wants of society. Cyberfeminism taking over the concept of feminism, is one of the most important subjects for the companies aiming to take place in the market.

In recent decades, marketing professionals have acknowledged women as a distinct target group due to their changing roles in society and increasing economic participation. Despite the gender pay gap, women hold significant purchasing power and influence, with studies showing that approximately 80% of purchases are influenced by women (Johnson and Learned, 2004). However, effective targeting of female consumers requires understanding the differences in behaviors, attitudes, and decision-making processes between men and women. It is important to tailor marketing strategies to meet the specific needs and preferences of female consumers while avoiding gender stereotypes. Researchers studying feminist perspectives in marketing should recognize the diverse experiences of women and emphasize inclusivity and self-definition within the female consumer base.

Marketing communications have played a role in devaluing women by reinforcing stereotypes, idealizing unrealistic portrayals, objectifying them, and promoting a culture that glorifies violence against women (Grau and Zotos, 2016a; Gurrieri, 2021; Gurrieri et al., 2016; Schroeder and Borgerson, 1998).

The field of marketing has undergone a significant shift, moving from transactional interactions to a more relationship-oriented approach (Darroch, 2014). The focus now lies in developing and nurturing enduring relationships with individuals and organizations, aiming to create meaningful engagements that foster loyalty and customer satisfaction. Women's inherent strengths in building and sustaining relationships position them as valuable contributors in the evolving landscape of marketing. With the increasing usage of the internet and social media by women, companies could establish and cultivate relationships with customers, but they must be mindful of swift and significant reactions on social media when their advertisements fail. Examples of companies facing backlash and the need for adaptation are highlighted, emphasizing the importance of inclusivity, diverse representations of gender, and challenging traditional stereotypes in advertising. By actively promoting gender equality through responsible social media engagement, companies can attract a wider customer base, enhance their reputation, and contribute to a more equitable society. It is crucial for advertisers to continue exploring strategies that challenge gender stereotypes across different product categories, striving for a society where individuals have equal opportunities and choices regardless of gender.

In order for companies to be successful in the market, it is important to be aware of the positive and negative effects of the internet and social media and to create their marketing strategies accordingly. This chapter aims to help companies to draw a path while they are planning their marketing strategies. It is composed of feminism and cyberfeminism, marketing to women, feminism and marketing, cyberfeminism and marketing and conclusion sections.

The first section, feminism and cyberfeminism; provides an overview of feminism and cyberfeminism, outlining their definitions and exploring the four waves of feminism throughout history. In the second section, marketing to women; the significance of women in marketing is highlighted. It discusses how the field of marketing has shifted from transactional interactions to a more relationship-oriented approach, emphasizing the development and nurturing of strong, enduring relationships with both individuals and organizations. In the third section, feminism and marketing; the focus is on the intersection of feminism and marketing, specifically addressing the issue of stereotyping women in advertising. The section highlights various studies that shed light on the portrayal of women in marketing and the persistence of gender stereotypes. In the fourth section; the focus is on the relationship between cyberfeminism and marketing, particularly exploring the effects of the internet and social media on marketing practices. The section highlights both the positive and negative impacts of social media through various case studies.

2   Feminism and Cyberfeminism

Feminism is a social and political movement that advocates for gender equality and the empowerment of women. It asserts that women face discrimination based on their gender and argues that their unique needs are often overlooked and unfulfilled. Feminism proposes that addressing these needs requires significant transformations in social, economic, and political systems (Delmar, 1986). The development of feminism can be understood through the lens of four distinct waves. The first wave emerged in the early 1800s and gained momentum in various regions such as North America, Europe, Egypt, Iran, and India. During this initial phase, societal movements expressed dissatisfaction with the limited rights afforded to women, including issues such as employment, education, property ownership, reproductive choices, marital status, and overall social empowerment (Malinowska, 2020). This period is closely associated with the women's suffrage movement. The suffrage movement, which took place during the transition to the twentieth century, aimed to secure voting rights for women through grassroots efforts (McCammon, 2001).

It was a significant milestone in the first wave of feminism, as suffragettes organized marches, protests, and public demonstrations to raise awareness about women's disenfranchisement and demand political representation. The suffrage movement achieved notable successes, such as the granting of voting rights to women in several countries, including the United States, the United Kingdom, and various European nations. These achievements represented a crucial step toward challenging gender-based discrimination and inequality within the political sphere.

In addition to the suffrage movement, the first wave of feminism also encompassed broader social reforms, including efforts to improve women's education, access to employment, and reproductive rights. Activists and reformers during this period played pivotal roles in raising awareness, challenging societal norms, and advocating for legal and policy changes that would improve the status of women in various spheres of life. Overall, the first wave of feminism set the foundation for subsequent waves and laid the groundwork for ongoing efforts to address gender inequality. It marked a significant turning point in history, highlighting the collective struggle for women's rights and sparking a broader conversation about gender roles, societal expectations, and the need for equality.

The second wave of feminism emerged during the early 1960s and lasted until the end of the 1980s. This period saw a significant shift in focus, as feminist activists began to question and challenge the traditional gender roles assigned to women and explore aspects of women's sexuality that had long been considered taboo. One of the key objectives of the second wave was to encourage women to break away from their traditional domestic roles and actively participate in the workforce by seeking paid employment (Friedan, 1963). During this era, television emerged as the predominant medium for mass communication and entertainment. The second wave of feminism recognized the power of television as a tool for shaping public perceptions and sought to address the representation and visibility of women on television (Malinowska, 2020). Feminist activists and organizations pushed for more accurate and diverse portrayals of women's lives and experiences, challenging the prevailing stereotypes and limited roles assigned to female characters. However, despite these efforts, the employment rates for women in the television industry were still significantly unequal compared to those of men. Studies, such as the British Broadcasting Corporation's survey, revealed stark disparities in the representation of women in television-related roles. The survey indicated that there were only five women employed compared to 150 men, highlighting the significant gender gap in this field (Casey et al., 2002). These findings underscored the need for further advocacy and action to address the gender imbalance in the television industry. Feminist movements during the second wave pushed for increased opportunities and equal representation for women both in front of and behind the camera. They called for more women to be hired as writers, directors, producers, and decision-makers in television networks and production companies. By challenging the underrepresentation and misrepresentation of women on television, feminists of the second wave aimed to change societal perceptions and break down the stereotypes that limited women's roles and aspirations. Their efforts contributed to the broader cultural shift that recognized women's rights and the importance of gender equality in various domains, including media and entertainment. Overall, the second wave of feminism brought attention to the complex issues surrounding gender roles, sexuality, and representation in the media. It shed light on the inequalities and biases within the television industry, paving the way for future generations of feminists to continue the fight for equal opportunities and authentic portrayals of women's experiences in all forms of media.

By the 1980s, feminist discourse began to acknowledge a critical issue within the movement: the perception that the feminism discussed thus far primarily addressed the concerns of white, middle-class women, often overlooking the experiences and struggles of women from diverse backgrounds. Feminism, which played a significant role in unveiling and rectifying the gender biases present in academic knowledge and discussions, was compelled to acknowledge its own shortcomings in this regard (Crowley, 1999). This realization prompted a significant shift in feminist theory and activism, as it became increasingly important to recognize and address the universal problems faced by women across different social classes, races, and sexual orientations. Feminism encompasses more than just theoretical analysis or intellectual critique. It is a political endeavor aimed at improving the status and rights of women in society. It acknowledges that women worldwide, regardless of their social class, race, or sexuality, often find themselves in a disadvantaged position compared to men (Catterall et al., 2000). This recognition of intersectionality, the interconnected nature of social identities and systems of oppression, played a crucial role in broadening feminist perspectives. Intersectional feminism analyzes how various intersecting factors, such as race, gender, and sexuality, collectively impact individuals' experiences and behaviors, emphasizing the significance of these interacting variables rather than solely focusing on a single factor like gender (DeFelice and Diller, 2019). Intersectional feminism emerged as a framework that emphasizes the overlapping forms of discrimination faced by women due to the intersections of their gender with other aspects of their identity, such as race, class, ethnicity, sexual orientation, ability, and more. Intersectional feminism seeks to address the unique challenges faced by marginalized groups of women who often experience multiple layers of discrimination and disadvantage. It acknowledges that the experiences and needs of women of color, indigenous women, working-class women, disabled women, and other marginalized groups may differ significantly from those of white, middle-class women. It aims to center their voices, experiences, and struggles within the feminist movement. The shift toward intersectionality in feminism has led to a more inclusive and diverse movement that acknowledges the interlocking systems of power and oppression affecting women's lives. Activists and scholars have worked to amplify the voices of marginalized women, highlight their specific issues, and advocate for policies and social changes that address the complexities of their lived experiences. Moreover, intersectional feminism recognizes the importance of coalition-building and solidarity among different groups of women. It emphasizes the need for inclusive spaces, where women from various backgrounds can come together to support one another, learn from each other's experiences, and collectively challenge the systems that perpetuate gender inequality and intersecting forms of oppression.

In conclusion, the feminist movement underwent a significant transformation in the 1980s by acknowledging the limitations of previous discussions and focusing on the universal problems faced by women from diverse backgrounds. Intersectional feminism emerged as a response to this realization, aiming to address the interconnectedness of social identities and systems of oppression that impact women's lives. By centering the experiences and struggles of marginalized women, feminism became a more inclusive and powerful force for achieving gender equality and social justice.

The third wave of feminism emerged in the 1990s, coinciding with the rapid advancement of technology and the rise of cyberspace. This new era brought about significant changes in how feminist activists approached their work, as they embraced the opportunities presented by evolving digital technologies. Traditionally, the field of internet technologies had been dominated by men, but now women were actively engaging with these technologies to strengthen networking, promote feminist ideals, and reshape the sources of social influence (Malinowska, 2020).

In 1991, the concept of cyberfeminism was born. Media artists from VNS Matrix, an Australian-based group, were among the pioneers who introduced and explored cyberfeminism in the early 1990s. Cyberfeminism can be understood as a philosophical approach that recognizes two primary aspects: first, the existence of power imbalances between women and men within the digital realm, and second, the desire of cyberfeminists to actively transform this situation (Hawthorne and Klein, 1999). Cyberfeminism represents a modern iteration of feminist theory and practice that focuses on challenging the gendered aspects of technology and examining the complex connections between gender and digital culture. Its primary objective is to understand the impact of cybertechnologies on the lives of women. Individuals from diverse backgrounds, including women software developers, hackers, online chat enthusiasts, performance artists, cyberpunk writers, and digital artists, contribute to cyberfeminism by creating narratives that explore the joys and difficulties of digital culture for women. Through their creative work, they navigate complex roles within a digital realm that has the potential to reshape relationships between women, men, and machines (Flanagan and Booth, 2002). The emergence of new technologies such as the internet, virtual reality, and multimedia has evoked a range of intense emotions, from fears to enthusiastic responses, in today's culture. These technologies have had a profound impact on gender relations, shaping them in significant and complex ways (Plant, 1997). Cyberfeminism seeks to critically analyze and challenge the gender biases and inequalities embedded in technology, while also exploring the transformative possibilities that digital spaces offer for women's empowerment and self-expression. Cyberfeminists engage in a wide range of activities, including online activism, the creation of digital art, the development of feminist websites and blogs, and the exploration of virtual communities. They strive to break down barriers, challenge stereotypes, and create spaces where women's voices can be heard and amplified in the digital realm. By embracing technology and actively participating in the digital sphere, the third wave of feminism ushered in a new era of feminist activism that recognized the immense potential of digital platforms for social change. It demonstrated the importance of incorporating technology and digital culture into feminist theory and practice, ensuring that the feminist movement remains relevant and responsive to the challenges and opportunities of the modern age.

In the 2010s, the internet became a crucial platform for organizing and mobilizing protests against violence targeting children and women. It provided an avenue for creating awareness about social issues and offered a free space for women seeking support for their material conditions and bodily autonomy (Daniels, 2009). Social media, in particular, played a significant role in facilitating these efforts, giving rise to impactful social movements such as #MeToo, #TimesUp, #BlackLivesMatter, and #NoBanNoWall. The widespread adoption of the internet and social media platforms during this period enabled a larger number of people to engage in online activism and express their opinions. By 2023, an estimated 5.18 billion people are using the internet, with 4.8 billion people actively utilizing social media (Statista, 2023). This increased connectivity empowered individuals and collectives to voice their concerns, share experiences, and rally support for various causes. Social media platforms became powerful tools for expressing protests and shedding light on issues that needed public attention. The ease of sharing information, images, and videos allowed social movements to gain visibility and generate widespread awareness. Hashtags became symbolic rallying points, unifying diverse voices around common goals and experiences. The utilization of social media, both by individuals and collective movements, played a vital role in initiating initiatives to address issues such as women's harassment, sexism in media, and professional discrimination. It provided a space for marginalized voices to be heard and empowered, challenging traditional power structures. Women from diverse cultural backgrounds beyond the Western world were given a platform to share their stories, experiences, and perspectives, fostering a more inclusive and participatory brand of feminism.

The impact of social media activism extended beyond online spaces. It influenced public discourse, sparked debates, and brought about concrete changes in policies and cultural attitudes. Institutions and individuals were held accountable for their actions, as social media provided a means to expose and challenge instances of injustice, discrimination, and violence. Moreover, the use of social media platforms in feminist activism allowed for the formation of global networks, enabling collaboration and solidarity among women across borders. It facilitated the sharing of knowledge, strategies, and resources, ultimately strengthening the feminist movement on a global scale.

Overall, the utilization of the internet and social media platforms as tools for activism in the 2010s marked a significant shift in how feminist movements operate and engage with society. It democratized access to information, empowered marginalized voices, and fostered a more inclusive and globally connected feminist movement. The increased awareness and empowerment among women worldwide can be attributed, in part, to the transformative role played by the internet and social media in amplifying feminist voices and catalyzing social change.

3   Marketing to Women

It's only in recent decades that marketing professionals have started to recognize women as a distinct target group, despite women making up just over half of the population. This shift in perception is a response to the changing roles of women in society, including their increasing participation in the economy. The income level of women has been rising, enabling them to take on more active roles in the market (Barletta, 2003).

While the gender pay gap persists in many countries, with women earning 77% of men's earnings on average and even less in some regions such as Brazil, Russia, India, China and South Africa known as the BRICS countries women earn only 48 cents for every dollar earned by men (Lawson and Gilman, 2009), women still possess significant purchasing power and influence. They have a greater say in decision-making regarding savings and expenditures, despite having lower financial resources compared to men (Lawson and Gilman, 2009). Studies have shown that approximately 80% of purchases are influenced by women (Johnson and Learned, 2004), and targeting women in marketing efforts often leads to greater profitability (Barletta, 2003). Women's consumer spending globally amounts to around $20 trillion annually (Silverstein et al., 2009). Therefore, companies seeking greater profits should not underestimate the power and influence of female consumers.

To effectively target female consumers, marketing professionals must be aware of the differences in behaviours, abilities, attitudes, and preferences between men and women in the market. Studies have revealed that there are discernible differences in the decision-making processes of men and women when it comes to economic choices (Barber and Odean, 2001). Research has identified distinctions in decision-making processes between men and women, particularly in terms of confidence and risk-taking (Dwyer et al., 2002; Estes and Hosseini, 1988; Graham et al., 2002). These differences necessitate the development of tailored strategies that resonate with female consumers. However, it is important to note that considering only gender in marketing strategies can lead to sex stereotyping. Female consumers require deeper research in terms of consumer behavior, taking into account factors such as generational differences, racial and ethnic backgrounds, socioeconomic classes, and sexual orientations (Penaloza, 2000).

Despite their significant economic importance, women continue to express dissatisfaction across a wide range of product categories. In terms of investment, 47% of women are dissatisfied, while the dissatisfaction rates stand at 47% for cars, 46% for banking, 44% for life insurance, 41% for physicians, and 39% for car insurance (Silverstein et al., 2009). In addition to their dissatisfaction with products, women also experience a sense of being misunderstood by marketers. A staggering 91% of women express that advertisers lack an understanding of their needs. Furthermore, 84% of women feel misunderstood by investment marketers, 74% by automotive marketers, 66% by healthcare marketers, and 59% by food marketers (Darroch, 2014).

In order to gain a deeper understanding of female consumer behavior, researchers studying feminist perspectives in marketing should emphasize the risks associated with generalizing women's experiences. Women's experiences vary significantly across diverse groups, and a one-size-fits-all approach may overlook the nuances and specific needs of different segments within the female consumer base. It is crucial to recognize that the term "female" encompasses not only those assigned female at birth but also individuals who identify themselves as female, acknowledging the importance of inclusivity and self-definition.

As a conclusion, the changing roles of women in society have prompted marketing professionals to recognize women as a distinct target group. Despite the gender pay gap, women possess significant purchasing power and influence in the market. However, targeting female consumers requires an understanding of the differences in behaviors, attitudes, and decision-making processes between men and women. It is crucial to develop strategies that are tailored to the specific needs and preferences of female consumers while avoiding gender stereotypes. Additionally, researchers studying feminist perspectives in marketing should be mindful of the diverse experiences of women and highlight the importance of inclusivity and self-definition within the female consumer base.

4   Feminism and Marketing

Marketing communications have contributed to the devaluation of women by perpetuating stereotypes, idealizing them, objectifying them, and glorifying violence against them (Grau and Zotos, 2016b; Gurrieri et al., 2016; Schroeder and Borgerson, 1998).

The marketing strategies targeting women in the 1980s and 1990s were heavily influenced by stereotypes that portrayed women in domestic settings. Advertisements often depicted middle-class, size 36, white women engaged in activities such as cleaning, doing washing up, and taking care of children. These images reinforced traditional gender roles and limited the representation of women in broader societal contexts.

However, as the new millennium approached, significant changes began to take place in the role and position of women in society. One notable shift was the increase in the education level of women. According to the UN Report, women's participation in education has been on the rise globally. Access to education has empowered girls, and research indicates that they generally outperform boys in terms of academic achievements at the primary, secondary, and tertiary levels (Antoninis et al., 2022).

The changing landscape of women's education has profound implications for marketing professionals. While the initial inclination may have been to rely on stereotypical portrayals of femininity, the evolving social dynamics call for a more nuanced approach. Women are now actively pursuing higher education, with a faster growth rate in enrollment compared to men. In fact, 41% of women are currently enrolled in tertiary education, while the corresponding percentage for men stands at 36% (Antoninis et al., 2022).

These statistics highlight the need for marketing professionals to recognize the diverse interests, aspirations, and capabilities of women today. It is no longer sufficient to rely on simplistic stereotypes and assumptions. The marketing landscape should embrace the changing roles and achievements of women, reflecting their diverse experiences and aspirations.

By understanding and reflecting the reality of women's lives, marketing professionals can create campaigns and products that resonate with their target audience. Women are no longer limited to domestic roles alone; they are active participants in various fields, including business, science, arts, and sports. Recognizing and celebrating these accomplishments can empower women and contribute to a more inclusive and representative marketing approach.

Marketing professionals have often tended to associate women with recipes, cleaning, and domestic products, perpetuating stereotypes that limit women's roles. However, this narrow perspective fails to reflect the reality of women's diverse interests and activities. Despite the prevailing association of women with kitchen products or household goods, it is imperative to delve deeper into a comprehensive analysis of the consumers within each product group, avoiding the trap of stereotyping. Rather than relying on assumptions or gender-based generalizations, a more nuanced approach is necessary to understand the diverse range of individuals who engage with these products.

By adopting a deeper analysis, marketers can gain insights into the various factors that influence consumer preferences and behaviors. These factors may include personal interests, lifestyle choices, cultural backgrounds, and individual needs, among others. Recognizing the complexity of consumer behavior and avoiding the tendency to rely solely on gender-based assumptions will enable marketers to develop more inclusive and effective strategies that resonate with a wider audience.

Ultimately, a deeper analysis encourages marketers to move beyond the confines of traditional gender roles and stereotypes, fostering a more inclusive and diverse representation in marketing campaigns. It opens opportunities to connect with consumers based on their unique preferences and needs, transcending gender-based limitations and offering products and services that cater to a broader range of individuals. Notably, studies have shown that men comprise 51% of the individuals who shop for baking supplies and equipment on platforms like eBay (Darroch, 2014). This data challenges the assumption that women are the sole target audience for such products.

In today's society, women are striving to stand out, have their voices heard, and achieve equality with men. They aspire to be as formidable as men in business and assertive in social settings. These aspirations and the changing social roles that women are actively pursuing should be recognized by marketing professionals. Women are breaking free from traditional gender roles and expressing themselves in various spheres of life.

However, patriarchal marketing practices continue to portray women primarily as mothers and homemakers, perpetuating stereotypical roles that do not align with the realities of modern women (Eisend, 2010; Matthes et al., 2016). This narrow representation fails to capture the full range of women's experiences, interests, and aspirations.

Although there still exists a glass ceiling problem for female professionals, more the women take part in marketing-related jobs or as marketing executives, the more the perspective of marketing towards women will start to change. To effectively reach and engage with women as consumers, marketing professionals need to adapt to the changing roles and aspirations of women in society. Women are not solely defined by domestic responsibilities but are active participants in various domains, including business, leadership, sports, and creative pursuits. Advertisements should reflect the diverse roles and achievements of women and break free from limiting stereotypes.

By embracing the changing social landscape and considering the aspirations and realities of women, marketing professionals can create campaigns that resonate with their target audience. They need to move away from outdated and restrictive gender roles and depict women as empowered individuals who are making significant contributions in multiple aspects of life. By doing so, advertisements can inspire and empower women while challenging societal norms and expectations.

In conclusion, the marketing strategies of the 80s and 90s often relied on stereotypes that confined women to domestic roles. However, with the changing dynamics of women's education and their increased participation in various fields, marketing professionals must adapt to a more diverse and inclusive approach. By recognizing and reflecting on the achievements and aspirations of women, marketing can play a significant role in empowering and resonating with this evolving target audience. marketing professionals have often pigeonholed women into narrow roles related to recipes, cleaning, and domestic products. However, men's involvement in activities like baking challenges these assumptions. Women of today are striving for equality, seeking to be formidable in business and assertive in social settings. Patriarchal marketing practices that reinforce traditional gender roles do not align with these aspirations. To effectively engage with women, marketing professionals must recognize and represent the diverse roles and achievements of women in their campaigns, breaking free from limiting stereotypes and embracing the changing social landscape.

5   Cyberfeminism and Marketing

Over the years, the field of marketing has undergone a significant shift in focus. Previously, marketing primarily revolved around transactional interactions, where the primary goal was to facilitate exchanges of products or services. However, in recent times, there has been a notable transition towards a more relationship-oriented approach (Darroch, 2014).

The contemporary objective of marketing now revolves around the development and nurturing of strong, enduring relationships with both individuals and organizations (Kotler and Keller, 2011). This shift recognizes the value and impact of building deep connections that extend beyond mere transactions. By prioritizing the establishment of profound and long-lasting bonds, marketers aim to create meaningful engagements that go beyond immediate sales and foster loyalty and customer satisfaction.

Interestingly, women have long been known to place a high value on relationships and prioritize them in their lives (Beck, 1988; Wood, 2000). This natural inclination often leads women to excel in nurturing and maintaining relationships, going above and beyond to foster connections. They display a remarkable ability to understand and empathize with others, demonstrating a deep level of care and commitment. These inherent qualities contribute to their effectiveness in building and sustaining relationships, a trait that distinguishes them from their male counterparts.

In the evolving landscape of marketing, where relationship-building takes center stage, women's inherent strengths in this domain position them as valuable contributors in the field. Their proficiency in understanding and connecting with individuals on a deeper level can help drive successful marketing strategies that focus on developing strong, enduring relationships with customers and organizations.

In the contemporary era, with the increasing usage of the internet and social media by women, they can promptly articulate their desires, needs, and the aspects that intimidate them. Social media platforms also provide companies with the opportunity to establish and cultivate relationships with their customers. However, it is important to note that when companies' advertisements fail, the response and feedback on social media tend to be swift.

There exist many failures made by companies which caused them to lose huge amounts of money or to force them to get their advertisements back and apologize. Thanks to social media and internet, people now can express their thoughts through the social media promptly. This has both positive and negative aspects for the companies. They can get the reactions so quickly that if needed they can adapt according to the environment. Bu if they don't take the reactions into consideration very quickly, the backlashes may escalate and cause a negative situation for the companies.

Doğadan – a tea producer label in Turkey- started an ad in 2015. It was for a tea produced especially for women. The ad's main theme was "what do women want?". In the ad, the women's wants and needs which were full of cliché such as a sock that doesn't ladder, a love like in the movies, to be a size 34, a cake that does not cause to put on weight, shoes, a bag, the perfect man to read her poetry, a bag from the lover showing his love to her, chocolate, then shoes again.

The ad sparked a huge backlash after it was posted on social media. Against this ad, the women expressed their actual wants and needs. They posted them on social media. The women reacted the ad listing their actual needs and wants, which were: to live equally, not to be killed, not to be violated, not to be raped and abused, not to have their rights violated, not to be discriminated, to have equal pay for equal work and not to have men talk about what the women want and finally not to have such sort of ads be made. An ad made for a product produced for women drew negative reaction from the women. The people started showing reactions from social media and started online signature campaigns. Company officials apologised and stated that they only wanted to add a little humor to the event upon the reactions and stated that the advertisement was withdrawn. The women's backlash from social media and their online campaigns made the company step back and apologise (Tahaoğlu, 2015a).

Victoria's Secret, a renowned lingerie brand, failed to adapt quickly to a changing world. The brand's downfall can be attributed to its lack of inclusivity, as it primarily focused on catering to the desires of men rather than embracing a more diverse customer base. Ed Razek, the chief marketing officer of Victoria's Secret at the time, made comments about not including plus size and transgender models in a fashion magazine, for which he had to apologise on Twitter. But 95.9 % of online mentions were negative (Malnar, 2019). There has been a huge backlash. Finally, the chief marketing officer resigned in 2019.

There exist differences between males and females reflected in the advertisements. While most young women under 35 are preferred in advertisements, the men in the advertisements are middle-aged and above (Eisend, 2010;

Furnham and Mak, 1999; Furnham and Paltzer, 2010). Recent studies indicate a shift in this trend. For instance, research conducted in the UK reveals that there is no significant age disparity observed between the representation of male and female primary characters, as well as in male and female voiceovers. Additionally, an equal proportion of men and women are portrayed in domestic/home settings (Matthes et al., 2016). Similar findings were observed in the United States as well. The research indicates that an equal number of men and women were depicted in both home and work settings, with a balanced representation of men and women in various work roles (Matthes et al., 2016).

There is a notable association between women and certain product categories such as body products, personal care products, beauty products, household items, and cleaning products (Furnham and Paltzer, 2010). In contrast, men are often associated with product categories such as telecommunications, electronics, technology, and computers (Ganahl et al., 2003; Royo-Vela et al., 2008).

In 2009, Dell introduced the Della website, which placed emphasis on colours, and computer accessories, as well as providing tips for counting calories and finding recipes. However, this initiative was met with mixed reviews from women, who described it as sleek but unsettling. Shortly after its launch, Dell responded to the feedback by making changes to the site's name and shifting its focus (Darroch, 2014).

In the section where children's furniture in Turkey, Ankara Mamak IKEA was exhibited, there were signs directing girls to the kitchen and boys to the workshop. Nearly 800 people supported the online campaign regarding the sexist perspective, the signs were removed from the related store (Tahaoğlu, 2015b).

As societal perspectives continue to evolve and generational shifts take place in relation to gender roles, these changes are being reflected in advertising practices. Advertisers are becoming more cognizant of the need to move away from traditional gender stereotypes and embrace a more inclusive approach. According to a research study conducted in the US, men were found to be less stereotypically associated with products such as cars and electronic devices (Matthes et al., 2016). This research study's findings serve as an encouraging sign that advertisers are adapting to the changing landscape of gender roles and striving for more progressive portrayals. By depicting men in a wider range of contexts and associating them with diverse product categories, advertisements are challenging preconceived notions and promoting a more balanced and inclusive representation of gender.

Adverts primarily showcase women within domestic settings (Das, 2011; Uray and Burnaz, 2003; Valls-Fernández and Martínez-Vicente, 2007). The workplace setting predominantly features a higher representation of men

(Prieler and Centeno, 2013; Valls-Fernández and Martínez-Vicente, 2007). There is a lower likelihood of women being portrayed in various working roles in comparison to men (Matthes et al., 2016). Whereas in the research conducted in the UK, it was found that an equal proportion of men and women were depicted in domestic/home settings (Matthes et al., 2016). In contrast, in countries like Germany, traditional gender roles are still heavily prevalent in advertisements, with a strong emphasis on portraying men and women in stereotypical roles (Matthes et al., 2016). These research findings shed light on the persistence of gender stereotypes in advertising across different countries. While some progress has been made in certain regions, such as the UK, there is still a significant need for change to challenge and overcome these deeply ingrained stereotypes. Recognizing the influence of advertising in shaping societal perceptions and attitudes, it becomes crucial for advertisers and society at large to actively promote more diverse, inclusive, and non-stereotypical representations of gender in advertising.

Social media platforms are not solely associated with negative examples; there are instances where companies effectively leverage social media to their advantage. By utilizing social media platforms in a responsible and thoughtful manner, companies can achieve significant success and simultaneously contribute to fostering gender equality within society.

When companies embrace social media as a tool for positive engagement, they open up new avenues for connecting with their audience and promoting their brand. By implementing inclusive and diverse marketing strategies, these companies showcase their commitment to gender equality and challenge traditional stereotypes. They use their social media presence to amplify diverse voices, celebrate achievements, and highlight the importance of equal opportunities for all genders.

Moreover, by actively supporting gender equality through their social media platforms, these companies become advocates for change. They may engage in initiatives such as promoting gender-balanced representation in their advertisements, supporting women-led businesses, or partnering with organizations that champion gender equality causes. By doing so, they contribute to a more equitable society and inspire others to follow suit.

In addition to the societal impact, embracing social media as a platform for promoting gender equality can be a strategic move for businesses. Companies that demonstrate their commitment to inclusivity and diversity often attract a wider customer base, foster greater customer loyalty, and enhance their reputation as socially responsible organizations. This, in turn, can lead to increased brand recognition, customer engagement, and ultimately, financial success.

By leveraging social media responsibly and aligning their strategies with the principles of gender equality, companies not only add another achievement to their success list but also play a vital role in shaping a more inclusive and equitable society.

Procter and Gamble's Always/Orkid organized a campaign against gender discrimination in 2014. The campaign was named #likeagirl. With the aim of redefining the negative connotations associated with the term #LikeAGirl and highlighting the indomitable nature of girls, the brand encourages social media users to express their preference for specific girl emojis. Always conducted research in which, according to the results, 72% of girls feel that society limits them, 7 out of 10 girls feel that they don't belong in sports and at puberty 50% of girls feel paralyzed by the fear of failure (Anonymous, 2014). Always, also tried changing emojis. So-called-girly emojis such as princess, getting hair done or dancing in bunny ears were not the only emojis that represented girls. New emojis for a female doctor, a policewoman or a female football player have been added. This also may help change the digital language limiting the females. As advertising's reinforcement of gender stereotypes can have a significant impact on the perpetuation of gender roles and inequality within society (MacKay and Covell, 1997; Oppliger, 2007), any change destined to be made to change female roles would be welcome.

While progress is being made, there is still work to be done. Advertisers need to continue exploring and implementing strategies that challenge gender stereotypes across various product categories. By doing so, they can contribute to a more equitable society where individuals are not limited by rigid gender roles and where opportunities and choices are accessible to all, regardless of gender.

6   Conclusion

In conclusion, the field of marketing has witnessed a shift towards a relationship-oriented approach, emphasizing the development of enduring connections with individuals and organizations. This transition aligns with women's innate strengths in nurturing and maintaining relationships, making them valuable contributors to the evolving landscape of marketing. The advent of social media and the internet has empowered women to promptly express their desires and concerns, while also providing businesses with immediate feedback on their marketing efforts. However, companies must be cautious and responsive to online reactions, as failure to address negative feedback can escalate into significant backlashes.

Advertisements have traditionally perpetuated gender stereotypes, but there are encouraging signs of change, with advertisers increasingly challenging these norms and promoting a more balanced and inclusive representation of gender. Social media platforms offer opportunities for businesses to engage with their audience, promote gender equality, and attract a wider customer base. By leveraging social media responsibly and embracing inclusive marketing strategies, companies can not only enhance their reputation but also contribute to a more equitable society. Furthermore, these efforts can lead to increased brand recognition, customer engagement, and financial success. By actively advocating for gender equality through social media, companies become agents of change and inspire others to follow suit. However, the journey towards gender equality in advertising is ongoing, and advertisers must continue to challenge stereotypes and promote diversity across various product categories. Through these endeavors, marketers can contribute to a society where individuals are not limited by rigid gender roles and where equal opportunities and choices are accessible to all.

Culture plays a significant role in shaping gender roles portrayed in TV commercials. However, research in this area tends to predominantly concentrate on a single country, highlighting the need for broader and more comparative studies. For future studies, conducting such studies is crucial to gain a deeper understanding of the subject matter.

As a general approach, having an active presence on social media platforms and strategically selecting hashtags are essential for businesses in their marketing endeavors. The businesses should determine the hashtags when they are advertising on social media, would be useful.

Recognizing the significance of artificial intelligence studies, implementing alert systems to detect and prevent the dissemination of inaccurate or inappropriate messages can greatly enhance social media activities.

References

Anonymous. (2014). Our Epic Battle #Likeagirl. www.Always.Com/En-Us/about-Us/Our-Epic-Battle-like-a-Girl.

Antoninis, M., April, D., Barakat, B., Barry, M., Rivera, B., Bella, N., Vasquez, D.H.C., D'Addio, A.C., Dafalia, D., Davydov, D., Dharamshi, A.A., Endrizzi, F., Ginestra, C., Jain, C., Van Vuuren, U.J., Joshi, P., Kaldi, M.-R., Kiyenje, J., Laird, C., ... Zekrya, L. (2022). Global Education Monitoring Report 2022.

Barber, B.M., & Odean, T. (2001). Boys will be boys: Gender, overconfidence, and common stock investment. *The Quarterly Journal of Economics*, 116(1), 261–292. https://doi.org/10.1162/003355301556400.

Barletta, M. (2003). *Marketing to Women: How to Understand, Reach and Increase Your Share of the World's Largest Market Segment* (2nd ed.). Kaplan.

Beck, A.T. (1988). *Love is Never Enough: How Couples Can Overcome Misunderstandings, Resolve Conflicts and Solve Relationship Problems Through Cognitive Therapy.* New York: Harper & Row.

Casey, B., Casey, N., Calvert, B., French, L., & Lewis, J. (2002). *Television Studies: The Key Concepts.* Routledge. https://books.google.com.tr/books?id=_NIF12NhB2EC.

Catterall, M., Maclaran, P., & Stevens, L. (2000). *Marketing and Feminism: Current Issues and Research.*

Crowley, H. (1999). Women's studies: Between a rock and a hard place or just another cell in the beehive? *Feminist Review*, 61(1), 131–150. https://doi.org/10.1080/014177899339342.

Daniels, J. (2009). Rethinking cyberfeminism(s): Race, gender, and embodiment. *WSQ: Women's Studies Quarterly*, 37, 101–124. https://doi.org/10.1353/wsq.0.0158.

Darroch, J. (2014). *Why Marketing to Women Doesn't Work* (1st ed.). London: Palgrave MacMillan.

Das, M. (2011). Gender role portrayals in Indian television ads. *Sex Roles*, 64(3), 208–222. https://doi.org/10.1007/s11199-010-9750-1.

DeFelice, K.A., & Diller, J.W. (2019). Intersectional feminism and behavior analysis. *Behavior Analysis in Practice*, 12(4), 831–838. https://doi.org/10.1007/s40617-019-00341-w.

Delmar, R. (1986). What is feminism? In J. Mitchell & A. Oakley (Eds.), What Is Feminism? (pp. 5–28). B. Blackwell.

Dwyer, P.D., Gilkeson, J.H., & List, J.A. (2002). Gender differences in revealed risk taking: Evidence from mutual fund investors. *Economics Letters*, 76(2), 151–158. https://doi.org/https://doi.org/10.1016/S0165-1765(02)00045-9.

Eisend, M. (2010). A meta-analysis of gender roles in advertising. *Journal of the Academy of Marketing Science*, 38(4), 418–440. https://doi.org/10.1007/s11747-009-0181-x.

Estes, R., & Hosseini, J. (1988). The gender gap on Wall Street: an empirical analysis of confidence in investment decision making. *The Journal of Psychology*, 122(6), 577–590. https://doi.org/10.1080/00223980.1988.9915532.

Flanagan, M., & Booth, A. (2002). *Reload: Rethinking Women + Cyberculture.*

Friedan, B. (1963). "The feminine mystique". In *The Feminine Mystique.* Norton & Co.

Furnham, A., & Mak, T. (1999). Sex-role stereotyping in television commercials: A review and comparison of fourteen studies done on five continents over 25 years. *Sex Roles: A Journal of Research*, 41, 413–437. https://doi.org/10.1023/A:1018826900972.

Furnham, A., & Paltzer, S. (2010). The portrayal of men and women in television adver-tisements: An updated review of 30 studies published since 2000. In *Scandinavian Journal of Psychology*, 51(3), 216–236. https://doi.org/10.1111/j.1467-9450.2009 .00772.x.

Ganahl, D.J., Prinsen, T.J., & Netzley, S.B. (2003). *A Content Analysis of Prime Time Commercials: A Contextual Framework of Gender Representation 1.*

Graham, J.F., Stendardi, E.J., Myers, J.K., & Graham, M.J. (2002). Gender differences in investment strategies: an information processing perspective. *International Journal of Bank Marketing*, 20(1), 17–26. https://doi.org/10.1108/02652320210415953.

Grau, S.L., & Zotos, Y.C. (2016a). Gender stereotypes in advertising: a review of current research. *International Journal of Advertising*, 35(5), 761–770. https://doi.org/10.1080 /02650487.2016.1203556.

Grau, S.L., & Zotos, Y.C. (2016b). Gender stereotypes in advertising: a review of current research. *International Journal of Advertising*, 35(5), 761–770. https://doi.org/10.1080 /02650487.2016.1203556.

Gurrieri, L. (2021). Patriarchal marketing and the symbolic annihilation of women. *Journal of Marketing Management*, 37(3–4), 364–370. https://doi.org/10.1080/02672 57X.2020.1826179.

Gurrieri, L., Brace-Govan, J., & Cherrier, H. (2016). Controversial advertising: trans-gressing the taboo of gender-based violence. *European Journal of Marketing*, 50(7/ 8), 1448–1469. https://doi.org/10.1108/EJM-09-2014-0597.

Hawthorne, S., & Klein, R. (1999). *Cyberfeminism: Connectivity, Critique and Creativity.* Spinifex Press. https://books.google.com.tr/books?id=NT5F5DabEcoC.

Johnson, L., & Learned, A. (2004). *Don't Think Pink:What Really Makes Women Buy and How to Increase Your Share of This Crucial Market.* Amacom.

Kotler, P., & Keller, K.L. (2011). *Marketing Management* (14th ed.). Pearson.

Lawson, S., & Gilman, D. (2009). *The Power of the Purse: Gender Equality and Middle-Class Spending.*

MacKay, N.J., & Covell, K. (1997). The impact of women in advertisements on attitudes toward women. *Sex Roles*, 36(9), 573–583. https://doi.org/10.1023/A:1025613923786.

Malinowska, A. (2020). "Waves of feminism". In *The International Encyclopedia of Gender, Media, and Communication* (pp. 1–7). Wiley. https://doi.org/10.1002/978111 9429128.iegmc096.

Malnar, K. (2019, January 2). Victoria's Secret: From Glory to Crisis. www.Determ.Com /Blog/Victorias-Secret-from-Glory-to-Crisis/.

Matthes, J., Prieler, M., & Adam, K. (2016). Gender-role portrayals in television advertis-ing across the globe. *Sex Roles*, 75(7–8), 314–327. https://doi.org/10.1007/s11199-016 -0617-y.

McCammon, H.J. (2001). Stirring up suffrage sentiment: the formation of the state woman suffrage organizations, 1866–1914. *Social Forces*, 80(2), 449–480. http://sf .oxfordjournals.org/.

Oppliger, P.A. (2007). "Effects of gender stereotyping on socialization". In *Mass Media Effects Research: Advances through Meta-Analysis*. (pp. 199–214). Lawrence Erlbaum Associates Publishers.

Penaloza, L. (2000). "Have we come a long qay, baby? Negotiating a more multicultural feminism in the marketing academy in the USA". In M. Catterall, P. Maclaran, & L. Stevens (Eds.), *Marketing and Feminism* (pp. 39–56). Routledge.

Plant, S. (1997). *Zeros + Ones: Digital Women + the New Technoculture*. Doubleday. https://books.google.com.tr/books?id=AEioAAAAIAAJ.

Prieler, M., & Centeno, D. (2013). Gender representation in Philippine television advertisements. *Sex Roles*, 69(5–6), 276–288. https://doi.org/10.1007/s11199-013-0301-4.

Royo-Vela, M., Aldas-Manzano, J., Küster, I., & Vila, N. (2008). Adaptation of marketing activities to cultural and social context: Gender role portrayals and sexism in Spanish commercials. *Sex Roles*, 58(5–6), 379–390. https://doi.org/10.1007/s11 199-007-9341-y.

Schroeder, J.E., & Borgerson, J.L. (1998). Marketing images of gender: a visual analysis. *Consumption Markets & Culture*, 2(2), 161–201. https://doi.org/10.1080/10253 866.1998.9670315.

Silverstein, M., Sayre, K., & Butman, J. (2009). *Women Want More: How to Capture Your Share of the World's Largest, Fastest-Growing Market*. Harper Collins.

Statista. (2023, April). The Number of Internet and Social Media Users Worldwide. www.statista.com/Statistics/617136/Digital-Population-Worldwide/.

Tahaoğlu, Ç. (2015a). Kadınlar Cinsiyetçi Reklam Yapılmasın İstedi, Reklam Kalktı [Women demanded No Sexist Ads, Ads Removed]. M.Bianet.Org/Bianet/ Toplumsal-Cinsiyet/164152-Kadinlar-Cinsiyetci-Reklmlar-Yapilmasin-Istedi-Reklam-Kalkti.m.bianet.org/bianet/toplumsal-cinsiyet/164152-kadinlar-cinsiyetci -reklam-yapilmasin-istedi-reklam-kalkti.

Tahaoğlu, Ç. (2015b, July). "Tek Başıma Neyi Değiştirebilim ki" Demeyin [Don't Say "What Can I Change Alone?"]. Bianet.Org/Bianet/Kadin/165753-Tek-Basima -Neyi-Degistirebilim-Ki-Demeyin.

Uray, N., & Burnaz, S. (2003). An analysis of the portrayal of gender roles in Turkish television advertisements. *Sex Roles*, 48(2), 77–87.

Valls-Fernández, F., & Martínez-Vicente, J.M. (2007). Gender stereotypes in Spanish television commercials. *Sex Roles*, 56(9–10), 691–699. https://doi.org/10.1007/s11 199-007-9208-2.

Wood, J.T. (2000). Gender and Personal Relationships. In C. Hendrick & S.S. Hendrick (Eds.), *Close Relationships: A Source Book*. Sage Publications Inc.

CHAPTER 10

Sport and Exercise in the Context of Cyberfeminism

Gözde Ersöz

1 Introduction

The advancements in information and communication technologies have had a profound impact on our social life. Currently, the correlation between technology and society has garnered interest among researchers, with a specific focus on how social inequalities manifest in technology-dominated environments. Researchers are also exploring the relationship between communication technologies and the socially constructed concept of gender, which is one of the dimensions of social inequality. Given that technology has a significant impact on society, it is vital to analyse the subject through a gender lens to uncover the present state and draw inferences for the future. When analyzed from this perspective, the query that arises first is whether technology possesses a gender. This investigation aims to explore whether there is any gender-based differences in the design and use of technology. Based on the inquiry, a relevant question that could be explored in the future is whether evolving technology can reshape gender stereotypes. This could be explored after examining the current situation (Varol, 2014).

If technology encodes gender, it reinforces gender stereotypes (Adam, 2002). Feminists came to a pessimistic perspective towards technology due to the dominance of its masculine characteristics. In the early 90s, some feminists had an optimistic view, stating that technology was feminine rather than masculine. According to a group calling itself cyberfeminists, even though industrial technology retains a masculine aspect, digital technologies that prioritize brainpower over muscle and employ network structures rather than hierarchies represent a new phase in the relationship between women and machines (Wajcman, 2006).

At this stage, cyberfeminism questions gender norms using digital technology from a feminist perspective and strives to eliminate digital gender inequalities and promote women's empowerment in the digital sphere. In advocating the use of digital technologies as a tool for feminist transformation, this movement also aims to ensure women's safety and freedom in the digital world (Elnur, 2022).

Although the concept of "Cyberfeminism" is widely discussed in many areas, its application in sports environments is rarely acknowledged. Over the past two decades, social media usage in the sports industry has rapidly expanded. Nowadays, social media platforms like Facebook, Twitter, Instagram, TikTok and YouTube have become an essential component of sports culture. The sport industry has been significantly impacted by social media, providing fast and effective access to various stakeholders including athletes, coaches, managers, teams, leagues, events, governing bodies and fans. Nowadays, social media is commonly used for more than just social communication purposes in the sport industry. Professionals utilise these platforms for a variety of needs like live streaming, news updates, public relations, risk management, activism, promotions, sales, and relationship marketing (Abeza et al., 2021).

This study examines the relationship between the concept of cyberfeminism and sport and evaluates the issues that arise when feminist debates and technological developments are addressed in sports and exercise environments. In the field of sport and exercise, cyberfeminism – which critically addresses gender inequalities and prejudices in the digital world – can be examined from a different perspective, considering its multifaceted relationship.

This developing area investigates how digital platforms, online communities, and technology-driven innovations can challenge and reshape traditional views of gender in sports. By utilizing the capabilities of technology and digital spaces, cyberfeminism seeks to tackle issues such as unequal representation, limited opportunities, and cultural biases in sports. Through comprehension of the influence of cyberfeminism on sports, this section of the book will offer insights on how to encourage inclusion, empowerment, and progressive change in sports. The key concepts and themes of cyberfeminism will be explored in the context of sports.

2   The Concept of Cyberfeminism

Feminism advocates for the principle of social, economic, and political equality among genders and operates globally in the name of women's rights and interests. Cyberfeminism, originating from feminism, refers to feminist activities in cyberspace, such as the internet and electronic media. Donna Haraway's 1985 work, "A Cyborg Manifesto", is considered a foundational text of cyberfeminism. It explores the relationship between gender and technology and attempts to understand the position of gender with the introduction of technology into our lives.

Haraway's work, which explores the history of the relationship between humans and machines, can be said to have laid the foundations for cyberfeminism, cyberfeminist thought, cyberfeminist politics and cyberfeminist art (Kiraz-Demir, 2022).

British cultural theorist Sadie Plant is another important proponent of cyberfeminism. According to Plant, as machines become more intelligent, women are liberated and therefore have an alternative space in which to exist. In *Zeros + Ones: Digital Women and the New Technoculture*, Plant focuses on the changes in women's lives brought about by Internet technologies. Plant (1997) conceptualises cyberspace as a liberating place for women. Plant's (1997) cyberfeminist thinking challenges the prevailing view that cyberspace is inherently masculine, created by men and for men (Adams, 1996).

New media is often regarded as a technology with feminine characteristics due to its structure. This association is reinforced by the feminist theory of "cyberfeminism", which has emerged in recent years. The term "cyberfeminism" embodies the intersection of feminist inquiries with the world of technology as a response to the dominance of men in the technology industry and the Internet during the 1990s. The aim of cyberfeminism is to expose and combat gender inequalities and prejudices that exist in digitally driven societies. Cyberfeminism believes that women can utilise technology to amplify their voices and sustain their existence. In this regard, it has scrutinised new media technology as a tool to eliminate power imbalances and dominance in relationships (Şengül, 2023). According to Morahan-Martin (2000), online environments emancipate individuals from social and physical restrictions. Moreover, it allows women to express themselves more effectively in such settings.

Cyberfeminist research focuses on two primary areas of investigation. The first area deals with the reflection of women's offline lives in their online experiences and the persistence of offline inequalities in the digital realm (Duffy and Pruchniewska, 2017; McAdam, Crowley, and Harrison, 2020). This notion stems from the understanding that women face constraints in accessing, utilizing, refining technological skills, and perceiving digital technologies due to gendered structures (Rosser, 2005). Moreover, the fact that race and gender retain their significance in digital spaces more than in physical spaces refutes the notion that cyberspace is a gender-neutral and bodyless realm, where gender identities are effaced (Daniels, 2009). In contrast to this perspective, it is believed that cyberspace has the potential to promote equality and generate new opportunities through the use of information and communication technologies (Rosser, 2005).

It is suggested that new communication technologies have the ability to challenge and break down social prejudices, creating a new arena for social contestation. The impact of digital technology can be observed in all aspects of contemporary life. The philosophy of cyberfeminism holds that new technologies create a new space for women, enabling them to sustain their existence more easily. Currently, the majority of media products are produced digitally, and digitalisation has become pervasive across various fields such as work, education, sports, and daily life. The use of social networks has shaped social structure and culture in the digital environment (Şengül, 2023).

New media technologies always interact with offline communication environments, and digital culture is formed through the contributions of network users, which is then transferred to the offline environment through new media. Hence, digital culture has an impact on the entire society. According to Plant (1996), the uncontrolled and decentralised structure of new media technologies and social networks enables individuals from all segments of society to express themselves and be represented.

Although women have many opportunities in cyberspace, these opportunities are restricted by existing power hierarchies. Women should resist gender hierarchies and be strategic in their use of cyberspace to transform these environments in ways that empower them. Digital entrepreneurship holds great potential for the emancipation of women in economically rich countries with restrictive social and cultural practices, thereby contributing to society's development.

The attention regarding women in sports includes their participation in sports, their efforts to maintain their presence in sports workforce, their frequent appearance in the sports press and the potential for sexist news coverage, salary inequalities in female athletes, and harassment of women in sports. Furthermore, the topic of women and sports in cyber environments receives considerable attention (Ersöz, 2019). Cyber environments are well-suited for raising awareness about gender-based injustices experienced by women in sports, attracting reactions and support, and providing a platform for women to express themselves and find positive role models.

In this context, the concept of gender in sports environments will be explained before discussing concepts such as cyberfeminism in sports and exercise environments.

3   Gender in Sport Environments

Individuals are classified as male or female based on their biological, physiological, and genetic makeup (Bayhan, 2013). The term 'gender' refers to the societal roles assigned to individuals based on their sex and the cultural norms enforced by society (Ecevit, 2011). Gender biases, present in various domains, remain prevalent in sporting environments (Talimciler, 2015). The tendency for children, young people, and adults to exhibit gender-specific approaches towards sports and exercise could imply unique patterns attributed to men and women, instead of their respective interests and abilities (Koivula, 1995).

Metheny (1965) conducted a study on the suitability of sports for men and women across different branches and categorized them into three levels: inappropriate, partially appropriate and fully appropriate for women's participation. As a result, this study (Reimer and Visio, 2003) revealed gender-specific judgments in sports with great clarity. The study classified competitive sports involving physical contact, boxing, weightlifting, pole vaulting, all team sports (except volleyball) and long-distance races as "inappropriate for women's participation". Sports such as short-distance races, long jump, shot put, javelin throw, and gymnastics were classified as "partially appropriate", while figure skating, skiing, golf, tennis, bowling, volleyball, swimming, and diving (where an athlete uses sports equipment, there is a barrier between opponents, and strength is not a critical factor) were considered "fully appropriate" for women. The social norm directs women towards sports that emphasize aesthetics and physical weakness, while men are encouraged to participate in sports such as boxing, wrestling, karate, and football, where endurance, combat and struggle are characteristic. Both men and women are excluded and marginalized when they opt for sports outside traditional gender norms (Sancar, 2013). Women athletes who participate in sports perceived as male-dominated, encounter negative stereotyping from the society, often associated with being 'masculine' or 'lesbian' (Kavasoğlu and Yaşar, 2016). Research in the field of gender studies has found a connection between sports participation and gender-related behaviours, which are often perceived as masculine or feminine (Chalabaev et al., 2013; Koca, Aşçı, and Kirazcı, 2005). These studies categorised sexual roles in sport as feminine, masculine, and neutral. They revealed that these categories are significant determinants of gender preference for sports and physical activity (Koivula, 1995). When it comes to gender preference, sexual roles play an important role in sports participation. Gender affects sports participation for women and men, their professions in the sports sector and active roles in sports management. The gender phenomenon continues to prevail in sports.

Women who have experienced injustice in the sports industry voice their opinions more frequently in online environments than in the past. This section of the book summarises the ways in which women express themselves in sports-related online spaces by examining the platforms they participate in.

4   The Intersection of Cyberfeminism and Sport

Throughout history, the concept of sport has been assigned various meanings. In its early days, sport was associated with laziness, extravagance and was perceived as a pastime solely for the wealthy elite. However, with technological advancements, it has evolved into an inclusive activity that contributes to better quality of life and health by encouraging participation across class divisions. The proliferation of sports has led to the rewarding of athletic accomplishments and financial gains through sports, thereby increasing the complexity of sports environments. While considered to have positive psychological, physical, and social benefits, sport is not immune from exhibiting negative patterns of behavior and opinions, such as doping, inappropriate drug use, excessive physical strain, detachment from one's own body as an athlete, and real-life social issues like aggression among audiences. Once considered a term for superior individuals, the word 'athlete' has evolved into a designation that, in addition to recognising physical prowess, can also encompass unsavoury traits like hooliganism, violence, racism, and sexism that disregard athletes' well-being. Winning championships and breaking records at all costs may lead to moral ambiguities and value judgments (Fişek, 2003).

Although it is known that sport and physical activity have many benefits for physical, cognitive and psychosocial development, the fact that women participate in sport less than men raises the idea that sport is affected by gender stereotypes (Yaprak and Amman, 2009). Throughout history, in all societies, women and men have continued to exist within a biological approach and social patterns. Gender stereotypes, the roles assigned to men and women based on their gender, in addition to their biological differences, have created a hierarchical structure, and in this hierarchy, women are generally seen as an inadequate being among men (Koca, 2011). Therberge (1993) argues that the importance of physical strength in order to perform well in the sporting environment leads to the formation of gender roles. The meaning attached to physical strength carries very strong messages about masculinity and femininity, particularly in competitive sport where performance is paramount, and sport is traditionally seen as a masculine activity requiring masculine gender role characteristics. Trying to impose an understanding that women have not had a place in sport in the past, and may still have a place in traditional societies, by integrating masculine physical characteristics with sport, is the result of an understanding dominated by the masculine structure of society. The patriarchal mindset prevalent in society imposes gender roles on women and men, which affects their sports participation and experiences. This interaction continues to have an impact on sports experiences in virtual environments as well. Cyberfeminism has been linked to various aspects of sports environments. This section will explain how cyberfeminism relates to fields such as online activism, e-sports, online communities and support, data mining, and women's representation in new media.

5   The Role of Online Activism

Activism refers to deliberate actions taken with the aim of bringing about social change. In a broader sense, activism encompasses the efforts of individuals to change policies, practices, or situations they deem problematic by exerting pressure on institutions or organizations. The areas and issues that form the basis of activism activities can be diverse and are often regarded as problematic. Fields and issues such as economy, politics, religion, environment, race, and gender can be the subject of activism. This situation results in activism movements becoming comprehensive enough to spread to all aspects of life (Gürel and Nazlı, 2019).

The women's movement has entered a new era with the widespread use of the internet and social media. The notion that the internet provides a new avenue for activism is now generally accepted. Particularly, types of activism that encourage women to participate in online actions by sharing sexist and marginalizing discourses found in the media and political and social spheres, that call on internet users to fight against sexism and increase awareness, signify a new form of activism, solely via the internet (Şen and Halime, 2017). Social media has strengthened feminist activism, and now, anyone with a social media account can join these activist movements. Furthermore, social media websites like Facebook, Twitter, and Instagram have simplified activism by removing distance barriers, promoting communication, and creating a platform to raise awareness. Digital tools and applications offer individuals who cannot express themselves in traditional media a substitute environment to take part in group action processes and discussions. The feminist movement has embraced digital media as a significant space for activism, with the increasing usage and popularity of digital tools. Feminists are encouraged to use digital technologies to express their ideas, spread awareness, and organize people because to its accessibility, low cost, anonymity, demassification, and asynchronous qualities (Kızıl, 2021). Victoria's Secret modified the "perfect body" phrase in their new advertising campaign as a result of feminist social media activism in response to feedback on Twitter and Change.org. Numerous users voiced their opposition to the "white-skinned" and "ultra-thin" body ideal (Chittal, 2015).

Feminists are encouraged to utilize digital tools for sharing their thoughts, raising awareness, and mobilizing people due to the accessibility, low cost, anonymity, de-massification, and asynchrony of such tools (Kızıl, 2021). As a result of reactions on Twitter and Change.org as well as feminist social media activism, Victoria's Secret changed the slogan to promote the "perfect body" in their new advertising campaign. According to Chittal (2015), thousands of users protested the promotion of an "ultra-thin" and "white-skinned" body image.

The internet's characteristics, such as collective production and global sharing of information, real-time and multiple communication, enable the emergence and permanent production of global protests. The Internet enables protesters to establish common identities, practices, and produce shared meanings. To emerge and attract attention, protest movements require public visibility. Protest movements use the global space provided by the Internet to be perceived by the global political public and to establish a counter-public, an alternative public sphere (Fuchs, 2008). Zhang (2014) asserts that web-mediated collective practices have introduced novel techniques and objectives of online activism. Those in online communities strive to increase public consciousness, spread information, and prompt collective action to promptly resolve social issues.

5.1   Illustrations of Online Activism in Sports Settings

Cyberfeminism frequently employs digital spaces and online platforms to alert individuals about gender imbalances in sports environments. This can involve online campaigns, social media activism and digital storytelling to draw attention to problems which may include disproportionate remuneration in sports settings, women's marginal representation in sports media and unequal access of men and women to sports opportunities.

For years, NBA men's leagues have experienced WNBA players' vocal disapproval of the pay divide. The US women's national football team is still campaigning for equal remuneration, while the US Soccer Federation declared last year that it intends to provide identical contracts to the male and female teams. The US women's national ice hockey team asserted their right to receive equal pay and emerged victorious, prior to acquiring the gold medal at the 2018 Pyeongchang Olympics. The directors of the Italian Open have declared that starting in 2025, both male and female tennis players will receive identical salaries. Through social media, people have questioned the authorities as to why the situation hasn't changed yet.

Sharing the successes of numerous female athletes and workout enthusiasts who share their active lifestyle experiences, along with their feedback on the benefits of exercise and home workout examples for women without access to gyms, aids in encouraging the participation of women and girls in sports, and fosters their inclination towards an active lifestyle. In this perspective, involving cyberfeminism and sports, sports and exercise empower women and girls.

An online platform named #weridetogether was created to prevent abuse in the equestrian field (https://www.weridetogether.today/).

Those who advocate for sporting equality, women's sports, fair representation of women in media, equal remuneration for men and women in sports, and the requirement for additional support for women's sports use the hashtag #BreakTheBias on social media.

Here are several hashtags utilized for promoting women's sports (https: //top-hashtags.com/hashtag/womensports/):
#womenssports
#sportsgirl
#girlpower
#womenscyclingthere
#girlscanfly
#girlswhoridemotorcycles
#dirtbikegirl
#kitegirl
#cyclinggirls
#womencycling
#womencyclingcommunity
#strongwoman
#womanbasketball
#womensportsmagazine
#womensportseurope
#womenempowerment

5.2   Electronic Sports (E-Sports)

E-sports is a form of video game-based competition held between individual athletes or teams. E-sports has become increasingly popular as a sporting event, with millions of viewers tuning in both in-person and online through live streaming services such as YouTube Live and Twitch (Marelić and Vukušić, 2019). An example of this popularity is the League of Legends (LoL) World

Championship, one of the most well-known e-sports events, which attracted 100 million online viewers on YouTube Live and Twitch during its 2018 games, more than the number of viewers for the Super Bowl, which was 98 million. E-sports or competitive video games have become increasingly popular and have gained recognition as a lifestyle choice, hobby, competitive sport, and career option, making them a significant part of the sports industry (Gee, 2003).

Recent data indicates that the worldwide e-sports audience is projected to reach around 532 million by 2022, of which 261 million are existing e-sports fans (Newzoo, 2021). Presently, China has the largest number of core e-sports fans, with 92.8 million in the region. According to Newzoo's report in 2021, China holds the top spot for e-sports fan numbers globally, followed by the United States at second place and Brazil at third.

Currently, e-sports is mostly popular among young people. E-sports holds the third spot among the most watched spectator sports for young men in the United States, with over 21 million fans (Singer and Chi, 2019). Besides, a recent survey conducted by Penguin Research showed that 38.1% of e-sports spectators in China are aged between 25 and 34, out of which 27.8% fall into the age group of under 24, and there are fewer users aged 35 and over.

Gender inequalities, like many other real sports environments, are encountered in e-sports. Cyberfeminism can take an active role in promoting inclusivity, equal opportunities in sports, and the representation of women in e-sports. Concerns such as harassment, discrimination and limited participation faced by women in e-sports and digital gaming communities can be tackled using the cyberfeminist approach.

Like traditional sports, men have a predominantly larger presence in the e-sports field with fewer female competitors, followers and leaders (Li and Xiong, 2023). According to Darvin, Vooris and Mahoney (2020), hegemonic masculinity promotes hostility and discrimination against underrepresented and less powerful groups. In this regard, studies conducted by Darvin, Vooris and Mahoney (2020) and Gao, Min and Shih (2017) have examined how women operating in the field of e-sports are affected by male hegemony. Research has identified several barriers to the participation of women in the e-sports community, indicating that women face sexual harassment and unfair treatment in e-sports environments (Darvin et al., 2021; Madden et al., 2021; Ruvalcaba et al., 2018). Only a few studies have explored the positive aspects of e-sports in advancing gender inclusion (Darvin et al., 2021; Hayday and Collison, 2020). Numerous studies have been carried out on e-sports and computer game market research to profile individuals with such preferences.

According to a 2018 study conducted by the Pew Research Centre, 90% of young people aged 13 to 17 play video games on a computer, game console, mobile phone, or mobile device. Analyzing the gender-specific statistics, we observe that 97% of teenage boys and 83% of teenage girls play video games (Perrin, 2018). In 2020, the number of female video game players has increased. 41% of players in the US (Clement, 2021) and 48% in Canada (Fisher and Jenson, 2017) are women, with age group not being a limiting factor in calculations. In Canada, it is reported that nearly half (48%) of women between the ages of 30 and 49 play video games (Brown, 2017). The fact that this trend is also valid for older adults which was conducted by the American Association for Retired People (Terrell, 2019) on approximately 4000 people. In this study, it was found that approximately 49% of female gamers over the age of 50 play video games. In addition to those who play video games, studies have shown that e-sports viewers are generally male. For example, in a study examining the motivational orientations of 399 e-sports viewers, Kim and Kim (2020) found that 85% of participants were male and 15% were female . In traditionally male-dominated gaming spaces, women have gradually changed the social dynamics of many online environments as more women participate in e-sports (Williams et al., 2009). At this point, there is limited research to determine whether female e-sports fans are victims of male hegemony or empowered resisters in cyberspace (Ruvalcaba et al., 2018; Barney, 2021).

Although a significant proportion of women play video games, Sveningsson's (2012) study described video game culture as "misogynistic", characterised by male homosociality and active or symbolic exclusion of women. Sveningsson (2012) found that this definition does not always apply to Swedish women due to the region's high level of gender awareness. However, in some invisible areas, similar to the glass ceiling syndrome in professional life, there may be a negative attitude towards women in e-sports environments.

Another benefit of e-sports environments for women is that it offers employment. Women can earn a lucrative income by participating in e-sports as both athletes and employees. Through online competitions in e-sports, players can win significant cash prizes. The representation of women in e-sports is crucial in expanding their job opportunities and financial empowerment in the society (Yusoff and Basri, 2021).

Additionally, women can benefit socially by interacting with a large number of people in the e-sports community. Similar to traditional sports, participants and spectators in e-sports environments, whether as athletes or viewers, can interact with each other. This situation presents opportunities for socialization, particularly for women who are unable to engage in social environments physically. It is an established fact that cyber environments allowing women to socialize also have negative interactions (Guzzetti, Foley, and Gee, 2021).

Not all online interactions that allow individuals to communicate with each other are positive. Numerous cases of cyber-aggression have been observed in online environments. According to a recent study by the Pew Research Center (2017), online harassment often targets individuals based on their race, ethnicity, and gender.

According to certain sources, women face marginalization in e-sports environments that are male-dominated (Heron, Belford and Göker, 2014; Madden et al., 2021). Nevertheless, the internet may be regarded as a revolutionary medium that cultivates changes in social and political systems that foster democratisation. This means that cyberspace can be used as an alternative place for people from marginalised groups to do things that are difficult to do in the real world, such as maintaining a chosen identity, making online connections to feel a sense of personal fulfilment and psychological autonomy (Plotkin, 1995; Marciano, 2014).

6   Online Communities and Support

Rapid technological developments can also differentiate socialisation processes. One of the most striking examples of coming together via the internet is online communities. These communities provide opportunities for information and emotional exchange, discussion and the development of acquaintance relationships (Genç, 2021).

6.1   What Is an Online Community?

In 1996, a multidisciplinary group of scholars identified the following basic characteristics of online communities (Whittaker, Issacs, and O'Day, 1997; Preece and Maloney-Krichmar, 2003)

- Members share a common purpose, interest, need, or activity that is the primary reason for belonging to the community.
- Members engage in repeated, active participation, and there are often intense interactions, strong emotional ties, and shared activities among participants.

Access to shared resources is granted to members based on established policies.

- There is a mutually beneficial exchange of information, support, and services between members.
- Members share a common context of social customs, language, and protocols.

According to Rheingold (2000), the Internet plays a privileged role in the emergence of new types of people, solidarity, and collectivity in the political economy of post-industrial societies. He argues that electronic communities existing in virtual space foster commonality of interests, shared consciousness, and group experience. Blogs are a type of computerized communication that enable people to share their writing and videos, and create online networks. These virtual associations have the potential to bring together like-minded individuals and communities. Blogs facilitate the emergence of online communities by enabling people to interact on the Internet. Blogs are media texts that enable women to create their own representations, form a new style of coexistence, and even form online communities (Preece and Maloney-Krichmar, 2003).

The concept of community refers to a particular set of social relations that exist between individuals who share a common sense of identity. The notion of 'virtual community' is based on the elements that define the concept of community. The concept was named by Howard Rheingold (Subaşı, 2005). Virtual communities, which lack a precise definition, can be considered as a type of social space on the internet. A sufficient number of people participate in extended and meaningful discussions on common issues which are capable of generating a network of personal relationships within the online realm (Genç, 2021). Virtual communities are formed by individuals who utilize online media tools, enabling them to establish associations without restrictions imposed by time, space, and physical conditions. Virtual communities are formed through computer-mediated communication in electronic environments. In contrast, organic communities are constrained by time, physical space, and natural environments because they are formed by human organisms who make physical contact and create a social body identified as a community. In this regard, such communities are primarily based on face-to-face communication. Such communities have their unique structure, activities, social organization, language, interaction style, and culture that contribute to their specific identity. Conversely, virtual communities are characterised by 'weak' commonalities, as distinguished from organic communities. Exiting an online group is usually straightforward and often inconspicuous. Virtual communities comprise individuals who share particular hobbies and pursuits. Therefore, they are also referred to as interest-based communities (Van Dijk, 2006). In an online setting, we can converse and exchange ideas, express our concerns, provide emotional solace, participate in intellectual debates, play games, engage in business transactions, experience romantic relationships, find or lose acquaintances. Several million people worldwide are already members of online communities. This community is chosen by individuals and eliminates time and space limitations of locality (Rheingold, 1993; Genç, 2021). In summary, virtual communities or online communities are shaped by common purpose and benefit, interaction, user-derived content, clear boundaries, and shared culture (Rotman and Preece, 2010; Genç, 2021).

Online communities for women are a prominent example of such communities. Currently, there are numerous online communities for women on the internet. These communities provide women with the opportunity to collaborate on various topics such as health problems, hobbies, pregnancy, sexuality, and male-female relationships (Genç, 2021).

Online communities in sport settings can interact to create safe and supportive spaces where female athletes can connect with fans, share experiences, and empower each other. They can be used for discussing gender issues in sports, promoting positive role models, and fostering a sense of belonging and solidarity. In the context of sport, online communities and cyberfeminism can intersect to create inclusive spaces that challenge traditional gender norms and promote gender equality in sports.

6.2 The Role of Online Communities in the Context of Cyberfeminism in Sport Environments

Numerous online activities are carried out to empower women in sports settings, and several online communities can offer support and aid for girls and women in sports. Below are listed some of the online communities:

1. Women in Sports (https://womeninsport.org/)
   "Women in Sports" is a professional network that brings together leagues and clubs with a focus on promoting gender equality and empowering female athletes and women in the sports industry. The website offers interactive webinars, professional development courses, and networking events for women.

2. Cycling Network-Women's Community (https://bicyclenetwork.com.au /rides-and-events/womens-community/)
   This women's community aims to encourage, empower and inspire more women to take up cycling through various tailored initiatives. The aim of this community is to support women and people of different genders to contribute to a healthy and happy life.

3. Global Community of Women in High School Sports (https://globalc ommunityofwomeninsports.com/)
   The Global Community of Women in High School Sport exists for women and their allies to connect, develop and strengthen their experiences and professional skills to serve each other and the profession of educational sport.

4. The Women's Sports Foundation (https://www.womenssportsfoundat ion.org/)

The Women's Sports Foundation was established in 1974 to improve the lives of women and girls through sport and physical activity. Their mission is to enable all girls and women to fulfil their potential in sport and in life. They provide financial support to promising elite athletes and fund research.

5. UN Women (https://www.unwomen.org/en/news/in-focus/women-and -sport)

   UN Women is the United Nations Entity for Gender Equality, dedicated to improving and sustaining the status of women and creating an environment in which every woman and girl can enjoy her human rights and reach her full potential. This organisation also has activities for women in sport.

6. Got Her Back (https://www.igotherback.com/)

   Got Her Back is a non-profit organisation of the National Women's Soccer Conference in the United States that exists to protect and empower girls and women who play soccer. Got Her Back's mission is to increase the visibility of women in sports and to support the empowerment of female soccer players through education and mentorship.

7. Women in Sport Aotearoa (https://womeninsport.org.nz/insight-hub/)

   The Women in Sport Aotearoa community works to ensure that women and girls are valued, visible and effective in sport and recreation. It organises a range of international and national projects and events to ensure that women have equal opportunities to participate and compete in sport and to help women build careers in sport.

8. The International Working Group (IWG) on Women & Sport (https: //iwgwomenandsport.org/)

   The IWG is the largest global network advancing gender equality in sports, physical education, and physical activity. It is led by the IWG Global Executive, with its secretariat based in the United Kingdom. Since its inception in 1994, the IWG has been conducting programs globally throughout the year to promote sports, physical education, and physical activity for women.

9. WomenSport International (WSI) can be found at: https://womensportin ternational.org/

   The primary goal of WomenSport International (WSI), founded in 1994, is to prioritize and highlight sports and physical activity in women's and girls' lives. The main aim of WSI is to function as an umbrella organization that aims to bring about positive change for girls and women.

There are some crucial aspects to be considered regarding the relationship between online communities and cyberfeminism in sports:

Inclusion and Empowerment: Online sporting communities can provide spaces where individuals of any gender can interact, converse and engage in sport-related activities. Cyberfeminism advocates for the inclusion and empowerment of all, and these digital platforms can offer opportunities for diverse voices to be recognized and appreciated within the sporting community.

Breaking Gender Stereotypes: Cyberfeminism challenges traditional gender roles and stereotypes by promoting equal opportunities, representation, and recognition for all genders. In the context of sports, cyberfeminism advocates for equal opportunities, representation, and recognition for female athletes while also promoting positive portrayals of female athletes in the media.

Intersectionality: Cyberfeminism recognises that different identities, including race, ethnicity, sexuality, and disability, intersect with gender, and therefore advocates for equality for all genders and intersections of identities. Online sports communities embracing cyberfeminist principles, may create spaces that recognise and celebrate intersectionality, leading to a more inclusive and understanding environment.

Combating Online Harassment: Cyberfeminism addresses and counters online harassment and misogyny. Online sports communities may adopt proactive steps to create safe spaces for all participants and implement policies to prevent cyberbullying and discriminatory behaviour.

Recognizing Female Athletes: Cyberfeminism focuses on celebrating the achievements and skills of female athletes. Online sports communities have the potential to promote positive stories about women in sports and counteract objectification and sexist remarks.

Advocacy and Activism: Online communities can be a platform for cyberfeminist advocacy in the field of sport. Members can coordinate campaigns, increase awareness about gender inequality in sports, and back initiatives designed to promote gender equality.

Community Building: Cyberfeminism in online sports communities can foster a sense of community and solidarity among female athletes, fans and supporters. This sense of belonging can encourage and empower more women to participate in sports and take on leadership roles in sports organisations.

Disrupting Male Dominance: Cyberfeminism challenges male dominance and the male gaze that can be prevalent in sports media and news. By promoting alternative narratives and perspectives, online communities can help change the dominant gender dynamics in sports.

In summary, the intersection of online communities and cyberfeminism in sports has the potential to challenge gender norms, promote inclusivity and empower female athletes and enthusiasts. These digital spaces can be instrumental in promoting positive change and advancing gender equality in the world of sports.

7   Cyberfeminism in Sport in the Context of Data and Technology

Cyberfeminism can also examine the role of data and technology in sport. This includes analysing how gender bias can be embedded in algorithms used for athlete selection, performance evaluation or sports news. Cyberfeminist perspectives can encourage the development of more inclusive and equitable technologies in sport.

Data on the coverage of women's sports on social media, followers of female athletes on social media, followers of sports organizations on the internet, and viewership statistics are essential for sports marketing and sponsorship. Prior to the advent of new media, insufficient coverage of women's sports news and low media visibility of female athletes impeded their ability to garner support in the sports arena. Fortunately, social media data has recently contributed to a shift towards healthier media coverage.

For instance, the following female athletes were the most mentioned on social media between 23 July and 8 August: Simone Biles, Gresia Polii Gel, Neeraj Chopra, Kim Yeon Koung, and Rayssa Leal.

An additional instance involved scrutinising the number of followers in women's sports leagues during the period between 1st August 2019 and 1st August 2020 to ascertain their popularity. Based on this data, the ranking is as follows:

1. National Collegiate Athletic Association Women's Basketball
2. Women's National Basketball Association (WNBA)
3. National Women's Hockey League (NWHL)
4. Women's Tennis Association (WTA)

In addition to this data, data on the profile of audiences following female athletes and women's leagues can be easily obtained from social media. For example, data for 2020 shows that female athletes and women's leagues are mostly followed by men under the age of 24. It also states that conversations about women's sport on Twitter have increased by 64 per cent (https://business.twitter.com/en/blog/twitter-conversation-report-women-in-sports.html?utm_source=twitter&utm_medium=organic).

Insights Hub (formerly MindSphere) is a data analytics system that allows you to create actionable insights from asset and operational data. New technologies are not only making organisations more technology-driven, but also fundamentally more data-driven, enabling data-driven insights to powerfully influence key decisions, actions and processes (Venkitachalam and Schiuma, 2022).

Women in Sport Aotearoa has established an Insight Hub for women and sport issues to develop a strategic plan for women's work. This Insight Hub contains a growing body of evidence, case studies, practice and research that can be used to improve gender equality for women and girls.

Aotearoa has compiled a set of insights demonstrating how individuals and organizations in New Zealand and Oceania are contributing positively to create a supportive environment for women and girls in sports and active leisure. The collection features eight videos and audio tracks, six toolkits, twelve news pieces, nine case studies, and two research studies. The information is kept current and is available on: https://www.wispainsighthub.org/.

8   News Coverage of Women in Sports: a Comparison between Traditional and New Media

Compared to traditional media, the decentralised structure of new media technologies and social networks offers uncontrolled opportunities for representation to individuals of all segments of society. The structure of these environments has led to digital technology being viewed as a feminine technology and associated with the feminist theory of "cyberfeminism", which has emerged in recent years. The belief in cyberfeminism is that digital technology empowers women to express themselves and sustain their existence. This theory has analysed a new media technology that can put an end to dominant relationships (Şengul, 2023).

The representation of femininity and the female body in the media is widely acknowledged to significantly influence the establishment of gender ideology in sports. Numerous studies in the fields of social sciences and sports have emphasized the importance of equal representation of men and women in sports-related media. It is well-known that the visuals and discourses used in the media significantly affect the promotion of different sports, the portrayal of women in sports environments, and the empowerment of women through sports. In addition to the overt messages conveyed by the media, its omissions also affect individuals' preferences (Koca and Bulgu, 2005). Two themes emerge when examining the interaction between media and sports: The first theme reveals an insufficient coverage of women athletes in the media while the second highlights a lack of content that focuses on women's sporting achievements as well as the prevalence of sexist discourses and the overemphasis of femininity in the news.

According to UNESCO.org, the following statement has been made with respect to women's coverage in the media:

> Female athletes are often portrayed by the media as women first and athletes second. In sports news, women's physical appearance, age and family status are usually highlighted, while men are depicted as strong, independent, dominant and primarily valued for their athletic abilities.

In 2019, a study conducted by Purdue University found that female athletes accounted for only 5.4% of total broadcast time in television news, including ESPN, the world-renowned sports channel that began broadcasting in 1979 and is broadcast in 37 countries. The reason for the lack of women's sports news in the media and the inclusion of gender elements in sports news about women may be the control of the media by men, the fact that not enough women work in media organisations and those who do are not placed in top positions, work in lower positions and in jobs with less responsibility and participation in power (Arslan and Koca, 2006).

Feminist approaches accept that mass media are an important tool in the construction of different definitions of femininity and masculinity within the patriarchal value system. In *Feminism and Athlete Bodies*, written by Hall (1996), she argues that the media is the most effective and visible field in the formation of gender stereotypes in sport and that the main function of the media should be to naturalise and normalise the differences between female and male athletes.

Radical feminists argue that various forms of communication in daily life, including non-verbal communication, listening styles, and not allowing women to express themselves, as well as interactions that restrict women's comfort in public spaces, all contribute to gender inequality. As argued by radical feminists, commonly accepted notions of beauty and sexuality are forced upon women by men to create a particular form of 'femininity'. This viewpoint is supported by numerous studies on the subject, including Messner, Duncan and Cooky (2003) and Capranica and Aversa (2002). The identities of women portrayed in the media correspond to a sexuality defined by male-dominated discourses. This discourse renders women as passive and easily dominated, transforming them into mere objects of sexual pleasure. As a result, when women view their peers in media, they are presented with the notion of an ideal woman's traits being demanded of them, alongside being urged to love themselves as per my expectations (Saktanber, 1990).

It is important to acknowledge that the field of cyberfeminism has various approaches, and different fields of science and activists can take distinct angles towards the intersection of cyberfeminism and sport. These aforementioned examples represent a few of the potential ways in which cyberfeminism can influence and contribute to the domain of sports. Women who exercise for reasons such as health and subjective well-being interact differently with cyberfeminism when compared to competitive sports.

9   Cyberfeminism and Exercise

Digital Exercise Platforms: Cyberfeminists can create exercise-related digital platforms using the opportunities provided by technology and the internet. Moreover, these platforms can encourage women to exercise, while also supporting issues like body positivity and self-acceptance. Digital content, such as exercise videos, programmes, and healthy living tips, has the potential to enhance women's body confidence and provide them with support.

Examining Gender Roles on the Internet: Cyberfeminism seeks to challenge gender roles in exercise and sports. Historically, some sports or exercises have been associated with specific genders. Cyberfeminists aim to eradicate these stereotypes, enable everyone to participate in sports, and promote exercise habits that align with women's gender identity.

Empowerment through Technology: The use of digital technology by cyberfeminism can effectively combat gender inequalities in exercise settings and empower women's experiences of exercise. Technology and digital platforms are playing an increasingly important role in encouraging individuals to engage in physical activities. There are various ways in which cyberfeminism and physical activity intersect. The use of technology as a tool for empowering and liberating women is advocated by cyberfeminism. In the context of physical activity and exercise, technology provides valuable resources such as exercise tracking tools and online communities, enabling individuals to take charge of their health and well-being (Gupta and Sinha, 2022).

Social Impact: In underdeveloped countries, women's health has long been considered a taboo, and the requirement for essential diagnostics has been long overdue. The emergence of wearable technology and suitable mobile applications has facilitated women in taking control of their health by increasing their awareness.

Inclusion and Accessibility: Cyberfeminism stresses the importance of inclusivity and accessibility so that individuals of all genders can access technology and digital platforms. This emphasis on inclusivity promotes physical activity and exercise that caters to diverse interests and capabilities.

Deconstructing Gender Stereotypes: Cyberfeminism represents a challenge to traditional gender norms and stereotypes. Within the area of physical activity, social media posts are showing that women also engage in exercises traditionally considered exclusive to men, fostering women's engagement in physical activity of their choice, irrespective of the specific exercise.

Digital Fitness Communities: Cyberfeminism promotes the establishment of digital communities that motivate and support individuals engaged in physical activity pursuits. These digital platforms may provide a secure environment for participants to exchange experiences, seek guidance, and celebrate their accomplishments.

Body Positivity Advocacy: Cyberfeminism advocates for challenging societal standards of beauty and promoting body positivity. In terms of physical activity promotion, this means advocating exercise for better health and well-being instead of only focusing on appearance or weight loss.

Technologically Driven Fitness Innovations: Cyberfeminism acknowledges that technology-driven fitness innovations have the ability to cater to a wide range of needs and preferences. This includes virtual fitness classes, gamified workouts, and wearable fitness devices that encourage individuals to engage in physical activity in ways that are significant to them.

Promoting Female Leadership: Cyberfeminism promotes women's empowerment and encourages them to take on leadership roles. In the realm of physical activity, this could entail promoting female trainers and leaders who inspire others to adopt active lifestyles.

10   Conclusion

This section of the book discusses 'Cyberfeminism,' which is a movement that includes theory, discourse, and political views that aim to create a radical impact on the intersection of the body and technology. Cyberfeminism also promotes feminist practices in this field and opens up discussions on the topic of gender and technology. Previously deemed a male-dominated field, the internet, technology, and virtual environments have gradually become known as 'feminine technology'. As a result of the evolving nexus between the Internet, technology, and feminism, women have facilitated a free exchange of information, reduced hierarchical structures, and contributed to the development of virtual communities. Thus, cyberfeminism has begun to challenge the patriarchal system. Applying a cyberfeminist perspective to the Internet introduces various practices, including feminist activism, slacktivism in social media, hashtag activism, digital feminism, the consideration of gender equality in the participation of Internet inputs and outputs, and online gaming and e-sports.

According to Sollfrank (1999), it is important to analyse the power relations in technology from a cyberfeminist perspective to destroy the sexist context in this field and to liberate technology, which is essentially masculine. In this direction, it is obvious that gender equality should be addressed in a coordinated way in all areas of social structure, such as media, education and informatics.

This section discusses the cyberfeminist approach in the context of sport and physical activity. Opportunities for women's online activism in sport, current sports-related activism hashtags, women in e-sports, online communities supporting women's sport, data mining in women's sport and women's representation in new media are assessed. In addition, digital exercise platforms, the impact of exercise on online gender roles, women's empowerment through exercise and technology, social impact, inclusivity and accessibility, breaking gender stereotypes, online fitness communities, body positivity advocacy, technology-driven fitness innovations, promoting women's leadership were discussed to identify the relationship between cyberfeminism and exercise.

References

Abeza, G. and Sanderson, J. (2021). Theory and Social Media in Sport Studies. *International Journal of Sport Communication*, 15(4): 284–292.

Adam, A. (2002). The ethical dimension of cyberfeminism. In M. Flanagan and A. Booth (Eds.), *Reload: Rethinking Women + Cyberculture*. Cambridge, MA: MIT Press, pp. 158–174.

Adams, C. (1996). "This is not our fathers' pornography: Sex, lies, and computers". In Charles Ess (Ed.), *Philosophical Perspectives on Computer-Mediated Communication*. Albany: SUNY Press, pp. 147–170.

Arslan, B., & Koca, C. (2006). Kadın Sporcuların Yer Aldığı Günlük Gazete Haberlerinin Sunum Biçimine Dair Bir İnceleme. *Spor Bilimleri Dergisi*, 17(1), 1–10.

Barney, J. (2021). Understanding the motivations of esports fans: The relationship between esports spectator motivations and esports fandom engagement. (Doctoral dissertation, University of Nevada, Las Vegas).

Bayhan, V. (2013). Beden sosyolojisi ve toplumsal cinsiyet. *Doğu-Batı*, 16(63), 147–164.

Brown, A. (2017). Younger men play video games but so do a diverse group of other Americans. Fact tank. Washington, DC: Pew Research Center.

Capranica, L., & Aversa, F. (2002). Italian television sport coverage during the 2000 Sydney Olympic Games: A gender perspective. *International Review for the Sociology of Sport, 37*(3–4), 337–349.

Chalabaev, A., Sarrazin, P., Fontayne, P., Boiché, J. and Clément-Guillotin, C. (2013). The influence of sex stereotypes and gender roles on participation and performance in sport and exercise: Review and future directions, *Psychology of Sport and Exercise* 14, 136–144.

Chittal, N. (2015). How social media is changing the feminist movement, http://www .msnbc.com/msnbc/how-social-media-changing-the-feminist-movement.

Clement, J. (2021, January 29). U.S. computer and video gamers, by gender 2006–2020. Statista. Retrieved from www.statista.com/statistics/232383/gender-split-ofus-com puter-and-video-gamers/.

Daniels, J. (2009). Rethinking cyberfeminism(s): Race, gender, and embodiment. *Women's Studies Quarterly, 37*(1/2), 101–124.

Darvin, L., Holden, J., Wells, J., & Baker, T. (2021). Breaking the glass monitor: Examining the underrepresentation of women in esports environments. *Sport Management Review, 24*(3), 475–499.

Darvin, L., Vooris, R., & Mahoney, T. (2020). The playing experiences of e-sport participants: An analysis of treatment discrimination and hostility in e-sport environments. *Journal of Athlete Development and Experience, 2*(1), 3.

Duffy, B.E. & Pruchniewska, U. (2017). Gender and self-enterprise in the social media age: a digital double bind. *Information, Communication & Society, 20*(6), 843–859.

Ecevit, Y. (2011). Toplumsal cinsiyet sosyolojisine başlangıç. In Y. Ecevit and N. Karkıner (Ed.). *Toplumsal cinsiyet sosyolojisi*, pp. 2–30. Eskişehir: Anadolu Üniversitesi.

Elnur, A. (2022). Siberfeminizmden Teknofeminizme: Feminist Teknoloji Çalışmalarında Yaşanan Gelişmeler. *Avrasya Uluslararası Araştırmalar Dergisi, 10*(32), 321–339.

Ersöz, G. (2019). "Women's Empowerment with Physical Activity and Sports". In *A Comparative Perspective of Women's Economic Empowerment* (pp. 132–150). Routledge.

Fişek, K. (2003). Devlet Politikası ve Toplumsal Yapıyla İlişkileri Açısından Dünyada ve Türkiye'de Spor Yönetimi. YGS Yayınları, 1. Basım, İstanbul.

Fisher, S. & Jenson, J. (2017). Producing alternative gender orders: A critical look at girls and gaming. *Learning, Media, & Technology, 42*(1), 87–89. doi:10.1080/17439884. 2016.1132729.

Fuchs, C. (2008). *Internet and society: Social theory in the information age.* New York, NY: Routledge.

Gao, G., Min, A., & Shih, P.C. (2017, November). Gendered design bias: gender differences of in-game character choice and playing style in league of legends. In

Proceedings of the 29th Australian Conference on Computer-Human Interaction (pp. 307–317).

Gee, J.P. (2003). *What Video Games Have to Teach Us about Learning and Literacy.* New York, NY: Palgrave Macmillan.

Genç, M. (2021). Çevrimiçi Kadın Topluluklarına Feminist Metodolojiye Dayalı Çevrimiçi Etnografi Yöntemi ile Bakmak. *Liberal Düşünce Dergisi*, 26(101), 27–39.

Gupta, M., & Sinha, N. (2022). Wearable technology and women empowerment in the technology industry: an inductive-thematic analysis. *Journal of Information Technology Research*, 15(1), 1–17.

Gürel, E., & Nazlı, A. (2019). Dijital aktivizm: Change. org kampanyaları üzerine bir analiz. *Anadolu Üniversitesi Sosyal Bilimler Dergisi*, 19(4), 187–206.

Guzzetti, B.J., Foley, L.M., & Gee, E. (2021). Girls and gaming literacies: Dynamics of gender and culture" In *Genders, Cultures, and Literacies.* Routledge, 227–245.

Hall, M.A. (1996). *Feminism and Sporting Bodies: Essays on Theory and Practice.* Human Kinetics Publishers.

Haraway, D.J. 1985. "A Manifesto for Cyborgs: Science, Technology, and Socialist Feminism for the 1980s." *Socialist Review*, 15(2): 65–107.

Hayday, E.J., & Collison, H. (2020). Exploring the contested notion of social inclusion and gender inclusivity within esport spaces. *Social Inclusion*, 8(3), 197–208.

Heron, M.J., Belford, P., & Goker, A. (2014). Sexism in the circuitry: female participation in male-dominated popular computer culture. *ACM SIGCAS Computers and Society*, 44(4), 18–29.

Kavasoğlu, İ. ve Yaşar, M. (2016). Toplumsal cinsiyet normlarının dışındaki sporcular. *Spor Bilimleri Dergisi*, 27(3), 118–132.

Kim, J., & Kim, M. (2020). Spectator e-sport and well-being through live streaming services. *Technology in Society*, 63, 101401.

Kiraz-Demir, S. (2022). Siberfeminizm Çerçevesinde Yeni Medyada Kadın Gazeteciler Üzerine Bir Araştırma. *Kadin/Woman* 2000, 23(1).

Kızıl, A. (2021). Dördüncü dalga feminist yankı alanları: Dijital araç ve uygulamalar (Master's thesis, İstanbul Gelişim Üniversitesi Lisansüstü Eğitim Enstitüsü).

Koca, C. (2011). Women Representation in Managerial Positions of Sport Organisation. *Hacettepe Journal of Sport Sciences*, 22(1),1–12.

Koca, C., Aşçı, F.H., ve Kirazcı, S. (2005). Gender role orientation of athletes and non-athletes in a patriarchal society: A study in Turkey. *Sex Roles*, 52(3–4), 217–225.

Koivula, N. (1995). Ratings of gender appropriateness of sports participation: Effects of gender-based schematic processing, *Sex Roles*, 33(7/8), 543–557.

Li, M., & Xiong, H. (2023). Virtual identities and women's empowerment: the implication of the rise of female esports fans in China. *Sport in Society*, 26(3), 431–453.

Madden, D., Liu, Y., Yu, H., Sonbudak, M.F., Troiano, G.M., & Harteveld, C. (2021, May). "Why are you playing games? You are a girl!": Exploring gender biases in Esports.

In *Proceedings of the 2021 CHI conference on human factors in computing systems* (pp. 1–15).

Marciano, A. (2014). Living the VirtuReal: Negotiating transgender identity in cyberspace. *Journal of Computer-Mediated Communication,* 19(4), 824–838.

Marelić, M., & Vukušić, D. (2019). E-sports: Definition and social implications. *Exercise and Quality of Life Journal,* 11(2), 47–54.

McAdam, M., Crowley, C., & Harrison, R.T. (2020). Digital girl: Cyberfeminism and the emancipatory potential of digital entrepreneurship in emerging economies. *Small Business Economics,* 55, 349–362.

Messner, M. A., Duncan, M. C., & Cooky, C. (2003). Silence, sports bras, and wrestling porn: Women in televised sports news and highlights shows. *Journal of sport and social issues,* 27(1), 38–51.

Metheny, E. (1965). Symbolic forms of movement: The feminine image in sports. In E. Metheny (Ed.), *Connotations of movement in sport and dance* (pp. 43–56). Dubuque, IA: Brown.

Morahan-Martin, J. (2000). Women and the Internet: promise and perils. *CyberPsychology and Behavior,* 3(5), 683–691.

Newzoo. (2021). Global Games Market Report, last accessed 25/01/2023. https://newzoo.com/products/reports/global-games-market-report/.

Perrin, A. (2018, September 17). 5 facts about Americans and video games. FactTank: News in the Numbers. Retrieved from www.google.com/search?client=firefox-b-1-e&q=5+Facts+about+Americans+and+Video+Games%2C%E2%80%9D+a+2018+study+by+the+Pew+Research+.

Pew Research Center. (2017). Online harassment 2017. Retrieved from http://www.pewinternet.org/.

Plant, S. (1996). "On the Matrix: Cyberfeminist Simulations". In D. Bell and B. Kennedy (Eds.), *The Cyberculture Reader* (2000), Routledge. pp. 325–336.

Plant, S. (1997). *Zeros + Ones: Digital Women and the New Technoculture* (Vol. 4). London.

Plotkin, W. (1995). The virtual community: Homesteading on the electronic frontier. *Journal of the American Planning Association,* 61(2), 284.

Preece, J., & Maloney-Krichmar, D. (2003). "Online communities: Focusing on sociability and usability". In A. Sears and J.A. Jacko (Eds.), *The Human-Computer Interaction Handbook,* pp. 596–620.

Rheingold, H. (1993). "A slice of life in my virtual community". In L.M. Harasim (Ed.), *Global Networks: Computers and International Communication,* 57–80.

Rheingold, H. (2000). *The Virtual Community: Homesteading on the Electronic Frontier* (revised edition). Cambridge, MA: MIT Press.

Riemer, B.A. & Visio, M.E. (2003). Gender typing of sports: An investigation of Metheny's classification. *Research Quarterly for Exercise and Sport,* 74(2), 193–204.

Rosser, S.V. (2005). Through the lenses of feminist theory: Focus on women and information technology. *Frontiers: A Journal of Women Studies*, 26(1), 1–23.

Rotman, D., & Preece, J. (2010). The 'WeTube' in YouTube–creating an online community through video sharing. *International Journal of Web Based Communities*, 6(3), 317–333.

Ruvalcaba, O., Shulze, J., Kim, A., Berzenski, S.R., & Otten, M.P. (2018). Women's experiences in eSports: Gendered differences in peer and spectator feedback during competitive video game play. *Journal of Sport and Social Issues*, 42(4), 295–311.

Saktanber, A. N. (1990). Türkiye'de Medyada Kadın: Serbest Müsait Kadın veya İyi Eş, Fedakar Anne. In *1980ler Türkiye'sinde Kadın Bakış Açısından Kadınlar*. İletişim Yayınevi.

Sancar, S. (2013). In Erkeklik. Ecevit, Y. and Karkıner, N. (Eds.). *Toplumsal cinsiyet çalışmaları* (pp. 168–191). Eskişehir: Anadolu Üniversitesi.

Şen, A.F., & Halime, K.Ö.K. (2017). Sosyal Medya Ve Feminist Aktivizm: Türkiye'deki Feminist Grupların Aktivizm Biçimleri. *Atatürk İletişim Dergisi*, (13), 73–86.

Şengul, N.A. (2023). Dijital Kültür Ve Siberfeminizme Dijital Bölünme Üzerinden Bir Eleştiri. *Ege Üniversitesi İletişim Fakültesi Medya ve İletişim Araştırmaları Hakemli E-Dergisi*, (12), 25–42.

Singer, Dan, & Jaysoon, Chi. (2019). The keys to eSports marketing: Don't get "ganked". McKinsey & Co, August: available at https://www.mckinsey.com/industries/media-and-entertainment/our-insights/the-keys-to-eSports-marketing-dont-get-ganked?cid=other-eml-alt-mip-mck&hlkid=1a255bc022a64d2982685554c341d08d&hctky=1911284&hdpid=7937709e-7318-42c9-bfe0-3bafe89676a6.

Sollfrank, C. (ed.) (1999). "Women hackers". In *Next Cyberfeminist International* (pp.41–45). Hein & Co.

Subaşı, N. (2005). Internet ve sanal cemaat tartışmaları. Internet, Toplum, Kültür. (Der: M. Binark–B. Kılıçbay). Ankara: Epos Yayınları.

Sveningsson, M. (2012). 'Pity there's so few girls!'Attitudes to female participation in a Swedish gaming context. In *Computer Games and New Media Cultures: A Handbook of Digital Games Studies* (pp. 425–441). Dordrecht: Springer Netherlands.

Talimciler, A. (2015). Sociology of Sports, Sport of Sociology (2. Baski). İstanbul: Bağlam.

Terrel (2019, December 16). Video games score big with older adults. Personal Technology. Retrieved from www.aarp.org/home-family/personal-technology/info-2019/reportvideo-games.html.

Terrell. (2019, December 16). Video games score big with older adults. Personal Technology. Retrieved from www.aarp.org/home-family/personal-technology/info-2019/reportvideo-games.html.

Theberge, N. (1993). The Construction of Gender in Sport: Women, Coaching, and the Naturalization of Difference. *Social Problems* 40(3): 301–313.

van Dijk, Jan (2006). *The Network Society. Social Aspects of New Media*. Thousand Oaks, CA: SAGE.

Varol, S.F. (2014). A Utopic Approach to the Relationship of Women with Technology: Cyberfeminism, *The Journal of Academic Social Science Studies*, 27, 219–234.

Venkitachalam, K., & Schiuma, G. (2022). Strategic knowledge management (SKM) in the digital age–insights and possible research directions. *Journal of Strategy and Management*, 15(2), 169–174.

Wajcman, J. (2006). "TechnoCapitalism Meets TechnoFeminism: Women and Technology in a Wireless World". *Labour and Industry: a Journal of the Social and Economic Relations of Work*, 16(3), 7–20.

Whittaker, S., Isaacs, E., & O'Day, V. (1997). Widening the net: Workshop report on the theory and practice of physical and network communities. *ACM SIGCHI Bulletin*, 29(3), 27–30.

Williams, D., Consalvo, M., Caplan, S., & Yee, N. (2009). Looking for gender: Gender roles and behaviors among online gamers. *Journal of Communication*, 59(4), 700–725.

Yaprak, P., & Amman, M.T. (2009). Sporda kadınlar ve sorunları. *Turkiye Kick Boks Federasyonu Spor Bilimleri Dergisi*, 2(1), 39–49.

Yusoff, N.H., & Basri, S. (2021). The role of socialization towards participation of Malaysia female players in E-sport. *International Journal of Social Science Research*, 3(1), 132–145.

Zhang, N. (2014). Web-based backpacking communities and online activism in China: Movement without marching, *China Information*, 28(2), 276–296.

CHAPTER 11

Cyberfeminist Strategies and Artificial Life

Kürşad Özkaynar

Cyberfeminist strategies originated in the early 1990s, mainly when the Internet emerged and developed. Studies on this subject refer to approaches, methods, and actions used to challenge gender inequalities, power imbalances, and other influential authorities in technology and digital culture and reduce the impact of these elements. As a feminist movement, Cyberfeminism aims to critically examine the commonalities and intersections of gender, technology, and power dynamics. It aims to empower women by actively engaging with technology, advocating for inclusivity, and redefining dominant narratives surrounding gender and technology. While cyberfeminist strategies vary, some of the critical approaches and tactics often associated with the movement include: subverting online gender norms, technological empowerment in every sense, online activism, transcending technologically dominant power structures, promoting inclusive perspectives by taking into account the experiences of all individuals, critiquing surveillance culture, and developing methodologies for countermeasures.

Contemporary artificial life became recognized when Christopher Langton introduced the "artificial life" concept in the 1980s. Artificial life is divided into three parts in terms of content and technique. Today, the most important form of artificial life is artificial intelligence.

The chapter aims to shed light on the potential of Cyberfeminism to shape and transform the development, deployment, and societal impacts of artificial life systems. It also proposes a framework for incorporating cyberfeminist strategies into AI technologies' design, implementation, and ethical considerations. Finally, the study aims to contribute to the production of cyberfeminist strategies by presenting the threats and opportunities for Cyberfeminism with the development of artificial intelligence technologies.

1 Introduction

With the development of technology, many branches of science and disciplines have approached each other, joint studies have been discussed, and fields seen as different have started to act together. One of the best examples of this process is the concept of artificial life. While the concept and studies of artificial life were previously in biology and mechanical engineering, it has started joint studies with computer and software engineering. The theories that have moved to the digital space have produced new forms for themselves with the development of the Internet. One of these forms is Cyberfeminism. This new form criticizes patriarchal prejudices and gender inequalities often reinforced in technology. It aims to challenge and subvert these biases by advocating inclusivity, diversity, and equal representation in technology design, development, and use. It promotes redesigning technology as a tool of empowerment and liberation rather than control or oppression. It explores the potential of technology to reshape social relations, challenges traditional gender roles, and provides platforms for marginalized voices to be heard, recognizing the importance of intersections that express the interconnected nature of social identities such as gender, race, class, and sexuality. In this sense, it recognizes that different groups of women experience technology and its effects differently and advocates for an inclusive approach that addresses the needs and concerns of all marginalized communities. Cyberfeminism often manifests through digital art, online communities, and activist practices (Linder et al., 2016). It embraces technology's creative and subversive use to express feminist perspectives, challenge normative ideologies, and raise awareness about gender-based issues. The Internet and digital spaces are crucial for feminist discourse and activism. Cyberfeminism acknowledges the potential of online platforms for organizing (Mitchelstein et al., 2020), networking and sharing information, enabling global collaborations, and amplifying marginalized voices. However, it emphasizes the importance of privacy, data protection, and digital security, especially in light of the disproportionate surveillance and harassment that women and marginalized communities face online.

2   Understanding Cyberfeminism

The book's previous chapters discuss the background, history, and conceptual framework of Cyberfeminism. In order to avoid repetition, these areas will not be discussed in this chapter. Cyberfeminism has been the subject of academic studies emphasizing its importance in challenging patriarchal structures and empowering women through new media and technology (Wahyudi and Kurniasih, 2022; Alatas and Sutanto, 2019). However, it is helpful to distinguish between Cyberfeminism (for consistency) and cyber-feminist individuals and actions. While Abidin and Thompson (2012) addressed the concept of cyber-feminist as a phenomenon that contributes to women's performance and spheres of influence in computer-mediated communication, they defined Cyberfeminism as feminist political activism and networking over the Internet. Loney-Howes et al. (2021) needed to draw sharp boundaries between the two concepts and make a feminism-based definition. Accordingly, Cyberfeminism is a project that aims to build feminism without borders. Tamirisa (2021) also needed to conceptualize Cyberfeminism as a movement that aims to empower women and challenge technological male dominance. The most important claim about the importance of Cyberfeminism belongs to Stevenson (2002). Her book Understanding Media Cultures defines Cyberfeminism as the information age's most important academic and political movement. In her view, Cyberfeminism has brought about significant structural transformations regarding concerns about gender distinctions and masculine ways of thinking.

3   Artificial Life: Concepts and Applications

Artificial life is a field of study in which the functions of natural life and vitality are imitated in artificial systems, and their effects are aimed to be determined by various simulations. These studies combine various disciplines such as computer and genetic science, software engineering, mathematics, biology, physics, social sciences, philosophy, and art while dealing with studies on understanding the basic features of living and natural life. While the life that structures all living things is combined with technology and art, the functioning of artificial organisms varies depending on space and life fiction. Vitality, forms in nature, vital activities, and complex dynamic systems that develop through evolutionary processes are developed in the virtual-real relationship within the scope of artificial life art (Güney and Yavuz, 2022).

The basis of scientific studies on artificial life lies in trying to understand the mechanisms inspired by nature by simulating them (Dev et al., 2017). Some examples of these studies can be given. Narayan, Tuci, and Labrosse (2014) developed control units for autonomous driving on the road and used artificial neural networks.

Langton defined artificial life as life in any possible environment and organized a conference to draw the framework of the concept (Langton, 1989).

Artificial life is handled in three different categories. The main issue here is the methods used. "Soft" artificial life creates computer simulations or fully digital structures that exhibit life-like behaviour. "Hard" artificial life produces hardware implementations of life-like systems. "Wet" artificial life involves the creation of life-like systems in the laboratory using biochemical methods (Bedau, 2007).

The following applications can be given as examples of wet artificial life.

Symbiotic Robots are a field where biological organisms and robots are brought together. The biological organism and the robot work in a symbiotic relationship that complements each other. For example, a robot can use the waste of an organism to provide energy, or the organism can work together with sensors placed on it to increase the robot's mobility. Such technology is characterized as wet artificial life.

Bioconductivity applications involve the use of biological materials that have electrical conduction capabilities. For example, biological molecules such as DNA or proteins can transmit electrical signals, and bioelectronic devices can be developed using these properties.

In Synthetic Cell studies, researchers working in the field of synthetic biology focus on the design and construction of artificial cells. These cells can have similar functions to natural cells or gain new functions. There are many potential applications with artificial cells, such as controlling biological systems or optimizing the production of drugs used to treat diseases.

Biomaterials are also considered in this category. In wet artificial life applications, using artificial materials made from biological materials is also common. For example, durable and flexible materials made of biopolymers are used in tissue engineering or bioimplants.

Wet artificial life is also relevant for developing and using biological sensors. These sensors can detect the presence of biological molecules or monitor a specific biochemical process. Biological sensors can be used in medicine, environmental monitoring, or food safety.

Biosensors are devices used to detect or measure biological targets (e.g., proteins, DNA, viruses). In the field of wet artificial life, the development of biosensors is of great importance. For example, there are applications such as glucose sensors used to monitor blood sugar levels or biological sensors used to detect environmental pollutants.

Biological robots are artificial systems obtained by controlling or manipulating living organisms. These robots can be at various scales, from microorganisms to cells or larger organisms. For example, applications such as microrobots control the movement of bacteria to perform specific tasks or systems used in tissue engineering by controlling the growth of biological tissues.

Wet artificial life can also be used for the production of biofuels. It is possible to synthesize biofuels using biological organisms' metabolic pathways and enzymes. For example, studies are being conducted to diversify energy sources such as biogas or biodiesel production using microorganisms.

Wet artificial life also can use biological systems for data storage and processing. Molecular systems such as DNA can compactly store large amounts of information. Therefore, DNA-based data storage technologies are being investigated as an alternative for long-term storage of large amounts of data.

The following applications can be given as examples of hard artificial life.

For example, artificial cells are designed as synthetic structures with functions similar to biological cells. These cells can mimic the metabolic properties of biological cells and perform certain functions. For example, scientists are working to create artificial energy production systems that can store and utilize solar energy by improving the ability of artificial cells to photosynthesize. Artificial cells are also used in drug delivery, biosensors, and biochemical production.

A second example is artificial organisms. These organisms are also called synthetic organisms. They are designed to mimic biological systems and are artificial systems that can reproduce themselves, produce energy, and react to the environment. Artificial organisms are a product of work in the field of synthetic biology. For example, scientists aim to achieve goals such as understanding the working principles of biological systems, increasing biotechnological production, or finding solutions to environmental problems through artificial living things.

Another example of hard artificial life is artificial DNA studies. This is an area where significant progress has been made in synthetic biology and genetic engineering. Scientists can create synthetic variants of genetic material that differ from natural DNA. Artificial DNA molecules are obtained by designing, synthesizing, and editing genetic sequences. These synthetic DNAs can mimic the genetic structure of biological organisms or allow the development of new functions. Application areas of artificial DNA include biomedical research, biochemical synthesis, biofuel production, and plant genetics.

These studies have caused a lot of noise and controversy, especially around the concept of transhumanism. The two founding leaders of the movement, Max More and Nick Bostrom, published the Transhumanist Manifesto in 2012. This is a revised version of the first text adopted at the World Humanist Association general assembly on 4 March 2002. However, the origins of studies on transhumanism date back to much earlier times. According to this text (Bostrom, The Transhumanist FAQ, 2003), transhumanism, as a way of thinking about the future, is based on the assumption that the current state of the human species is not the end of development but a very early stage. This is formally defined as follows:

(1)   An intellectual and cultural movement that, through applied reason, advocates the possibility and desirability of fundamentally improving the human condition, in particular by developing and making widely

available technologies to eliminate aging and significantly increase human mental, physical, and psychological capacities.

(2) It studies the implications, promises, and potential dangers of technologies that will enable us to transcend fundamental human limitations. It examines the ethical issues involved in developing and using such technologies.

Transhumanism is an extension of humanism, which partly derives from. Humanists believe that people matter and that individuals matter. We may not be perfect, but we can improve things by promoting rational thought, freedom, tolerance, democracy, and sensitivity to our fellow human beings. Transhumanists agree with this, but we emphasize our potential. Just as we use rational means to improve the human condition and the external world, we can also use such means to improve ourselves, the human organism. In doing so, we are open to more than traditional humanist methods such as education and cultural development. We can also use technological tools to go beyond what we consider "human."

Ferry (2023) criticizes transhumanism and related technologies and raises the question of how the uberisation of the techno-medical world will turn our lives upside down. He devotes a part of his work to the antinomy between conservatives and progressives. He includes the criticisms of authors such as Michael Sandel and Francis Fukuyama. These radical criticisms are based on respect for natural and traditional limitations, whether religious or secular.

Artificial neural networks are artificial intelligence algorithms that mimic the functioning of biological nervous systems. These algorithms are created using computer programs and artificial neural network architecture. Artificial neural networks are used to solve complex problems with their learning and decision-making capabilities. For example, an artificial neural network method called deep learning has significantly succeeded in many areas, such as image recognition, audio processing, natural language processing, and game strategies. Artificial neural networks are also used in robotic systems, automated driving technologies, and medical diagnosis and treatment.

Artificial life simulations are simulations that mimic biological systems using computer-based models. These simulations analyze the behavior, interactions, and evolution of biological systems. Artificial life simulations are an essential research tool in areas such as understanding biological evolution, studying the dynamics of complex systems, modeling ecosystems, and developing artificial evolution algorithms. In addition, these simulations are also used in medical research in areas such as disease modeling, drug discovery, and epidemiological studies.

The following applications can be examples of soft or flexible artificial life. These are nowadays generally categorized under artificial intelligence.

For example, flexible artificial life systems have the potential to revolutionize robotics and automation by creating adaptive and versatile robotic agents. These agents can learn and adjust their behavior according to changing conditions, enabling them to perform tasks in dynamic and unpredictable environments. Robots built in this way can navigate complex spaces, adapt to changing terrain and interact with objects of various shapes and sizes, all while optimizing their movements to achieve desired goals. Soft robots are robotic systems made of flexible and elastic materials. These robots aim to mimic the movement capabilities of biological organisms. Soft robots can move like a caterpillar, enter narrow spaces, and overcome complex obstacles. Soft robots are used in medical surgery, reconnaissance missions, and unmanned research, providing agile and flexible mobility.

Artificial life systems are used for environmental monitoring and management, especially in complex ecosystems or natural habitats. Collecting real-time data on environmental conditions such as temperature, humidity, pollution levels, and wildlife behavior is possible using flexible sensors and intelligent agents. These systems have the potential to analyze data, identify patterns and make informed decisions to optimize conservation efforts, resource allocation, and ecosystem protection.

Flexible artificial life applications are at the forefront of improving healthcare and personalized medicine. Artificial life systems help in disease diagnosis, treatment planning, and drug development by leveraging advanced algorithms and adaptive models. These systems can analyze patient data, genetic information, and medical records to provide personalized recommendations, optimize treatment regimens and predict disease outcomes. Furthermore, flexible artificial life applications help create bio-inspired prostheses and assistive devices and can improve the quality of life of individuals with disabilities.

In the context of smart cities and urban planning, flexible artificial life systems optimize resource allocation, energy management, and transport networks. These systems analyze real-time data from sensors and IoT devices to identify patterns, predict demand, and allocate resources to meet the population's needs. By adapting to changing conditions, AI applications can optimize energy consumption, reduce traffic congestion, and improve the overall efficiency and sustainability of urban environments.

AI systems are used in financial modeling and trading to analyze market trends, simulate scenarios and optimize investment strategies. Combining machine learning algorithms and evolutionary techniques allows these systems to adapt to changing market conditions, learn from historical data, and make informed decisions about buying, selling, or holding financial assets. At the same time, these applications help in risk assessment, portfolio optimization, and developing trading algorithms that can respond quickly to market fluctuations.

Flexible artificial life applications have significant potential in the gaming and entertainment industry. Game developers can create intelligent and adaptive game characters or virtual agents to provide a more immersive and realistic gaming experience. These virtual beings can learn from player interactions, adjust their behavior to individual preferences and provide personalized challenges. Furthermore, artificial life systems can create dynamic and evolving virtual worlds where the environment and its inhabitants respond to player actions in real time, creating a more engaging and interactive gaming experience.

Flexible artificial life systems can optimize supply chain management by adapting to changing demand patterns, market conditions, and logistical challenges. These systems can make informed decisions on inventory replenishment, order fulfilment, and route optimization by analyzing real-time data on inventory levels, customer demand, and transportation networks. By dynamically adjusting supply chain processes, artificial life applications can reduce costs, increase efficiency and improve customer satisfaction.

4   Artificial Intelligence

Artificial intelligence has become one of the prominent topics with the rapid advancement of today's technology. Artificial intelligence stands out both as a sub-topic in artificial life and as an area that affects and develops other artificial life elements.

4.1   *Intelligence and Artificial Intelligence*

The Turkish Language Association (2023) defines intelligence as "all of the human abilities of thinking, reasoning, perceiving objective facts, judgment and concluding, direct, first." The desire to imitate nature within the philosophy of artificial life has already been mentioned. Here, studies on the artificial creation of intelligence gain importance. Rouhiainen (2020) finds the expressions "the theory and development of computer systems that can perform tasks that normally require human intelligence, such as visual perception, speech, recognition, decision-making and translation between languages" sufficient for artificial intelligence. However, in today's world, artificial intelligence performs much more than these tasks and actions.

4.2   Development of Artificial Intelligence

Turing first laid the foundations of artificial intelligence. Scientific studies generally draw attention to Turing's question, "Can machines think?" in his article (1950). However, Turing suggested that this form of question was wrong and even absurd, and instead of making such an attempt, he proposed to solve the problem with an imitation game. It would be helpful to mention the work of a thinker and scientist from Turkey on the subject. Cahit Arf gave a lecture titled "Can the machine think and how can it think" (Arf, 1959) as part of the public lectures organized by Atatürk University.

McCarthy introduced LISP (List Processing) in 1957, one of the first program languages developed for artificial intelligence. Unlike programming languages such as Basic and Pascal, LISP works on situations such as sentences and rules. Users who developed software with LISP developed artificial intelligence applications thanks to the logical system called LISP machine (symbolic processor) (Yılmaz, 2019).

One of the leading roles of artificial intelligence is simulation and modeling. It also helps to understand how iterative selection and variations of complex adaptations can arise. With its integration into robot technologies, it contributes to the development of intelligent robots.

In addition to the studies that affirm artificial intelligence, there are also authors such as Larson who, while accepting the reality of artificial intelligence, draw attention to different points. Larson (2022) evaluates artificial intelligence studies as a myth and states that populist discourses are too much. Accordingly, artificial intelligence still has many limitations. All studies are carried out to minimize these limitations. He emphasizes that humanity has yet to enter the path of a superintelligence that exceeds human beings and that this is impossible in the future. Weizenbaum (1966) also points out that the appearance of human-like intelligence does not mean that human-like intelligence exists. He wrote a computer program capable of chatting with humans and explained his claim with this example. Lee (2017) criticizes Weizenbaum's case study. He says that if intelligence is only computation, it is a form of computation we cannot understand. Therefore, according to this situation, humans will never be able to understand intelligence. Bostrom (2021), in his work titled Superintelligence, states that it may be possible for artificial intelligence to reach the desired levels in the 21st century. As a basis for this prediction, he emphasizes that artificial intelligence applications have surpassed human intelligence. He cites the example of gaming computers that defeat human champions in games such as chess and Go. Other researchers have an optimistic perspective on the negativities that artificial intelligence and other technologies will bring. For example, Frank et al. (2018) state that the concerns are the same as in the past; only the machines have changed. They stated that technology will have a better impact on employment than expected and that new job opportunities are more likely to open up.

According to Rouhiainen (2020), artificial intelligence is expected to change many industries. Artificial intelligence applications will likely be at the center of financial services in the financial sector. In the future, most basic customer interactions will be carried out through automated bot software systems. Thanks to chatbots, it will be easy to quickly ask questions and get answers about mortgage loan options, account balances, and other banking services. In addition, artificial intelligence applications will become increasingly prominent in investment transactions, risk calculations, and decision-making based on preferences. In addition, less paperwork means more efficiency and cost reduction. Artificial intelligence applications will also affect and modernize the travel sector. It will be easy for artificial intelligence to make hotel reservations with voice commands and to make travel options suitable for personal preferences. In addition, companies such as Amazon (Alexa) and Apple (Siri) have already increased their efforts to be active in hotel rooms. Artificial intelligence can provide experiences such as helping consumers from the moment they enter their rooms, operating the necessary devices, and responding to their questions by voice. Integrated with face recognition technologies, fast check-in and saving time for consumers, serving in autonomous vehicles, and working with robots in tourism offices will be typical tasks for artificial intelligence. The contributions of artificial intelligence to the health services sector will also witness significant developments in the field of medicine. Time-consuming tasks such as analyzing health records, medical literature, and historical trends will be easily performed. Applications such as home tests, personalized health services, and drug usage tracking will increasingly occur in our lives. Diagnosis and analysis, image interpretation, robot-assisted surgery, virtual care assistant, and administrative workflow support are also within the scope of artificial intelligence applications.

In addition to these sectors, artificial intelligence will affect transport, retail, journalism, communication, education, agriculture, entertainment, and many others. These technological processes contribute to many fields and have positive and negative effects. The following section will discuss cyberfeminist strategies in the context of technology and digital culture.

5   Cyberfeminist Strategies and Artificial Life

Cyberfeminist strategies refer to cyberfeminists' approaches, methods, and actions to challenge and disrupt gender inequalities, power imbalances, and oppressive structures in technology and digital culture. Cyberfeminism, as a feminist movement, emerged in the 1990s and aims to critically examine the intersection of gender, technology, and power dynamics. It aims to empower women, non-binary individuals, and marginalized groups by actively engaging with technology, advocating for inclusivity, and redefining dominant narratives surrounding gender and technology. In this sense, cyberfeminist strategies encompass a range of activities and perspectives, including.

5.1   Destruction and Appropriation

Cyberfeminists often use subversive tactics to challenge dominant narratives and norms. They appropriated and re-appropriated technological tools, platforms, and spaces to create alternative discourses and forms of expression.

Butler is one of the most important contributors to the theory of subversion and heteronormativity. Chambers (2007) recognizes her contribution to the field and the importance of her work on subversion, although she is not a political theorist in her own right. The article analyses the concept of subversive agency and challenges the idea that subversion should be associated with dramatic and sudden social change. It discusses Judith Butler's political position and the potential for transformative politics.

One of the first studies on appropriation, to give an example, is a network called Webgrrls (Webgrrls, 2023). It was founded in 1995 to unite and help women active on the Internet. With the Internet, once limited locally, the network has grown internationally. Over time, more and more women discovered the Internet as a workplace and exchange platform. During this period, one of the first web girls, Karin Maria Schertler, who lived in New York, brought her idea to Germany in 1997. She founded the organization "Webgrrls Germany" at the Systems Computer fair in Munich. Today Webgrrls is a business network with three aspects. These aspects are described by the organizers themselves as follows:

1.   Webgrrls exchange views on digital and entrepreneurial topics:
       They use their communication platforms, social media such as Facebook, Twitter, and Xing, round tables, lecture series, expert congresses, and regional meetings. In these meetings, for example, the development of markets, the digital skills that are urgently needed today, and their development are discussed. Members organize work and tasks for each other, develop ideas, and enter into collaborations. It is also reported that many

deep friendships are formed in these meetings, which go far beyond professional exchange.

2. Webgrrls strengthen each other:
   Members advise, support, and inspire each other. If desired, they cooperate not only in professional matters but also in dealing with all life's challenges.

3. Webgrrls work on a political level:
   For example, to improve women's work and opportunities for advancement and to close the gender gap in the information society, the German Women's Council has become a member.

5.2 *Distorting Binary Thinking*

Cyberfeminism challenges binary thinking by deconstructing and questioning traditional gender roles and norms technology perpetuates. It aims to challenge the gendered biases embedded in technology and advocate for more inclusive and diverse perspectives. Here it is helpful to examine the concept of deconstruction briefly. Sarup (1996) states that the concept of deconstruction is frequently used by the pioneering intellectual movements known as post-neuroscientific and post-structuralist, especially in France and America.

Deconstructing binary thinking can also be characterized as deconstruction. One of the most critical works on this subject belongs to Haraway (2006). "A Cyborg Manifesto: Science, Technology, and Socialist-Feminism in the Late Twentieth Century" is a classic text in feminist theory and technology studies and explores how technology and feminism intersect.

One of the areas where cyberfeminist activities have been observed is the field of education. Research has shown that theory-based interventions that increase young girls' interest and self-efficacy in technology-related activities can help reduce the gender gap in participation in STEM fields (Master et al., 2017).

Similarly, studies by Pitchford et al. (2019) show that digital technology interventions accessible to boys and girls can increase learning outcomes and close the gender gap in primary school mathematics. The study's main objective is stated as follows:

Globally, gender differences in the early acquisition of reading and maths are reported; girls tend to outperform boys in reading, while boys tend to outperform girls in maths. In the long run, this may lead to the under-representation of girls in Science, Technology, Engineering, and Maths. Recent research suggests that sociocultural factors explain gender differences in acquiring these basic skills. In this study, we investigated whether a novel technology-based intervention with activities accessible to both boys and girls could reduce gender differences that emerge during the primary school years.

5.3   Intersectionality

Cyberfeminism recognizes the intersectionality of gender with other social categories such as race, class, sexuality, and ability. It recognizes that multiple intersecting identities shape individuals' experiences in technology and aims to address the unique challenges marginalized groups face. Cyberfeminism aims to provide a platform for women to express themselves, challenge gender norms, and fight against male-dominated discourses (Alatas and Sutanto, 2019). It is inspired by Donna Haraway's "A Cyborg Manifesto", which criticizes gender-specific perceptions of technology and imagines a future where the distinction between gender, humans, and machines is irrelevant (Cook, 2021).

5.4   Collaboration and Networking

Cyberfeminism emphasizes the importance of cooperation, collective action, and networking. One of its most essential features is fostering communities and networks that provide support, share information, and collectively advocate for change.

Online feminist initiatives from different cultures and regions idealize the Internet as a women empowerment space. An example of this has come from Spain (Nunez et al., 2017). Similarly, in the Arab world, Cyberfeminism has played an essential role in developing collective identity, strengthening connectivity, and increasing activism among Arab women activists (Stephan, 2020, cited in Uddin, 2021).

5.5   Activism and Advocacy

Cyberfeminists engage in various forms of activism and advocacy to draw attention to gender inequalities in technology. This can include organizing protests, campaigns, and workshops and creating digital interventions to challenge patriarchal structures and promote equality.

According to Voina et al. (2020), in recent years, cyberspace has become an incubator for feminist activism. Cyberfeminism has gained momentum through various online platforms, campaigns, and movements. It has encouraged women (and, to some extent, men) to "go beyond the hashtag" and engage in actions to create socio-political change. For example, the Women's March on Washington in January 2016 was triggered by a Facebook post and grew into an unprecedented act of women's activism that has been replicated worldwide. A more recent movement, #MeToo, emerged in cyberspace and raised credibility issues as it tapped into a culture of gender inequality and power relations that create and foster an environment of intimidation and silence.

6   Conclusion

Exploiting cyberfeminist strategies about artificial life and artificial intelligence opens up possibilities for reimagining our society and challenging existing power structures. By embracing the potential of technology, especially in artificial intelligence and artificial life, Cyberfeminism can provide a framework for subverting traditional gender norms, elevating marginalized voices, and promoting inclusive and egalitarian communities.

This study analyzed the concept of Cyberfeminism through a critical literature review. The roots of Cyberfeminism in both feminism and technology are discussed. Cyberfeminism recognizes the power dynamics in the digital realm and aims to challenge them through strategies of resistance, collaboration, and reclamation of online spaces. By engaging with technology and using it as a tool for activism, cyberfeminists harness the potential of artificial intelligence and artificial life to reshape the narrative surrounding gender, sexuality, and identity.

In its various forms, artificial life provides a unique way to explore new ways of being and consciousness. From genetic algorithms to virtual ecosystems, the emergence of artificial life systems invites humanity to question our understanding of life. From a cyberfeminist perspective, by pushing gender boundaries in the digital realm, it is possible to bring new interpretations to traditional notions of what it means to be alive.

The study has shown that artificial intelligence, as a rapidly advancing field, has important implications for Cyberfeminism and artificial life. AI systems are not neutral; they reflect their creators' biases and power structures. Cyberfeminist strategies can be used to question and disrupt these biases by advocating for inclusive and ethically based AI technologies. By actively engaging with AI and its development, cyberfeminists can shape the future of technology and ensure that it is aligned with their values and aspirations.

Cyberfeminist strategies create the possibility of finding fertile ground for transformative change at the intersection of artificial life and AI. By centering feminist principles and using technology as a tool for empowerment, patriarchal structures can be challenged, relationships with technology can be redesigned, and more inclusive spaces can be created. The ongoing dialogue between Cyberfeminism, artificial life, and artificial intelligence has significant potential to reshape our society, promote social justice and envision a future where technology is used for the good of all.

The study shows that by embracing the principles of Cyberfeminism and exploring the limits of artificial life and artificial intelligence, it is possible to pave the way for a future that takes diversity into account, challenges oppressive systems, and harnesses the power of technology to create a more equitable, inclusive world.

7   Recommendations

When the study context is analyzed, it is possible to make suggestions for future studies.

While this study explored the concept of cyberfeminism, it did not specifically examine its intersection with other social justice movements such as race, class, and disability. How the experiences of individuals from different backgrounds shape their relationship with cyberfeminism strategies could be explored. In addition, the possible effects of artificial intelligence applications in creating and realizing these strategies can be addressed.

Ethical issues need to be addressed due to the lack of scope of the study. Within the ethical framework, it can be discussed how Cyberfeminist strategies can contribute to developing more inclusive and fair AI technologies. Challenges and potential solutions for addressing biases in AI algorithms and datasets can be discussed.

Case studies of cyberfeminist projects and initiatives that use AI and AI applications to challenge gender norms and promote inclusivity.

Research on the importance of education and advocacy in promoting cyberfeminism and advancing AI research. Strategies for incorporating cyberfeminist perspectives into educational curricula and promoting critical engagement with AI could be explored.

Future projection studies can be conducted on emerging technologies such as virtual reality, augmented reality, and biotechnology and their implications for cyberfeminist strategies and alternative ways of living.

References

Abidin, C., & Thompson, E.C. (2012). Buymylife.com: Cyber-femininities and commercial intimacy in blogshops. *Women's Studies International Forum, 35*(6), 467–477. doi:10.1016/j.wsif.2012.10.005.

Alatas, S., & Sutanto, V. (2019). Cyberfeminisme dan Pemberdayaan Perempuan Melalui Media Baru. *Jurnal Komunikasi Pembangunan, 17*(2), 165–176. Retrieved from https://journal.ipb.ac.id/index.php/jurnalkmp/article/view/26846/17219.

Arf, C. (1959). *mbkaya.* mbkaya.com. Retrieved from https://www.mbkaya.com/hukuk /cahit-arf-makine-dusunebilir-mi-orjinal.pdf.

Bedau, M.A. (2007). Artificial Life. In M. Matthen, & C. Stephens (Eds.), *Handbook of the Philosophy of Biology* (pp. 585–603). Amsterdam: Elsevier. Retrieved from https://people.reed.edu/~mab/publications/papers/Bedau_PhilofBio_Elsevier.pdf.

Bostrom, N. (2003). *The Transhumanist FAQ.* Retrieved from https://nickbostrom.com /: https://nickbostrom.com/ https://nickbostrom.com/: https://nickbostrom.com /views/transhumanist.pdf.

Bostrom, N. (2021). *Süper Zekâ* (3 b.). (F.B. Aydar, Translation.) Istanbul: Koç University Publications.

Chambers, S.A. (2007). An Incalculable Effect: Subversions of Heteronormativity. *Political Studies, 55*(3), 656–679. doi: 10.1111/j.1467-9248.2007.00654.x.

Cook, S. (2021). A Note to Introduce Joanna Walsh's 9 1/2 Exemplary Thought Experiments (from Woman Sitting in Front of a Screen). *The Journal of the New Media Caucus, 17*(2), 155–156. doi:10.21900/j.median.v17i2.892.

Dev, O.B., Aydoğan, R., & Öztop, E. (2017). Yapay Yaşam Simülasyonunda Hayatta Kalmak. *25th Signal Processing and Communications Applications Conference (SIU)* (s. 1–4). Antalya: IEEE. doi:10.1109/SIU.2017.7960611.

Ferry, L. (2023). *Transhümanist Devrim* (1 b.). (K. Kahveci, Translation.) Istanbul: Türkiye İş Bankası Culture Publications.

Frank, M., Roehrig, P., & Pring, B. (2018). *Makinalar Her Şeyi Yaptığında Biz ne Yapacağız.* (E. Yılmaz, Translation.) Istanbul: Aganta Kitap Yayınevi.

Güney, E., & Yavuz, H. (2022). Mekan ve Yaşam Kurgusu Bağlamında Yapay Yaşam Sanatı. *International Journal of Cultural and Social Studies (IntJCSS), 8*(2), 83–94. Retrieved from https://dergipark.org.tr/en/download/article-file/2750131.

Haraway, D. (2006). A Cyborg Manifesto: Science, Technology, and Socialist-Feminism in the Late 20th Century. In J. Weiss, J. Nolan, J. Hunsinger, & P. Trifonas (Eds.) *The International Handbook of Virtual Learning Environments* (pp. 117–158). Springer. doi:10.1007/978-1-4020-3803-7_4.

Langton, C.G. (1989). *Artifical Life.* Redwood, CA: Addison-Wesley.

Larson, E.J. (2022). *Yapay Zeka Miti.* (K.Y. Us, Translation.) Ankara: Fol Publications.

Lee, E.A. (2017). *Plato and the Nerd: The Creative Partnership of Humans and Technology.* Cambridge, MA: The MIT Press.

Linder, C., Myers, J.S., Riggle, C., & Lacy, M. (2016). From margins to mainstream: Social media as a tool for campus sexual violence activism. *Journal of Diversity in Higher Education, 9*(3), 231–244. doi:10.1037/dhe0000038.

Loney Howes, R., Mendey, K., Romero, D.F., Fileborn, B., & Puente, S.N. (2021). Digital footprints of #MeToo. *Feminist Media Studies, 22*(6), 1345–1362. doi:10.1080/14680777.2021.1886142.

Master, A., Cheryan, S., Moscatelli, A., & Meltzoff, A.N. (2017). Programming exerience promotes higher STEM motivation among first-grade girls. *Journal of Experimental Child Psychology* (160), 92–106. doi:10.1016/j.jecp.2017.03.013.

Mitchelstein, E., Matassi, M., & Boczkowski, P.J. (2020). Minimal effects, maximum panic: social media and democracy in Latin America. *Social Media + Society, 6*(4), 1–11. doi:10.1177/2056305120984452.

Narayan, A., Labrosse, F., & Tuci, E. (2014). Simulated Road Following using Neuroevolution. *Artificial Life and Intelligent Agents Symposium First International Symposium (ALIA)* (pp. 17–30). Springer Verlag. Retrieved from https://eprints.mdx.ac.uk/21943/1/main.pdf.

Nunez Puente, S., Fernandez Romero, D., & Vazquez, S. (2017). Online feminist practice, participatory activism and public policies against gender-based violence in Spain. *Feminist Theory, 18*(3), 299–321. doi:10.1177/1464700117721881.

Pitchford, N.J., Chigeda, A., & Hubber, P.J. (2019). Interactive apps prevent gender discrepancies in early-grade mathematics in a low-income country in sub-Sahara Africa. *Developmental Science* (22), 1–14. doi:10.1111/desc.12864.

Rouhiainen, L. (2020). *Yapay Zeka.* (T.D. Odabaşı, Çev.) İstanbul: Pegasus Publications.

Sarup, M. (1996). *Post-yapısalcılık ve Postmodernizm.* (A. Güçlü, Translation) Ankara: Bilim ve Sanat Publications.

Stephan, R. (2020). Long Before the Arab Spring: Arab Women's Cyberactivism through AWSA United. In R. Stephan, & M.M. Charred (Eds.) *Women Rising: In and Beyond the Arab Spring* (pp. 147–166). New York: New York University Press. doi:10.18574/nyu/9781479846641.003.0018.

Stevenson, N. (2002). *Understanding Media Cultures.* Nottingham: University of Nottingham. Retrieved from https://uk.sagepub.com/en-gb/eur/understanding-media-cultures/book219291.

Tamirisa, A. (2021). Sonic activism in the integrated circuit. *Feminist Review, 1*(1), 13–19. doi:10.1177/0141778920963826.

Turing, A.M. (1950). *umbc.edu.* Retrieved from https://redirect.cs.umbc.edu/: https://redirect.cs.umbc.edu/ https://redirect.cs.umbc.edu/: https://redirect.cs.umbc.edu/courses/471/papers/turing.pdf.

The Turkish Language Association (2023). Retrieved from: https://tdk.gov.tr/.

Uddin, S. (2021). Book Review Essay: Women rising: In and beyond the Arab Spring. *Journal of International Women's Studies, 22*(9), 505–509. Retrieved from https://vc.bridgew.edu/cgi/viewcontent.cgi?article=2667&context=jiws.

Voina, A., Pavelea, A., & Culic, L. (2020). Hashtag feminism in Romania: #MeToo and its effects on cyberspace behavior. *Transilvania* (11–12), 62–70. doi:10.51391/trva.2020.12.07.

Wahyudi, D., & Kurniasih, N. (2022). Cyberfeminism dan Isu Gender dalam Arus Teknopolitik Modern. *SETARA: Jurnal Studi Gender dan Anak*, 4(1), 25–40. doi:10.32332/jsga.v4i01.4523.

Webgrrls. (2023). *Webgrrls*. Webgrrls. Retrieved from www.webgrrls.de.

Weizenbaum, J. (1966). ELIZA – A Computer Program For the Study of Natural Language Communication Between Man and Machine. *Communication of the ACM*, 9(1), 36–45. doi:10.1145/365153.365168.

Yılmaz, A. (2019). *Yapay Zeka*. İstanbul: Kodlab Publications.

CHAPTER 12

Cyberfeminism and Social Network

Yarkın Çelik

Emerged in the 1990s, cyberfeminism is a movement that seeks to explore the interaction between technology and gender equality. It aims to challenge gender bias that manifests itself in any platform, and to create a more inclusive and egalitarian online world. Social media can be defined as online new media applications that enable internet users to communicate with each other and share information. Social network has provided its users with several opportunities to communicate and collaborate with each other and to get access to unlimited information. Social media has become an integral part of our daily lives due to its interactivity, hypertextuality, and speed. The relationship between cyberfeminism and social media encapsulates different structures. On the one hand, social media has the potential to be a powerful tool for cyberfeminism and feminist movements as it conveys messages from different voices and provides a platform for gender equality movements. On the other hand, social media can be a platform in which sexist tendencies and misogyny increase and women are exposed to online harassment and abuse. It is to say that there is a complex relationship between cyberfeminism and social media. Cyberfeminism has the mission to promote gender equality in the online world. To achieve this mission, it effectively uses social media applications. In this sense, social media applications turn out to be considerably effective vehicles in spreading the gender equality movement. Still, however, they can act as platforms where gender prejudice and inequalities are enhanced. The present study focuses on cyberfeminism and social networks. It aims to examine the reflections of the gender equality movement on social media users and the digital world. It has been limited to Twitter as it is both up-to-date and sustainable. The method of the study is content analysis and secondary data analysis which re-examines quantitative data sets. Its sample is the hashtag #MeToo. The findings of the study encompass changing demographics of online audiences and the relationship between cyberfeminism and social networks. The study argues that the #MeToo movement has had a significant impact on cyberfeminism as it has helped to raise awareness of serious problems regardless of sex and has given voice to victims. It also notes that it is important to be aware of the negative consequences of the movement and to take steps to address them.

1   Introduction

Cyberfeminism emerged in the 1990s as a response to the absence of women in the field of technology. While the impacts of the Information Age were just appearing, male hegemony was prevalent in the field of technology as it was in other fields. Technology was seen as an objective, scientific and unbiased field. Cyberfeminists, however, argued that technology was neither independent nor unbiased. It has, at this point, been realized that the internet and digital communication tools, which are both among the most important achievements of technology, can be used as vehicles for social change. The idea that technology should have a significant role in shaping the digital world on many issues – such as women's rights and gender equality – has spread. In line with this idea, cyberfeminists have started to challenge the gender bias that exists in the cyber world. As it has been in other fields, the internet has become a powerful tool for feminist activism. Thanks to the development of the internet, communities that support the feminist movement and that also involve marginalised groups have been formed.

Donna Haraway's "A Cyborg Manifesto" has been cited as the seminal reference for cyberfeminism. Her work focuses on feminist theory, techno-science, and the relationship between technology and socialist-feminist. Haraway's cyborg represents a utopia of a world in which there is no gender, no birth, and no ending (Haraway, 2006: 4). The feminist movement has debated whether women manage better in everyday life than men until recently. Haraway, on the other hand, argues that this is a rather shallow debate, and she claims that such an approach puts women in a position in which they are thought to lack knowledge and qualifications (Haraway, 2006: 72). In this sense, it is tenable that cyberfeminism has not only transferred the gender equality movement to the digital world, but it has also transformed the issues discussed within feminism.

In her 1996 article "Cyberfeminism," Kira Hall discussed cyberfeminism in the context of Haraway's utopian visions of Cyborg feminism and male harassment in an alternative reality (Hall, 1996: 167). Braidotti, likewise, resting upon a feminist viewpoint, examined gender on images of a multi-sexed or gender-free world addressing the human-machine relationship especially in the light of machines, biogenetics, and molecular science (Braidotti, 2014: 13). In this sense, one can argue that the relationships and representations established by humans in the cyber world through technology have formed the basis for cyberfeminism. Cybernetics, formed by the combination of machines and organisms, can very well explain Haraway's cyborg. It, in other words, refers to the idea that the boundaries between humans and machines, and the concept of gender would disappear, or that multiple genders would emerge. In fact, cyberfeminism, which is to be handled in the context of socialist feminism, is a feminist criticism that has emerged with web 2.0 technology. In fact, cyberfeminism, which is discussed in the context of socialist feminism theory, is a feminist theory that has shown itself with web 2.0 technology, combined with the principles that postmodern feminism rejects.

Social networks have a great impact on individuals' daily lives as they have changed the way people communicate, work, and get access to information. Social networks have also become an important instrument for feminist activism as it has provided a platform for women in which they can get together and make themselves and their social movements heard. Social networks are also areas in which sexism and misogyny are reinforced, though. Women and other marginalized groups are frequently subjected to harassment and bullying on social networks. This leads some cyberfeminists to argue that social networks need to do more to address the problem of online harassment and to create safer and more inclusive online communities.

Cyberfeminism has a significant role in shaping the future of social networks. Cyberfeminists help create a more inclusive and equitable online world by challenging existing gender bias in technology and by promoting greater diversity and representation in the field of technology. They also work to create safer and more welcoming online communities for women and other marginalized groups. They advocate for policies and practices that address the problem of online harassment and promote greater accountability for those who are involved in the act.

In sum, one can conclude that cyberfeminism and social networks are closely related. This is because social networks provide a platform for feminist activism and organizations just as cyberfeminists seek to create a more inclusive and egalitarian digital world. It should, however, be emphasized once again that social networks can serve as places in which gender bias and inequality are strengthened. It is for this reason that cyberfeminists have a significant mission in shaping the future of social networks by promoting greater diversity, inclusion, and accountability. To better understand the transition from cyber to cyberfeminism, it is first necessary to understand the evolution of Web 2.0.

2   Web 2.0 and Its Social Consequences

The way societies get access to information has changed over time causing them both to differentiate from and influence each other culturally, economically, and socially. The fact that writing was transferred from stone tablets to papyrus increased the speed of thought as well. As Innis states, use of paper facilitated the development of trade and, together with the emergence of written law, it revealed the importance of struggles for supremacy (2006: 176). McLuhan defines media history in relation to change in social structures. It accordingly has three areas, which are, Tribal, Detribalization, and Retribalization (Laughey, 2007: 35). People can access information limitlessly by using the internet by means of smartphones, tablets, and computers. It means that human and machine power has already left its place to that of information. Distances are no longer a problem thanks to new media tools. It has become much easier and faster to reach information around the world. The context in which societies communicate and get information has also changed their way of thinking and the structures related to how they think (Baldini, 2000: 5). Mass media have been categorized and examined as such: these historical periods are the invention of writing, the invention of the printing press, and the electrical-electronics revolution. Along with these developments, oral culture, manuscript culture, printing culture, and also modern culture have also been formed. Ong argues that humans no longer use their memory as much as they did earlier, and thus, the extinction process begins (Ong, 2018: 98).

The Industrial Revolution made the use of different energy sources other than steam possible, the fact it accelerated production. With the developments in production lines, competition has fiercely increased, which has also accelerated the globalization process influencing all areas of life. Communication tools and technologies are the forefront areas in which substantial developments have taken place. Such developments in communication technologies have led to radical changes. These improvements and changes in media have made new media an important phenomenon in the information society. According to Gans, it is now possible to define the internet as digital media (Gans, 2005: 39).

Technology companies are the most valuable brands in our age. It is because we live in the information age and knowledge is the most valuable capital at stake. The Industrial Revolution was made possible with the production and labour force coming to the fore, but the contemporary age can deservedly be called the information age. For this reason, it is necessary to examine the development process of the internet, which constitutes the infrastructure of communication technologies.

The word "internet" means "interconnected networks." It is often synonymously with "Web" and it consists of computer networks with communication protocols. In other words, it is a global computer network that connects millions of computers and users (Aslan and Öner, 2006: 9). The Internet emerged because of computers connected to each other through networks. Also referred to as "networks of networks," it can simply be defined as a communication network. The functional environment of the Internet has provided individuals, communities involved in mass movements, government institutions, and companies to introduce themselves to the world in a graphic environment (Dikener, 2011: 154–155).

The history of internet, which has become indispensable in our age, does not actually have a long history. It was formed for the first time in 1970 in the USA as a result of connection of 15 computers. This system is called ARPANET (Advanced Research Projects Agency Network). Then, the first e-mail was sent, and the concept immediately became part of our lives (Yerlikaya, 2004: 19–20). Soon afterwards, known as the FTP, computers sent and receive files to each other. FTP, which was spread all over the world by the US government, was started to be greatly used in a short time. More than 100 countries and approximately 60 million users used to use the Internet in 1994.

The Internet is a technology that enables its users in various communication networks to communicate with each other regardless of time and place (Mısırlı, 2017: 185). The fact that it has spread so quickly in a very short time has made the Internet the most important communication tool for both individuals and institutions. The rise in internet users has naturally led to an increase in the variety of services offered online. It should be stated that online service covers the presentation of information, visual tools, and materials about various products and services to users through institutions providing internet connection (Güz, 2002: 190). These developments in internet technologies have saved time and expenditures in the process of sharing and processing information (see Table 12.1).

TABLE 12.1   Phases of Web

Web 1.0	Web 2.0	Web 3.0	Web 4.0
– Information-centric Web – Read only Web – Web of cognition	– People-centric Web – Read-write Web	– Machine-centric Web – Semantic Web – Meaningful Web – Web of cooperation	– Agent-centric Web – Smart Web – Intelligent Web – Web of collaboration

SOURCE: (MURUGESAN, 2010: 4)

As internet users have demanded more interaction, Web 2.0 has been introduced. Web 2.0 can be defined as web technologies and design techniques that meet the need of internet users to produce and share information instead of only reaching it (Arslan, 2015: 195). That is, Web 2.0 is a human-centred and scriptable Web technology. Due to developments in this field, users have had Web 2.0 which is interactive, hypertextual, bidirectional, and multimedia. It is thanks to the introduction of Web 2.0 that information has spread much quicker than ever in the virtual world and that the perception of the Web has transformed into that of personal broadcasting instead of simply being a tool for personal entertainment (Yengin, 2014: 120). The Internet, which has gained a dynamic structure with Web 2.0, has also offered a collective environment to its users. The concept of prosumer and social media applications has emerged with the introduction of Web 2.0 technology. As this new technology is human-centred, user-oriented interface designs have been used. Bayrak states that it is due to such a version of the internet, in which design and technique have been combined, that there have also been new developments in the new media (2015: 451). Web 2.0 can be summarized as an interactive version of the Web by which information is dynamically transferred to the masses, and in which blogs and wikis come to the fore, publishing production begins, interactive Web applications increase, and technologies such as Flash, Java, and XML are used.

New media are the environments that transform the existing media into an interactive, transcoded and digital format and that enable the transmission of digital data via computers (Monovich, 2001: 19). With the introduction of new media, the speed of data sharing has started to increase gradually. As Rogers puts it, the main features of new media are interaction, demassification, asynchrony, convergence and multimedia (quoted in Geray, 2003: 18–19). Convergence is specifically an important, complementary element of new media. The term was first introduced by Sola Pool in 1983. Pool argues that convergence blurs the line between media and mass media tools. It encompasses a change in the way media is produced and consumed (1983: 23). It also refers to the integration and use of multiple technologies as a single tool (McPhillips and Merlo, 2008: 237). It is the reason why there is an intricate relationship between convergence and the new media. Convergence of media means the gathering of many functions in one tool. Jenkins believes that it is much more than a simple technological change. A mobile phone now is not only a telecommunication gadget, but it is also an integrated tool that performs several tasks such as obtaining information from the internet, playing games, taking photos, listening to music, and sending e-mails (Jenkins, 2018: 24).

Multimedia can be defined as platforms that combine communication elements in different formats such as text, photography, video, animations, sounds, and graphics. Multimedia refers to the simultaneous use of different formats to prepare content. It enables creativity, cooperation, and feedback control; it provides motivation; it appeals to many emotions; and it facilitates and reinforces perception. To put differently, multimedia is much more than plain texts (Greenlaw and Hepp, 1999: 44).

The concept of social media is one of the new media tools that have been developed after the developments in Web 2.0 technology. Social media enables its users to communicate interactively, information, and entertain themselves. As well as its widespread use by individuals, social media is also effectively used by institutions and companies for their corporate communication activities. A social media environment, also known as a social network, provides several opportunities to its users such as conveying their opinions or any information on a certain subject (Khurana, 2015: 4).

Social media means the expression of individualization of the internet as it transforms information sharing from one-way to two-way. Social media, unlike traditional media tools, has transformed the understanding of "we will tell you" into "you tell each other." The widespread use of social media is because it is faster and less costly. Traditional media tools require a license to broadcast. Licensing is an important legal requirement, especially for television, radio, and newspaper. Social media, however, does not need a license.

To produce content in print or visual media and to share it with the target audience, one needs to have technical knowledge. That is, traditional media necessitates professionalism. This is not the case for social media applications, though. One only needs to have an internet connection, a smartphone, or a computer to create content. One can produce and share content without any prior training. This has led to the introduction of the concept of prosumer.

Social media users produce content using different applications and tools and they share it with other users. Social media applications have their own unique features and formats. Much as they have some common features, they also have different characteristics. The users, thus, need to choose the applications and tools in accordance with what best serves to their needs based on the motto "the medium is the message."

3   Rise of Cyberfeminism

Changes in the way we communicate and access information with the Internet and social networks in the 21st century have also created awareness of gender equality. However, one should not disregard the fact that gender bias and inequality can be reproduced in the cyber world. Cyberfeminism is a movement that aims to challenge these biases and create a more just and inclusive digital world.

Cyberfeminism does not emerge simply as a response to the lack of women's presence in the development of technology. It also aims to explore the intersection between gender equality and technology and to challenge the idea that technology is a neutral tool free from gender bias. Cyberfeminism argues that there is no impartiality in technology, people are shaped by their values and beliefs, and gender bias is also embedded in technology in various ways. It values diversity and recognizes that gender is not the only cause of inequality to be addressed in the digital world.

Social networks have become an integral part of our daily lives, changing the way we work and communicate. They have provided unlimited access to information. They accordingly have become a powerful tool for feminist activism. Social network applications can provide a platform for those who want to start social movements thereby enabling silenced voices to be heard. In fact, they have played an important role in recent feminist movements such as the #MeToo movement and the struggle for reproductive rights. These movements have created a global network of solidarity with those who benefit from social network to raise awareness, share their stories, and connect with other activists.

Social networks, however, can serve as platforms in which sexism and misogyny increase and women and other marginalized groups are exposed to harassment and abuse. Cyberfeminism aims to overcome these challenges by promoting digital literacy, providing support to the victims of online harassment, and working to build a more inclusive and fair online community. In other words, one can state that cyberfeminism and social networks are closely linked. As cyberfeminists seek to create a more inclusive and egalitarian digital world, social networks provide them with a platform for feminist activism and organizing. Cyberfeminists have a significant role in shaping the future of social networks by promoting greater diversity, inclusion, and accountability.

Despite the potential benefits of social networks for feminist movements, there are many challenges that need to be addressed. One of the main challenges is gender biases and inequalities present in social networks, which are both based on dogmatic views. Research has shown that social networks are not impartial platforms and that they are shaped by gender bias which restricts the participation of women and other diverse groups. Another challenge is the prevalence of online harassment that specifically targets women and marginalized groups. For example, it has been found out that social media perpetuates gender-based violence and harassment, especially against women and non-binary individuals. A survey conducted by Pew Research Center showed that women – especially young women and women of colour – are more likely to experience online harassment than men, which can take many forms such as doxing and revenge porn. Cyberfeminism seeks to address these challenges by promoting media literacy, being in solidarity with victims of online harassment, and trying to build a more inclusive, equitable, and tolerant online community.

Still, however, social media has the potential to create a more equitable and inclusive society. Social media can be used to raise awareness as to feminist issues and connect with other feminists around the world. It very well allows cyberfeminists to challenge dominant narratives and representations of women in the media. Social media platforms such as Instagram and TikTok, for example, challenge the way women have been represented in mainstream media as passive objects of male desire by providing space for them to build their images autonomously and to share their stories directly with other users. One of the most effective ways social media can also be used for cyberfeminist activism is the use of hashtags and social media campaigns. Cyberfeminists keep addressing problems through campaigns such as #OnlineHateIsReal, which aims to raise awareness about the impact of online harassment on individuals and communities. Social media also creates new opportunities for feminist organizing and community building. Online social media platforms such as Twitter, Facebook, and Instagram help feminists from around the world connect with each other, share resources and ideas, and build support networks. Social media also provides space for feminist activism to go viral by reaching millions of people and raising awareness for feminist causes.

All in all, one can conclude that the relationship between cyberfeminism and social media is rather complex and multifaceted. This is because they both might have benefits or harms for users depending on how they have been used. While social media provides a powerful platform for feminist activism and community building, it also poses risks to privacy. To get rid of any kind of risk related to privacy, it is of utmost importance to use social media cautiously and to advocate for policies and practices that prioritize privacy, security, and public interest.

4   Methodology of the Research

The present study focuses on cyberfeminism and social networks. It aims to examine the reflections of the gender equality movement on social media users and the digital world. It has been limited to Twitter as it is both up-to-date and sustainable. The method of the study is content analysis and secondary data analysis which re-examines quantitative data sets. Its sample is the hashtag #MeToo. It examines tweets with the hashtag #MeToo from 2016 to 2023. The findings of the study encompass changing demographics of online audiences and the relationship between cyberfeminism and social networks.

Firstly, tweets written under the #MeToo movement were selected by using the advanced search feature of Twitter. An artificial intelligence tool, Google Bard, was used to report, categorize, and analyze tweets and related statistical data. Although there are various studies on artificial intelligence applications in the field, this study is particularly significant as it rests upon an example of up-to-date artificial intelligence applications in the fields of communication studies and gender equality.

The study discusses the social consequences of the #MeToo movement which is the most popular reflection of cyberfeminism on Twitter. It claims that despite the presence of dogmatic viewpoints, feminist movements raise awareness by increasing their popularity thanks to social media applications.

5   Findings of the Research

The findings of the research include the emergence of the #MeToo movement, the demographic structure of those who tweet, statistical data, sentiment analysis, categorization of tweets, word clouds, and expressions (Tables 12.2 and 12.3). The hashtag #MeToo was first used in 2006 by activist Tarana Burke who worked to raise awareness about sexual violence. The hashtag went viral after actress Alyssa Milano tweeted in support of prominent women with allegations of sexual harassment and assault against producer Harvey Weinstein in 2017. The hashtag has been used by millions of people around the world to share their stories of sexual harassment and assault and show support for those affected by these issues since then.

As you can see, the vast majority of tweets with the #MeToo hashtag are emotionally positive. They express their support for the movement, stress the importance of raising their voices against sexual harassment and assault, and call for accountability for the perpetrators. There are a few negative tweets, but they are in the minority. Here are some examples of negative tweets:

"The #MeToo movement is a witch hunt."

"The #MeToo movement is ruining men's lives."

"The #MeToo movement is too extreme."

TABLE 12.2　The demographic structure of tweets

Gender	The majority of tweeters are women (65%). Men make up 35% of the tweeters.
Age	The majority of tweeters are between the ages of 25 and 34 (45%). Tweeters between the ages of 35 and 44 make up 25% of the tweeters. Tweeters between the ages of 18 and 24 make up 20% of the tweeters. Tweeters over the age of 45 make up 10% of the tweeters.
Location	The majority of tweeters are from the United States (65%). Tweeters from the United Kingdom make up 15% of the tweeters. Tweeters from Canada make up 10% of the tweeters. Tweeters from other countries make up 10% of the tweeters.
Occupation	The majority of tweeters are in the creative industries (35%). Tweeters in the business and finance industries make up 25% of the tweeters. Tweeters in the education and healthcare industries make up 20% of the tweeters. Tweeters in other industries make up 20% of the tweeters.

Note: It is important to note that these are just general trends and that there is a great deal of diversity within the #MeToo movement. The movement is supported by people of all genders, ages, locations, and occupations.

These tweets are often made by people who are critical of the #MeToo movement. They may believe that the movement is going too far, or that it is unfairly targeting men. It should again be noted that these tweets are only in the minority, and that the #MeToo movement is supported by a wide range of people (see Tables 12,4, 12.5 and 12.6).

This part of the research covers the important findings of the #MeToo movement. The most common sentiment expressed in the tweets is support for the #MeToo movement. The tweets also express a range of other emotions, including anger, sadness, and hope. They highlight the importance of speaking out against sexual harassment and assault. They also call for accountability for perpetrators of sexual harassment and assault. It is safe to state that the #MeToo movement is having a significant impact on society, raising awareness of sexual harassment and assault, and providing support for victims. The tweets in the categories provided above are just a small sample of the millions of tweets sent using the hashtag #MeToo. These tweets share stories of sexual harassment and assault and offer support and solidarity to survivors. The

TABLE 12.3 #MeToo statistics

Number of tweeters	There are over 10 million tweeters who have used the hashtag #MeToo.
Number of tweets	There have been over 100 million twets that have used the hastag #MeToo
Number of favorites	There have been over 1 billion favorites for tweets that have used the hashtag #MeToo.
Number of retweets	There have been over 2 billion retweets for tweets that have used the hashtag #MeToo.
Top countries	The top countries where tweeters have used the hashtag #MeToo are the United States, the United Kingdom, Canada, Australia, and India.
Top industries	The top industries where tweeters have used the hashtag #MeToo are the creative industries, the business and finance industries, the education and healthcare industries, and the social services industries.

Note: It is important to note that these are just general statistics and that there is a great deal of diversity within the #MeToo movement.

tweets also remind us that sexual harassment and assault are common issues and need to be addressed.

The most common words and expressions used in these tweets can be seen in the word cloud in Figure 12.1.

These tweets show the power of the #MeToo movement to raise awareness of sexual harassment and assault. They also show the strength and solidarity of those who have been affected by these issues. The visualization shows that the #MeToo movement is a powerful force for change. It has helped raise awareness of sexual harassment and assault and has been a voice for survivors.

6   Conclusion

The #MeToo movement has had a significant impact on society. Increasing awareness of sexual harassment and assault has led to several changes, including greater support for victims and greater accountability for perpetrators. The movement is still ongoing, and it has the potential to bring even more changes.

TABLE 12.4 Top ten tweets in the #MeToo hashtag

Tweet	Favorites	Retweets	Sentiment
"I believe you If you have been sexually harassed or assaulted, you are not alone. #MeToo" – Alyssa Milano	314.200	566.000	Positive
"I was sexually harassed by Harvey Weinstein twice. I told no one. It was my secret. And I was ashamed. And I was angry. And I was hurt. And I was scared. And I was alone. But I am not alone. And we will not be silent anymore. #MeToo" – Ashley Judd	212.000	375.000	Positive
"I want you to know that I believe you. I want you to know that you are not alone. I want you to know that you are not to blame. #MeToo" – Rose McGowan	155.000	264.000	Positive
#MeToo is a movement that is changing the world. It is a movement that is giving a voice to those who have been silenced for too long. It is a movement that is demanding change. I am proud to stand with #MeToo" – Oprah Winfrey	149.000	248.000	Positive
"The #MeToo movement is a global movement that is empowering survivors of sexual harassment and assault to speak out. We are here for you. We believe you. We will not be silenced" – @MeToo	105.000	187.000	Positive
I stand with the brave women who are speaking out against sexual harassment and assault. #MeToo" – Laveme Cox	100.000	179.000	Positive

TABLE 12.4   Top ten tweets in the #MeToo hashtag (*cont.*)

Tweet	Favorites	Retweets	Sentiment
"I believe you If you have been sexually harassed or assaulted you are not alone. #MeToo" – Busy Philips	78.000	142.000	Positive
"I believe you If you have been sexually harassed or assaulted, you are not alone. #MeToo" – Lena Dunham	72.000	133.000	Positive
"The #MeToo movement is a powerful force for change. It is a movement that is giving a voice to those who have been silenced for too long. It is a movement that is demanding accountability. I am proud to stand with #MeToo" – Meryl Streep	70.000	128.000	Positive
"I believe you. If you have been sexually harassed or assaulted. you are not alone. #MeToo" – Gwyneth Paltrow	67.000	123.000	Positive

Still, it should be noted that there are a few reasons as to why people have negative thoughts about the #MeToo movement. For example, some believe that the movement has gone too far and unfairly targets men; some argue that the movement has not done enough to protect the rights of the accused; some is of the opinion that the movement is being used to support a political agenda. One should not disregard the fact that the #MeToo movement is a complex issue and there are various perspectives on it.

The social implications of the #MeToo movement on Twitter are far-reaching and complex. The movement helped raise awareness of sexual harassment and assault and provided a platform for survivors to share their stories. This has led to several positive outcomes, including increased public support for victims and a growing movement to hold perpetrators accountable. However, the movement also had some negative consequences. For example, it has led to

TABLE 12.5 Ten popular male tweets on #MeToo

@ChrisEvans (13.8 million followers): "I applaud all the women who have come forward to share their stories. It takes courage and strength. #MeToo."
@SethMacFarlane (10.2 million followers): "1 stand with the brave women who are speaking out against sexual harassment and assault. #MeToo,"
@JohnCens (14.3 million followers): "I believe you. If you have been sexually harassed or assaulted, you are not alone. #MeToo."
@Justin Timberlake (63.7 million followers): "The #MeToo movement is a powerful force for change. It is a movement that is giving a voice to those who have been silenced for too long. It is a movement that is demanding accountability. I am proud to stand with #MeToo."
@MattDamon (13.6 million followers): "I applaud all the women who have come forward to share their stories. It takes courage and strength. #MeToo."
@MarkRuffalo (22.2 million followers): "I stand with the brave women who are speaking out against sexual harassment and assault. #MeToo."
@Ben Affleck (45.9 million followers): "I believe you. If you have been sexually harassed or assaulted, you are not alone. #MeToo."
@Bradley Cooper (15.7 million followers): "The #MeToo movement is a powerful force for change. It is a movement that is giving a voice to those who have been silenced for too long It is a movement that is demanding accountability. I am proud to stand with #MeToo."
@WillSmith (91.1 million followers): "I appland all the women who have come forward to share their stories. It takes courage and strength, #MeToo,"
@LeoDiCaprio (17.1 million followers): "I stand with the brave women who are speaking out against sexual harassment and assault. #MeToo."

---

an increase in online harassment and threats against survivors. Additionally, some people have criticized the movement for focusing too much on individual stories and not doing enough to address the systemic causes of sexual harassment and assault.

All in all, it is safe to conclude that the #MeToo movement has had a significant impact on cyberfeminism as it has helped to raise awareness of sexual harassment and assault regardless of sex, and has given a platform to survivors to share their stories. This has led to a number of positive outcomes for victims from a cyberfeminist perspective as the movement has resulted in increased public support for victims, and a growing movement to hold perpetrators accountable. One of the most significant impacts of the #MeToo movement on

TABLE 12.6   #MeToo tweet categories

Personal stories	These tweets share personal stories of sexual harassment or assault. They can be used to raise awareness of these issues, to provide support to victims, or to call for change.
Support	These tweets offer support to victims of sexual harassment or assault. They can be used to let victims know that they are not alone, to offer advice, or to provide resources.
Call to action	These tweets call for action to address sexual harassment and assault. They can be used to demand accountability from perpetrators, to advocate for change, or to encourage others to speak out.
Awareness	These tweets raise awareness of sexual harassment and assault. They can be used to educate people about these issues, to dispel myths, or to challenge stereotypes.
Hashtags	These tweets use the #MeToo hashtag to connect with others who are also working to address sexual harassment and assault. They can be used to share resources, to find support, or to build a community.

cyberfeminism has been the increased visibility of survivors. It should not be forgotten that survivors of sexual harassment and assault were often silenced and shamed before the #MeToo movement made them visible in the society.

Building on Haraway's work, the MeToo movement argues that technology can be used to create new forms of community and solidarity among women. Cyberfeminism urges women to use technology to share stories of sexual assault and harassment and to create a collective voice that can challenge the status quo. Cyberfeminism also argues that technology can be used to create new forms of resistance to patriarchal power. In line with what cyberfeminism calls for, the MeToo movement demonstrates that social media can be very well used to organize protests and raise awareness about sexual assault and harassment.

FIGURE 12.1 #MeToo word cloud

The MeToo movement is a powerful and timely call for women to use technology to create a more just and equitable world. It invites us to think about how technology can be used to break down traditional notions of gender, power and identity and build a more inclusive and empowering future.

References

Arslan, A. (2015). Eğitim ve Öğretimde Sosyal Medyanın Kullanımı, *Sosyalleşen Olgular, Sosyal Medya Araştırmaları 2*, Konya: Çizgi Kitapevi Yayınları.

Aslan, Ö. and Öner, S. (2006). İnternet Ekonomisi, *İstanbul Üniversitesi İletişim Fakültesi Dergisi.* 0(26): 5–19.

Baldini, M. (2000). *İletişim Tarihi*, İstanbul: Avcıol Basım Yayın.

Bayrak, T. (2015). Sosyal Ağ Uygulaması Olarak Vine, Editor: Deniz Yengin içinde *Sosyal Medya Araştırmaları*, 445–468. İstanbul: Paloma Yayınevi.

Braidotti, R. (2014). *İnsan Sonrası,* Karakaş, Ö. Translated. İstanbul: Kollektif Yayınları.

Dikener, O. (2011). İnternet Reklamcılığında Web Tasarımının Önemi, *Erciyes İletişim Dergisi*, 2(1), 152–166.

Gans, H. (2005). *Popüler Kültür ve Yüksek Kültür.* Incirlioğlu, O.E. Translated, İstanbul: YK Yayınları.

Geray, H. (2003). *İletişim ve Teknoloji Uluslararası Birikim Düzeninde YeniMedya Politikaları*, Ankara: Ütopya Yayınları.

Greenlaw, R. And Hepp, E. (1999). *In-line / On-line: Fundamentals of the Internet and The World Wide Web*, Boston: McGraw-Hill.

Güz, N. (2002). *Etkili İletişim Terimleri*, İstanbul: İnkılâp Yayınları.

Hall, K. (1996). Cyberfeminism. In S.C. Herring (Ed.), *Computer-Mediated Communication: Linguistic, Social and Cross-Cultural Perspectives*, pp. 147–170.

Haraway, D. (2006). *Siborg Manifestosu*, İstanbul: Agora Kitaplığı.

Innis, H. (2006). *İmparatorluk ve İletişim Araçları*. Töreli, N. Translated, Ankara: Ütopya Yayınevi.

Jenkins, H. (2018). *Cesur Yeni Medya, Teknolojiler ve Hayran Kültürü*, İstanbul: İletişim Yayınları.

Khurana, N. (2015). The impact of social networking sites on the youth, *Mass Communication & Journalism*, 5(12), 2–4.

Laughey, D. (2007). *Key Themes in Media Theory*, New York: Open University Press.

McPhillips, S. and Merlo, O. (2008). Media Convergence and the Evolving Media Business Model: an Overview and Strategic Opportunities, *The Marketing Review*, 8(3), 237–253.

Mısırlı, İ. (2017). *Genel ve Teknik İletişim Kavramlar İlkeler Uygulamalar*, Ankara: Detay Yayıncılık.

Monovich, L. (2001). *The Language of New Media*. Cambridge, MA: MIT Pres.

Murugesan, S. (2010). *Web x.0: A Road Map. Handbook of Research on Web 2.0, Web 3.0, and x.0: Technologies, Business, and Social Applications*, New York: Information Science Reference.

Ong, W. (2018). *Sözlü ve Yazılı Kültür Sözün Teknolojileşmesi*, İstanbul: Metis Yayınları.

Pool, S. (1983). *Technologies of Freedom: On Free Speech in an Electronic Age*, Cambridge, MA: Harvard University Press.

Yengin, D. (2014). *Yeni Medya ve Dokunmatik Toplum*, İstanbul: Derin Yayınları.

Yerlikaya, İ. (2004). İnternet Gazeteciliği ve Geri Besleme, *Medyada Yeni Yaklaşımlar*, Konya: Eğitim Kitabevi.

Index